Margaret Case Harriman

The Vicious Circle

THE STORY

OF THE ALGONQUIN ROUND TABLE

Illustrated by Al Hirschfeld

Rinehart & Co., Inc.   NEW YORK : TORONTO

COPYRIGHT, 1951, BY MARGARET CASE HARRIMAN
PRINTED IN THE UNITED STATES OF AMERICA
ALL RIGHTS RESERVED

I know the Table Round, my friends of old;
All brave, and many generous, and some chaste.

—TENNYSON: Idylls of the King.

Acknowledgment

Grateful acknowledgment is made to the following for permission to use the material indicated:

MARC CONNELLY, New York, N. Y. and HOWARD E. REINHEIMER, New York, N. Y., Attorney for George Kaufmann: Excerpts from *The Morning-Evening*.

EDNA FERBER, New York, N. Y.: An excerpt from *A Peculiar Treasure*, by Edna Ferber.

JANET FLANNER, New York, N. Y.: An excerpt from a letter written by Janet Flanner to Alice Leone Moats.

DORIS FLEISCHMAN, New York, N. Y.: Letter which she sent to the Secretary of State, in 1925.

JACKSON, NASH, BROPHY, BARRINGER & BROOKS, New York, N. Y., Attorneys for "The Press Publishing Company": Review of *No Sirree!*, by Wilton Lackaye, which appeared in Heywood Broun's column in the former New York *World*, May 1, 1922; Review of *The Forty-Niners*, by Alexander Woollcott, which appeared in Heywood Broun's column in the former New York *World*, in November, 1923; and a quotation from a column of Heywood Broun's, which appeared in the former New York *World*, in 1927, following the execution of Sacco and Vanzetti.

THE NATION, New York, N. Y.: An excerpt from an article by Heywood Broun which appeared in *The Nation*,

ACKNOWLEDGMENT

about four months after the execution of Sacco and Vanzetti in 1927.

THE NEW YORKER, New York, N. Y.: Excerpts from Douglas Watt's review of *The Consul,* which appeared in *The New Yorker* of March 25, 1950; and excerpts from a burlesque of the Enquiring Reporter, which appeared in *The New Yorker* of August 29, 1925.

THE NEW YORK TIMES, New York, N. Y.: A Review by Laurette Taylor of *No Sirree!,* by Wilton Lackaye, which appeared in the *Times* of May 1, 1922.

BERRY ROCKWELL, New York, N. Y.: Excerpts from reviews by Robert Benchley from the old *Life* magazine.

HAROLD ROSS, New York, N. Y.: Appendage to a letter to Alexander Woollcott; letter to Margaret Case Harriman about the *Stars and Stripes* staff; and the text of the prospectus, "Announcing a New Weekly Magazine."

MURIEL A. RUSSELL, San Francisco, California: Letter from Gertrude Atherton to Frank Case (1938); and excerpts from *Black Oxen* by Gertrude Atherton.

THE VIKING PRESS INC., New York, N. Y.: Letter from Alexander Woollcott to Lucie Christie Drage, from page 83 of *The Letters of Alexander Woollcott;* Letter from Alexander Woollcott to Harold Ross; and quotations from pages 112 and 120 of *While Rome Burns,* by Alexander Woollcott.

§ viii §

CONTENTS

1	How Did It All Begin?	3
2	A Glance Over the Shoulder	21
3	Actresses, Attitudes, and Other High Ideals	39
4	Crusaders and Infracaninophiles	59
5	Fun and Feuds	81
6	Abide with Me	111
7	Manners, Maneuvers, and Married Maidens	133
8	Onward and Upward	153
9	The Birth of The New Yorker	171
10	The Sophisticates and the Logrollers	199
11	How To Be a Wit	219
12	As the Girl Said to the Sailor	233
13	Merrily We Roll Along	251
14	How To Run a Fortune Into a Shoestring	267
15	Whatever Became of Tootsie Rolls?	287
	Index	303

§ ix §

The Vicious Circle

CHAPTER ONE

How Did It All Begin?

ONE DAY in 1919, just after World War I, two rotund young men entered the Algonquin Hotel on West 44th Street in quest of angel cake. The tall, serene gentleman was a theatrical press agent named John Peter Toohey; the short, explosive one was Alexander Woollcott, then drama critic of *The New York Times*. Toohey had earlier discovered the wares of Sarah Victor, the Algonquin's pastry cook, and knowing his friend Woollcott's sweet tooth, had brought him there for lunch.

The cosy combination of a critic lunching with a press agent was to become a familiar one around the Algonquin, and was to lead to some lively accusations of "logrolling" from certain jaundiced observers; but all that came later. On this particular day, it is safe to say that Woollcott and Toohey had nothing on their minds more sinister than angel cake.

Seated at a table for two, Woollcott focused his revolving stare upon the room. He was then thirty-two years old and already a striking combination of hero-

§ 3 §

THE VICIOUS CIRCLE

worshiper and Madame Defarge. On this, his first visit to the Algonquin, his roving appraisal found food for speculation as rich as Sarah's cake. As on most days at the luncheon hour, there was Ethel Barrymore sitting at a corner table, perhaps with her brother Jack or her uncle, John Drew. At other tables were Laurette Taylor, Jane Cowl, Elsie Janis, Rex Beach, Commander Evangeline Booth of the Salvation Army, Irvin S. Cobb, Ann Pennington, Constance Collier . . . all the stimulating array of people that had already made the hotel famous. Woollcott's starry-eyed gaze sharpened into the knitting needles of Madame Defarge only when it encountered the two columnists in the room, O. O. McIntyre and S. Jay Kaufman. McIntyre was gently dismissed as a kindly old corn-fed writing slob by Woollcott's generation of newspapermen, but they really hated S. Jay Kaufman, a more debonair type who ran a column in the *Telegram* called "Around the Town." No one now knows the exact reason for this dislike. Some say that the boys considered Kaufman's city slicker airs a little too grand and glossy, a touch pretentious; others trace the distaste to the fact that S. Jay once referred to their pal, Marc Connelly, in his column as "poor Marc" after a play of his had failed, and they found this sympathy patronizing. At any rate, their disinclination for Mr. Kaufman is notable because it was a feature of the first gag to be pulled off by the Algonquin Round Table as a group, at what might be called its first luncheon.

It is hard to say just when the first luncheon of the Round Table took place, or just which *was* its first lunch-

§ 4 §

How Did It All Begin?

eon. Like any other group which meets mainly for companionship, with no formal organization, no bylaws, and no dues, it came into being gradually. Many of its members—Bob Benchley, Brock and Murdock Pemberton, Toohey, Heywood Broun—had lunched at the Algonquin singly or together for some years before there was a Round Table. Franklin P. Adams, one of its oldest patrons, had originally gone there to call on his friend Samuel Merwin, the novelist. Adams, Woollcott, and Harold Ross had known one another during the war in France where they were all attached to the A.E.F. and to the staff of the *Stars and Stripes;* as F.P.A., a former captain, wrote in his *Diary of Our Own Samuel Pepys* in 1926, "To my office, and remember that nine years ago this day we had declared war against Germany, and if it had not been for that, methought, Private Harold Ross never would have carried my gripsacks through the streets of Paris, and called me 'Sir.' "

None of these men ever said to any other, "Hey! Let us start a regular lunch-group at the Algonquin and call it the Round Table." Nobody ever said anything like that. The whole thing just bloomed as slowly and pleasantly as any June moon, so it's difficult to pin down its moment of inception. Perhaps it was Toohey's introduction of Aleck Woollcott to the angel cake. But more probably it was the occasion of Toohey's next lunch with Woollcott a few weeks later, in company with Heywood Broun, the Pembertons, Laurence Stallings (who was yet to write *What Price Glory?*), Deems Taylor, Art Samuels (then editor of *Harper's Bazaar*), Adams, and Bill Mur-

§ 5 §

THE VICIOUS CIRCLE

ray, a music critic on the Brooklyn *Eagle* who was later to become an ex-husband of Ilka Chase and one of the heads of the William Morris Agency.

This luncheon was a Welcome Home to Woollcott from the Wars, tendered by the above long-suffering friends who had been listening to him tell about his experiences ever since his return from France some months earlier. "From my seat in the theatre of War . . ." he would begin, taking a long breath, and this had once goaded Bill Murray into muttering "Seat 13, Row Q, no doubt?" Fresh from a Woollcott recital at lunch one day, Murdock Pemberton and Murray repaired to the Hippodrome across the street where Murdock, the Hippodrome's press agent, had his office. There, they set a covey of stenographers to typing out announcements of a great rally at the Algonquin in honor of Woollcott the Warrior, and hopefully designed to shut him up for a while. Knowing Woollcott's extreme touchiness about the correct spelling of his name (three o's, two l's, two t's, *if* you please), they laboriously spelled it wrong in all possible ways throughout the announcement—Wolcot, Woolcot, Wolcott, and Woolcoot. Having mailed this document to all their friends, and Woollcott's, they got the Hippodrome's wardrobe department to make a huge red felt flag, lettered in gold as follows:

A W O L

cot

and, conscious of his aversion to S. Jay Kaufman, the man-about-town columnist, they thoughtfully added:

§ 6 §

How Did It All Begin?

S. JAY KAUFMAN POST NO. 1

This banner, on the appointed day, they hung over the luncheon table in the Algonquin. It was a table in the dining room now called the Oak Room and then known as the Pergola, and economically decorated with murals of the Bay of Naples along one wall and mirrors along the other, so that you saw the Bay of Naples twice for the cost of one mural. All the invited guests turned up, and the luncheon was such a success—although it never achieved its aim of stifling Woollcott—that somebody said, "Why don't we do this every day?" According to most people's recollection, it was Toohey who said it. As far as anyone knows, the Round Table was born then and there.

At first, the group had no name, and it didn't meet at a round table. After some months at a long table in the Pergola, it moved to another long table in the Rose Room, up front near the door. As more people kept coming they overflowed into the aisles and upon adjoining tables, so my father, Frank Case (who operated but did not yet own the hotel in those days), had Georges, the headwaiter, move them for greater comfort to a large round table in the center of the room, toward the rear. This was the table they made famous. Father, who liked them individually and loved faithfulness in anyone, gave them one or two extra little attentions—free olives and celery and popovers, and their own pet waiter named Luigi. The nearest the group had come to a name was when certain members referred to it lightly as The

§ 7 §

THE VICIOUS CIRCLE

Board, and to the luncheons as Board Meetings. With the regular appearance of Luigi it was no time at all, of course, before they took to calling the table the Luigi Board.

Their own favorite name for themselves soon became The Vicious Circle, but as the members grew in prominence and achievement, and began entertaining even more famous people at lunch, other guests in the Rose Room fell to pointing them out to their own guests; "There's Mrs. Fiske over there, between Woollcott and Benchley at that round table"—or "That's Arnold Bennett sitting over there next to Heywood Broun, at the round table." Columnists and out-of-towners would drop in to ask Georges, "Who's at the round table today?" About 1920, a cartoonist named Duffy on the Brookyln *Eagle* published what was probably the first caricature of the group, seated at a luncheon table which he called the Algonquin Round Table. Soon newspaper columns began featuring quips and other items that originated at the Algonquin Round Table. Although other tables in the Rose Room still had their own smaller groups of celebrities, these altered from day to day, and the unchanging circle in the center of the room became its focal point.

The Round Table became a focal point, too, to the people who lunched at it. They were hard-working young people who led busy and scattered lives, but they were a group close-knit by common tastes, common standards, and the same kind of humor, and they enjoyed one another's company better than anybody else's

§ 8 §

HOTEL ALGONQUIN
NEW YORK
Dinner

Imported Russian Caviar, Individual 1 50

Blue Points 40	Robbin Island 60	Cape Cods 50	Clam Juice Cocktail 35
Little Neck Clams 80	Cherrystones 40	Shrimp Cocktail 85	Sea Food Cocktail 1 00
Crab Meat Cocktail 95	Lobster Cocktail 1 25	Oysters or Cocktail Sauce 10 Cents Extra

RELISHES
Tomato Juice Cocktail 30　Sauerkraut Juice 25　Vegetable Juice Cocktail 30
Grape Fruit Cocktail 60　Fresh Fruit Cocktail 75　Melon Cocktail 60
Canape Anchovy 60　Canape Algonquin 80　Canape Caviar 1 00　Scallions 25　Radishes 25
Celery 40　Stuffed Celery 60　Green Olives 30　Stuffed Olives 40　Ripe Olives 40
Bismark Herring 40　Sardines 50　Tunafish 75　Assorted Hors d'Oeuvres 1 00

SOUPS
Fresh Vegetable, Paysanne 40　Cream of Cauliflower aux Croutons 40
Jellied Tomato Bouillon 40　Consomme Nicoise 35　Clam Broth, Cup 40

CARTE DU JOUR
Boiled Kennebec Salmon, Hollandaise, Steamed Potatoes 2 00
Broiled Bluefish, Maitre d'Hotel, Lattice Potatoes
Lobster Saute, Newburg en Cassolette 1 75
Creamed Chicken, Tetrazzini au Gratin 1 25
Calf's Liver and Bacon Saute, Mashed Potatoes 1 25
Fresh Vegetable Plate Dinner, Poached Egg 1 00
Minced Tenderloin of Beef a la Deutsch, Home Fried Potatoes 1 25
Stewed Fresh Mushrooms with Fresh Tomatoes and Chives on Toast 1 25
Broiled Veal Chop, New Lima Beans, French Fried Potatoes 1 40
Roast Lamb, Mint Sauce, Baby Carrots, Boulangere Potatoes 1 50
BLUE PLATE DINNER—(Half) Broiled Spring Chicken on Toast,
Cauliflower Hollandaise, Buttered Beets, French Fried Potatoes 1 65

FROM THE GRILL
(Half) Broiled Guinea Hen 1 65　Filet Mignon, Algonquin 1 95
Broiled Pork Chops, Apple Sauce　Broiled Sweetbreads Virginia 1 50

COLD BUFFET
Algonquin Dutch Lunch 10　Tomato Stuffed with Shrimps, Cocktail Sauce 90
(Half) Roast Chicken, Fruit Salad 1 40
Sliced Chicken and Virginia Ham, Celery Knob Salad 1 50
(Half) Boiled Lobster, Sliced Tomato, Mayonnaise 1 50
Kennebec Salmon, Sliced Cucumber, Mayonnaise 95

FRESH VEGETABLES
String Beans 50　Artichoke 50　Broccoli 75
Fried Egg Plant 40　Butter or Hollandaise 60　Au Gratin 60
Creamed Baby Onions　Spinach Plain 45　Creamed 50　with Egg 65
California Giant Asparagus, Drawn Butter or Hollandaise 65　French Peas 50
Haricots Verts Beans 50　Flageolets Beans 50　Baby Carrots 50

POTATOES
Cottage Fried 40　Lyonnaise 35　Julienne 25　Au Gratin 35
French Fried 25　Mashed 30　Saratoga Chips 25　Fried Sweets 30
Hashed Browned 30　Hashed in Cream 30　Candied Sweets 40

SALADS
Fruit 75　Fresh Vegetable 65　Shrimp 1 25　Lobster 1 75　Chicken 1 25　Chiffonade 65
Cucumber 45　Bartlett Pear, Cream Cheese and Pecans 75　Alligator Pear 65　Kuroki Salad 65
Sliced Tomatoes 45　Lettuce and Orange 60　Dates, Cream Cheese and Nuts 65　Celery Knob 65
Elda 65　Waldorf 70　Combination 65　Romaine and Grape Fruit 60　Celery and Watercress 50
Fresh Pear with Roquefort Cheese 70　Algonquin Fruit Salad 70　Chicory with Egg and Beet 65
Escarole, Pineapple and Apple 65
Egg, Russian or Roquefort Dressing 20 Cents Extra, Mayonnaise 15

FRUITS AND SWEETS
Stewed Apricots 30　Sliced Fresh Pineapple 40　Stewed Fresh Pear 40
Preserved Figs with Cream 50　Fresh Stewed Peaches 40　Compote of Fruit 40
Grape Fruit (Half) 40　Huckleberries 50　Table Apple or Pear 20
Sliced Peaches with Cream 50　Honey Ball 50　Raspberries 60
Persian Melon 60　Honey Dew Melon 60　Cantaloupe 40
Baked Apple with Cream 40　Stewed Rhubarb 40

Lemon Layer Cake 30　Macaroon Custard Pudding 35
Fresh Peach Pie 35　Green Apple Turnover, Whipped Cream 35
Rice Pudding 30　Macaroon 35　Pie In Mode 60　Lady Fingers 30　Pound Cake 35
Chocolate, Coffee or Vanilla Eclair 25　Green Apple Pie 35　Cup Custard 30

ICE CREAM
Ice Cream Cake　Chocolate Sauce 65
Spumoni 40　Neapolitan 40　Coupe St. Jacques 60　Fresh Peach 40
Meringue Glace 60　Nesselrode 40　Raspberry Sherbet 30　Pear Melba 60　Peach Melba 60
Biscuit Glace 40　Chocolate 40　Burnt Almond 40　Fresh Strawberry 40　Vanilla 40　Coffee 40
Orange Sherbet 30　Macaroon Glace 60
Pistachio Parfait 50　Chocolate Ball, Algonquin 55

CHEESE
Roquefort 40　Liederkrans 35　Swiss Gruyere 35　Imported Swiss 35　Cream 25
Port du Salut 35　Camembert 35　Cream Cheese with Bar-le-Duc or Guava Jelly 60
McLarens 35　Danish Cheese 35　Toasted Crackers Served with All Orders
Assorted Cheese Tray

COFFEE, TEA, ETC.
Coffee, Special Algonquin Blend, Pot for one 25　Demi-tasse 15　Kaffee Hag 40
Individual Bottle Milk 15　Buttermilk 15　Cream per glass 10　Half and Half 20
Ceylon, English Breakfast, Oolong or Orange Pekoe Tea, Pot for one 25　Acidophilus Milk 20
Bread or Rolls and Butter 15　Toasted Rolls and Butter 20

TUESDAY, SEPTEMBER 24, 1929

FRANK CASE

How Did It All Begin?

in the world. At the Round Table they were sure to find it, at least once a day, and they gravitated to it like skiers to a fireside.

The charter members of the Round Table were Franklin P. Adams, Deems Taylor, George S. Kaufman, Marc Connelly, Robert Benchley, Harold Ross, Heywood Broun, Art Samuels, Alexander Woollcott, John Peter Toohey, the Pembertons, Bill Murray, Robert E. Sherwood, John V. A. Weaver, Laurence Stallings, and a couple of theatrical press agents named David Wallace and Herman J. Mankiewicz; and, on the distaff side, Dorothy Parker, Jane Grant, Ruth Hale, Beatrice Kaufman, Peggy Wood, Peggy Leech, Margalo Gillmore, Edna Ferber, and Neysa McMein. F.P.A. was generally considered the dean of the group since he was, in 1920, one of its few solvent members, with a steady job and a large reading public. His column, "The Conning Tower," ran in the New York *Tribune,* and a good part of his fellow lunchers' waking thoughts were devoted to trying to write something good enough to "land" in it. Once a year Adams gave a dinner and a gold watch to the contributor who had landed the greatest number of verses or bits of prose in the column during the year, and one year, the proud winner of this award was Deems Taylor, then music critic of the *World,* who contributed under the name of "Smeed." When somebody once asked Adams why he gave a prize for the *most* contributions, and not for the best single one, he threw back his head and closed his eyes in his familiar gesture of thought, and intoned, "There is no such thing as the

§ 11 §

THE VICIOUS CIRCLE

'best' contribution. The fact that any contribution is accepted by me means that it is peerless."

Another constant, and fairly peerless, contributor to "The Conning Tower" in the days when the Round Table started was "G.S.K.," or George S. Kaufman. Kaufman was drama editor of *The New York Times*— a job he held on to long after his plays were successful— but in 1920, he was known as a playwright only as co-author, with two men named Evans and Percival, of a majestic failure called *Someone in the House*. The only thing that anyone now remembers about *Someone in the House* (aside from the inevitable cracks about there being no one in the house where it was playing) is that Kaufman, during the influenza epidemic in New York when the health authorities urged people to stay away from crowds, commanded the show's press agent to send out an urgent behest to all New Yorkers to hurry to the theatre where *Someone in the House* was on view. "Only place in town you can be absolutely safe from a crowd," he pointed out.

Marc Connelly, with whom Kaufman was to write *Dulcy, Merton of the Movies,* and many other hits, was a newspaper reporter from Pittsburgh who also had written a play. It was *The Amber Empress,* and if anybody asks Marc about it now he just says, "Oh, God. But, you know—I kind of *liked* that show."

None of the charter members of the Round Table was much more of a celebrity than Kaufman and Connelly, in fact, in 1920 when Duffy published his cartoon. Broun was a sportswriter on the New York *Tribune*.

§ 12 §

How Did It All Begin?

Laurence Stallings, a reporter from the Atlanta *Journal*, who had lost a leg in the war, was a long way from writing *What Price Glory?*, or even from his collaborator, Maxwell Anderson, who was then an editorial writer for the New York *World*. Harold Ross was editor of the *American Legion Weekly*, and mainly known for his crew cut which, measured one day by a friend in a statistical mood, proved to be an inch and a half high. Johnny Weaver had not yet written *In American*, the poems that were to make him famous, and Brock Pemberton was an assistant producer to Arthur Hopkins.

The girls at the Round Table were doing a little better than the men, in 1920. Edna Ferber had already written *Dawn O'Hara* and the Emma McChesney stories, Peggy Wood was making a hit in musical comedies like *Marjolaine* and *Sweethearts*. Jane Grant, a *Times* reporter who later married Harold Ross, and Ruth Hale, a Selwyn press agent who married Heywood Broun, had made good in jobs that were not usually open to women in 1920; and they had, besides, made so much noise about Votes for Women that they were instrumental in getting the Woman Suffrage Act passed in 1920. In contrast to these militant gals, there was Neysa McMein, the ultrafeminine, the siren, who painted magazine covers and illustrations and had begun to be successful, in a softer way, in 1920. There were Peggy ("Peaches-and-Cream") Leech, who wanted to be a writer, Margalo ("The Baby of the Round Table") Gillmore, who wanted to be an actress, and Beatrice Kaufman, who just wanted to lunch with her husband,

THE VICIOUS CIRCLE

George. In order to be eligible to the Round Table as a professional worker, Bea took a job as reader for Horace Liveright, the publisher, a man so generally disliked that the Round Table hated him even ahead of S. Jay Kaufman. For some time Horace Liveright, a daily luncher at the Algonquin, had to watch his employee, Mrs. Kaufman, slip into her accustomed seat at the Round Table—which he was never asked to join. One day he spoke to Mrs. Kaufman about it in his office.

"Look here," he said, "those kids at what you call the Round Table are starving to death. I could *publish* them."

Bea looked at him. "Do you think so?" she said.

The three glossiest members of the group were Bob Benchley, Bob Sherwood, and Dorothy Parker; not because they were any more prosperous than the others, but because they all worked on *Vanity Fair,* as managing editor, drama editor, and drama critic respectively. There was a great prestige in working for *Vanity Fair* in those days, if not much money. What presently happened to these three proved that the Round Table friends, although they could—and later did—bicker and even quarrel violently among themselves, had an unswerving loyalty to one another in time of trouble.

In 1920, Dorothy Parker reviewed in *Vanity Fair* a Maugham play called *Caesar's Wife,* starring Billie Burke. "Miss Burke," wrote Mrs. Parker, "is at her best in her more serious moments; in her desire to convey the girlishness of the character, she plays her lighter

§ 14 §

How Did It All Begin?

scenes rather as if she were giving an impersonation of Eva Tanguay." When this tribute appeared on the newsstands, Florenz Ziegfeld threatened to tear the offices of *Vanity Fair* apart, and what was more drastic, to remove his advertising from all Condé Nast publications unless Mrs. Parker were fired. Mrs. Parker was fired. Without a moment's hesitation her friends Benchley and Sherwood quit too, in sympathy and protest, and all three repaired to lunch at the Round Table, where they calmly announced their unemployment. Everyone at the table applauded the Benchley-Sherwood gesture but took it, as they themselves did, as a matter of course; injustice had been done and a pal roughly treated—what else could anyone do but string along with her?

Such loyalty meant a real sacrifice to Benchley and Sherwood at that time. They had no money to speak of, and no other jobs, and neither had yet had much success in selling his own stuff. Sherwood, before long, got a job as an associate editor on the old *Life*, but Benchley and Mrs. Parker, disdaining the career of wage slaves, rented an "office" in the loft building over the Metropolitan Opera House and set up joint shop as free-lance writers. Little work got done in this atelier, mainly because of their habit of subscribing to undertakers' trade journals and other hilarious publications, and whiling away the mornings reading them until it was time to go up to the Algonquin for lunch. They nearly always found the money for a taxi, especially for open cabs in fine weather, and on at least one Spring day the journey was enlivened by Dottie's leaping to her feet and shriek-

§ 15 §

THE VICIOUS CIRCLE

ing wildly to passers-by, "Help! Help! This man is abducting me!" while Benchley whipped off his scarf and proceeded to gag her with it.

After some months of free lancing Benchley gave in to financial pressure and took a job as drama editor on *Life*, but Mrs. Parker announced that she would stay on alone in the office over the "Met" and get some real work done. She was a gregarious soul, however, and the loneliness began to get her. When nobody had dropped in to see her for a week, she finally hit upon a way to acquire the visitors she craved; she tacked a large cardboard sign on her office door that read simply: MEN.

Dottie Parker was then—and is still—a little dark-haired woman with bangs and an almost overpowering air of dulcet femininity. She was married to Edwin Parker, a young insurance man generally liked but seldom seen. She wore bows on her shoes, spoke in muted tones, and had a way of resting a hand confidingly on yours when she talked to you. From this honeyed exterior, like the bee sting from the rose petal, regularly issued, of course, a gunfire of devastating cracks. One day, another lady writer, pausing at the Round Table (although not invited to sit down), was congratulating herself at some length on the success of her marriage and the virtues of her husband, whom the Round Table privately considered a rather dull fellow.

"I've kept him these seven years!" crowed this happy matron complacently.

"Don't worry," cooed Dottie, "if you keep him long enough he'll come back in style."

§ 16 §

DOROTHY PARKER

How Did It All Begin?

Toward the end of lunch that same day she said, "Excuse me, everybody, I have to go to the bathroom." Halfway out of her chair, she added, "I really have to telephone, but I'm too embarrassed to say so."

A wave of easy laughter followed her as she left. The Round Table wasn't trying to impress anybody, and they had no thought of treasuring any member's remark for the anthologies. They met purely for enjoyment, and their humor was the product of minds geared to high activity by hard work and ready to relax for an hour in the company of friends. They were no different from any group of plumbers, advertising writers, bankers, or farmers, except for one thing: their minds were born to think of things in an unusual way.

All of their humor was casual in the early days, and much of it was merely pensive . . . almost like a man talking to himself. Once, F.P.A. took Harold Ross tobogganing on a country weekend, and on Monday, at lunch at the Round Table, somebody asked him how Ross had looked, tobogganing. Adams looked across the table, at Ross's clown face and rigid crew cut.

"Well," he said, thoughtfully, "you know how he looks *not* tobogganing."

Talk at the Round Table was mostly like that in 1920—easy, unrehearsed, and full of unexpected pleasures. It took Herman J. Mankiewicz, the press agent (now a gold-plated Hollywood producer), to put his finger on the bitter fact that none of this fun was bringing in any money. Mank watched his friends leaving the Algonquin one day after lunch: Benchley, Sherwood,

§ 19 §

THE VICIOUS CIRCLE

Parker, Ross, Kaufman, Connelly, Broun, Stallings, and so on. Mank shook his head sadly.

"There," he said to Murdock Pemberton, "goes the greatest collection of unsalable wit in America."

§ 20 §

CHAPTER TWO

A Glance Over the Shoulder

THE ALGONQUIN ROUND TABLE came to the Algonquin Hotel the way lightning strikes a tree, by accident and mutual attraction. Actors and writers always enjoyed staying with Father as much as he enjoyed having them, and he himself had an explanation for this contagious liking, in his own book, *Tales of a Wayward Inn.* "If a man should stand in Times Square with his heart simply bursting with love for bricklayers," he wrote, "I don't doubt that in time the bricklayers would sense it and gather round."

The Algonquin already had its legend in 1920, when the Round Table started. Eleven years earlier Paul Armstrong had written *Alias Jimmy Valentine* there (in exactly nine days); Eugene Walter had written *The Easiest Way,* and Montague Glass had turned out many of his *Potash and Perlmutter* stories under its roof; and Booth Tarkington and Harry Leon Wilson had completed the last act of *The Man from Home* in one of its rooms. Gertrude Atherton, Charles Hanson Towne,

§ 21 §

THE VICIOUS CIRCLE

Lady Gregory, Rex Beach, Richard Harding Davis, and Alfred Noyes had all done at least some of their work there; and among theatre people, DeWolf Hopper, Raymond Hitchcock, John Drew, the Barrymores, Elsie Janis, Constance Collier, Frank Craven, Ina Claire, and countless others had studied their parts within its friendly walls. To writers and actors it had come to be not only a quiet little hotel where they could write or study in peace; it was a place that produced success. The younger ones grew superstitious about it, and would come back and ask for the same rooms that had brought them good luck last time. And to the very young ones, of course, it was sheer heaven just to ride in the same elevator with Elsie Janis or John Drew.

(They couldn't miss riding in the same elevator, since the Algonk had only one.)

The list of famous names grew so long that even Father, who was never blasé, reeled only slightly when a new night clerk came rushing up to him one time and excitedly told him that Mark Twain, William Makepeace Thackeray, and Edgar Allan Poe had just registered and gone upstairs together. Investigation proved that Frank Ward O'Malley of *The Sun* had come in late from a newspapermen's dinner and whiled away a few fanciful moments at the ledger.

It was O'Malley, too, who, registering on another occasion, found "Richard Harding Davis, and man" written in the space above his own, and loftily inscribed underneath: "Frank Ward O'Malley, and Two Men."

As the innkeeper's daughter I grew up among famous

§ 22 §

A Glance Over the Shoulder

people so gradually that I came to take them with a great, and perhaps regrettable, calm. I don't recall ever standing aghast before any celebrity except Zip the What-Is-It, a pinheaded "aborigine" in Barnum & Bailey's sideshow to whom Frank O'Malley formally introduced me when I was ten years old. I remember gravely handing Zip a cigar, which he ate. *Him* I stared at.

John Drew was the first person to tell me the proper pronunciation of the word "miscellany"—accent on the second syllable, according to Mr. Drew. The first woman I ever saw smoke a cigarette in public—or anywhere else—was Lady Gregory, the Irish author, who ordered her after-dinner coffee in the lobby one evening and, to Father's horror, tranquilly lit up a gasper and puffed away. The ordeal of asking an old and distinguished party like Lady Gregory to cut it out was so horrid that Father put it off for days . . . until it was solved in an instant by the kind of quick exchange that sometimes occurs between two nice people.

"Dear Mr. Case, I do hope my cigarette doesn't distress you," she said one night when Father stopped at her particular corner to say good evening.

"Dear Lady Gregory, there is only one thing that *you* could ever do that *would* distress me," said Father with the old eagle eye on the cigarette.

She smiled at him like an angel, doused the cigarette, and from then on smoked in her room.

During my schooldays my younger brother Carroll and I often had lunch with Douglas Fairbanks, Jr., who was about Carroll's age and lived at the Algonquin with

§ 23 §

THE VICIOUS CIRCLE

his father and mother; and I would feel very elderly as I helped Deedie, Douglas's nurse, urge the two little boys to use their silver pushers *nicely,* and not try to scoop up peas with their bare hands. Afternoons and some Saturday mornings I used to skip rope on the hotel roof with Douglas's father, Fairbanks Senior, who had long since worn out my own father by his endless pursuit of new and more violent excercise. Mr. Fairbanks had just started his movie career with (I think) a picture called *The Lamb,* which—like most films in those days—was made in New York. I do remember, most distinctly, that the picture opened the new Strand Theatre on Broadway, and that I was allowed to stay up late and go to the opening with Father. We sat in a box. After the picture we came home in a taxi with Mr. and Mrs. Fairbanks and a lot of people, all of whom were exclaiming, "Well, the picture's all *right,* Doug. As good as any moving picture *can* be. But for god's sake, Doug, you're an *actor* . . . you can't be thinking of going in for this thing *seriously?"*

All except Father. Father just kept still. He was a man who not only never spouted advice, but had a great gift for saying absolutely nothing at just the right time.

During our rope-skipping on the Algonquin roof Mr. Fairbanks, after several thousand turns of the rope, generally began exploring for new adventures, and that is how Mr. Fairbanks and I once came to be stuck for some fifty minutes in the dead end of a hollow cornice that ran along the front of the roof. This cornice had a door at one end, God knows why, about the size of an old-fashioned dumbwaiter door, and the minute Mr.

§ 24 §

A Glance Over the Shoulder

Fairbanks spied this mysterious entry he naturally had to get into it. "Come on," he said to me, prying open the rusty hatches, and just as naturally I followed. If he had stood on the edge of the roof, flapped his arms, and said, "Come on, let's take off," I would have followed him.

The door to the secret tunnel was so small that I had to get in first and ease Mr. Fairbanks in after me. After we both got in the tunnel there was no room to change places, so I crawled along ahead of Mr. Fairbanks who followed me, also on his hands and knees. The tunnel was so small that the top of it scraped my back and its sides scraped my elbows. Behind me, Mr. Fairbanks kept saying enthusiastically, "Keep going, Margaret, keep going!"

I know now, perfectly well, that Douglas Fairbanks expected with his whole heart to find a dragon or a pixie in that tunnel at the age of thirty, just as much as I did at the age of twelve. I have sometimes wished, since, that I had been old enough, and wise enough, to *invent* a dragon or a pixie for him during that crawl through the tunnel. All I need have done was say, "OOH, LOOK!" and he would have been at the ready, as he so enjoyed being. As it turned out, the danger that actually threatened us was rather dull. Just asphyxiation.

When we got to the dead end of the tunnel we found it was too small to turn around in. Mr. Fairbanks said, "We'll have to back up." This turned out to be a bad idea, partly because I kept kicking Mr. Fairbanks in the face, but mainly because we had dislodged so many pieces of metal, shale, and old tin—or whatever the cornice was

§ 25 §

THE VICIOUS CIRCLE

made of (and it was never meant for people to crawl into)—that a whole pile of it had fallen down and blocked the door.

"Well," said Mr. Fairbanks, "we seem to be in a little trouble here. Better turn around and face it."

"I *can't* turn around!" I wailed.

"Sure you can," he said. "Just let all your breath out, fall on your stomach, roll over, take a deep breath, and sit up facing in the opposite direction. Look—I'll do it first."

He did, and somehow I managed to do it too. It was a little better that way, at least less humiliating than facing suffocation with our rear ends in the air, but we were still trapped in the tunnel. Nobody, not even Father, would have thought of looking for us in a piece of architectural trimming that was merely a part of the Algonquin's façade hanging out over 44th Street. Mr. Fairbanks and I were like the Bride in the Box—mysteriously gone forever.

We hollered and hammered with bits of shale on the metal sides of the tunnel for what seemed hours before Oscar, the hotel carpenter, who had mercifully come out on the roof for a quiet pipe, finally heard us. (What his emotions must have been on hearing faint human cries from *inside* the cornice, I cannot think.) It took Oscar and two men from the engine room a good half hour to get us out; and it took another ten or fifteen minutes to pledge the three men to secrecy. If Father had ever heard of that adventure there would have been an end to my rope-skipping.

§ 26 §

A Glance Over the Shoulder

It was a later exploit, in fact, that was the cause of the only coolness, I think, that ever occurred between Father and Douglas Fairbanks throughout their long friendship. One day on the roof Mr. Fairbanks (whom, incidentally, I never called by his first name until I was a wife and mother) dared me to climb a spidery iron ladder that was clamped flat against a brick wall, and led from the main roof to a higher roof where the chimneys were. It was obviously an emergency ladder, to be used only by firemen, chimney sweeps, or any other monkeys loose in the vicinity besides Mr. Fairbanks and me. But did I know that, or care? Certainly not . . . up I went.

That night at dinner I described this accomplishment with relish, and innocently added, "Gosh, Father, I almost let go halfway up, when I looked down and saw *nothing* below me but Forty-Fourth Street thirteen stories down, with all the little people running around like ants!" Father left the table immediately in search of Mr. Fairbanks. What passed between them I never knew . . . but the next time I skipped rope on the roof with Mr. Fairbanks, we just skipped rope.

With all of these heady incidents in my everyday life it was small wonder that I came to take them for granted. If I thought about it at all, I probably assumed that the girls I knew at Gardner School had the same kind of life with *their* fathers' friends. However, my father was a sage parent, and I was never allowed to grow sophisticated (that new word), at least outwardly. I went to bed at nine-thirty until I was fifteen, and curt-

§ 27 §

THE VICIOUS CIRCLE

sied to my elders until I was so tall that they formally
objected. Father censored the books I read and the plays
I saw . . . I remember that *An American Tragedy* was
forbidden, and among plays, *A Pair of Silk Stockings*
and even *The Jest* although, for some reason, I was per-
mitted to read Oscar Wilde and Ibsen (possibly because
Father hadn't got round to reading them himself). He
also engaged for my brother and myself a series of rather
forceful governesses who taught us to eat potatoes for
breakfast (German governess), love Viennese waltzes
(Austrian governess), take cold-water baths (English
governess), leave nothing on our plates (French governess), and dance the tango (Brazilian governess). Combined with the Algonquin, it was a fairly inclusive education.

One thing I learned during that tremendously happy
childhood and adolescence at the Algonquin was that
famous people in general are just as uninspired when
talking to children as your Aunt and Uncle Gussie are.
With the exception of John Drew, Frank Ward O'Malley,
Douglas Fairbanks, and one or two other rare souls, they
all said the usual things: "How you've *grown!*" and so
on. A great favorite with them in my own youth was,
"And this is Margaret! My dear, I've known you since
you were *this* high!" And they would hold a hand about
two feet off the floor. I must have inwardly rebelled, because I recall the intense pleasure I took in a certain
exchange one day in my twenties when Bee Drew Deveraux, John Drew's daughter, came in with her son
Jackie, aged five or six. (This was the same John Drew

§ 28 §

A Glance Over the Shoulder

Deveraux who later played the eldest Day boy in *Life With Father* and also became a notable paratrooper in the recent war.)

"You know Jackie, don't you, Margaret?" Mrs. Deveraux said to me.

"Do *I* know *Jackie?*" I boomed. "Why, I've known Jackie since he was *this* high!" And I leaned over and put my hand flat on the floor.

That little incident naturally reminds me of the now-familiar remark by Bob Benchley, when someone asked him if he knew the six-foot-seven Bob Sherwood. Benchley climbed on a chair and extended a hand just below the ceiling. "Why, I've known Bob Sherwood since he was *this* high!" he said.

And so we come back to the Round Table. . . .

It will be clearly evident that the Algonquin was no ordinary hotel when the Round Table came into being there. And Father's attitude, at first, was no more fulsome than that of any other host who welcomes one more likely looking party to the picnic ground. Certainly he didn't expect to make any money out of the Round Table, since nobody there had any and the lunch each member usually ordered consisted of hamburger or ham and eggs, apple pie, and coffee.

But Father was a man easily won by laughter. And although his liking for the Round Table arose mainly from the fact that it was a group of young and struggling writers, for whom he was ever a pushover, it probably crystallized into affection when they began playing "I-

§ 29 §

THE VICIOUS CIRCLE

Can-Give-You-a-Sentence" with him on the way to and from lunch.

"I-Can-Give-You-a-Sentence," possibly the first of the many word games that were to engross the Round Table, consisted of saying to someone (for instance), "I can give you a sentence with the word 'burlesque.'" Courteous attention was required of your opponent as you added, "I had two soft-burlesque for breakfast." Simple fun, and a little corny today; but it was highly popular in the 'Twenties, and it definitely started at the Round Table. I believe Franklin P. Adams began it one Yuletide when he went around wishing everybody "a meretricious and a happy New Year."

The chief charm of the game, as with other Round Table pastimes, was the complete gravity and rigid politeness with which it was played. When anybody came up to you and said he could give-you-a-sentence, you simply ceased existing for yourself, you were all his until the gem was unleashed. And, by an unwritten rule, you *never* topped it immediately, even if you could; you just laughed, bowed slightly, and waited for your own chance.

One day George Kaufman, whose face was perfectly constructed for seriousness of this kind, stopped Father in the lobby and said he could give him a sentence with the word "punctilious." "I know a farmer who has two daughters, Lizzie and Tillie," said George. Father waited, in the proper attitude of expectancy. "Lizzie is all right," George continued carefully, "but you have no idea how punctilious."

§ 30 §

A Glance Over the Shoulder

Father confided to me later that the topper for that one, or at least a companion piece, flashed into his mind instantly and he went through considerable agony waiting the proper interval until George came *out* from lunch.

"Hey, George," he said then. "I know two sisters who are in a quandary." Kaufman waited, this time the wholehearted straight man. "Bettina devil Anna deep blue sea," said Pa.

That, as far as I know, was the start of the Name Game, which was added on to the Word Game, and attained such favor that Alexander Clark, the actor, once climbed to the top of a Fifth Avenue bus he saw me riding, sat down next to me, and pointed to a blonde in the front seat.

"That's Iris," he said.

"Iris who?" I innocently asked.

"Iris I was in Dixie," Alex sang, and got off the bus at the corner.

It was Alex Clark and Johnny Weaver who had a private form of salutation when they met in the lobby that, for some reason, always had me in the aisles. It consisted only of stopping dead and silently forking two fingers at each other's eyes. Alex never lunched at the Round Table, but as a good friend of Weaver's and Bob Benchley's he had a large share in its lighter moments.

I never lunched at the Round Table either, a fact I feel I should make plain before proceeding further with this book. (Actually I am the last person to write this book, in more ways than one, since I believe the pub-

THE VICIOUS CIRCLE

lishers unsuccessfully approached at least one authentic member of the group before asking me.) Although I am now at the tender age where I am beginning to feel a little tender about what my age is, I was still in school when the Round Table started; and even later, I certainly did nothing remarkable enough to warrant being included. The thought simply never occurred to me, any more than it did to the Round Table, and that is why I am always skeptical when I hear people say that this person or that was "envious" of the Round Table, or "mad" at not being asked to join, and therefore made cracks about it. It's my belief that when anybody, at any table in the Rose Room, made a crack it was because he, or she, had thought up a good one and enjoyed delivering it . . . and for no more complicated reason than that. The atmosphere of the room was witty—how could it be anything else with Irvin S. Cobb, Jack Barrymore, Laurette Taylor, and so on, lunching at its various tables, *and* with the Round Table at rear center? But the idea was only to amuse your own table-companions; not, as many people still think, to aim your shaft at the Round Table. Those other starlit lunchers were too much wrapped up in themselves and their own busy lives to cast any envious glances at a little group of newcomers at a round table. At first, the Round Table wasn't important enough. Later, when it mysteriously became the greatest force in literature and the theatre in all New York, the actors at the other tables still gave it only half an eye—the half that was terrified of Alexander Wooll-

§ 32 §

A Glance Over the Shoulder

cott's reviews—and the writers never looked at it at all.

This is because actors and writers have the happy privilege of living in a withdrawn world where all that is important is themselves. Or at least, I think so. And that is why I think the idea that the Rose Room was seething with jealousy during the rise and reign of the Round Table is silly. The people at the other tables were just as wrapped up in themselves as the Round Table was.

I know *I* was. I lunched every day at the family table—to the left, just inside the velvet rope—and I usually had a couple of girls with me and (on big days) two or three John-Type-Held college boys. We talked about proms, and dates, and the new way of making Hawaiian music by easing a "whisky" glass along the strings of a banjo-mandolin. It was Prohibition then, and although some of us were familiar with bathtub gin and orange juice, having been sick on it, we didn't know that glasses came in sizes, or by name. We didn't know what a "whisky" glass was. So naturally, when Father came over to talk to us for a minute I put the problem to him. "We need a 'whisky' glass, Father," I said. Father turned white with rage, and sat down at our table in no uncertain way.

"Which one of you boys has a flask in his pocket?" he said. And when Father asked a question, it could be like thunder shaking the hills.

"Gee, Mr. Case," said Johnny, truthfully and with

§ 33 §

THE VICIOUS CIRCLE

great anxiety, "none of us here have a flask in their pocket."

"Golly, Mr. Case," said Jimmy, "we just want the whisky glass because Johnny can't reach the heighth of some chords without running a whisky glass up and down the strings."

Fortunately, Johnny's grammar and Jimmy's mispronunciation diverted Father's wrath into another channel. He gave them each a long cold look.

"None of us here *has* a flask in *his* pocket. Also, the word is *height*," he said, "and that doesn't mean that you have to pronounce its opposite 'deb-bt' either." And excusing himself pleasantly, he got up and strolled away.

Father, with no great formal education, nevertheless took a scholar's interest in the English language, and was most particular about it. He broke me of saying "Look" or "Listen" before almost every sentence, and of replying "Fine, thanks" to inquiries about my health; ("I'm well, thank you" fell more pleasingly on the ear, he suggested); and it really hurt him when anyone said things like "Why dincha open the winda?" Summers, at Sag Harbor, we were always great ones for leaping up from the dinner table to fetch the dictionary or encyclopedia and thrash out some moot point of fact or pronunciation then and there, so I grew up to be pretty bookish myself. At sixteen or seventeen (I forget which) I actually "landed" in F.P.A.'s "Conning Tower" with a verse which I shall quote here simply for the pleasure it gives me . . . (the title was F.P.A.'s, but the rest all mine):

§ 34 §

A Glance Over the Shoulder

THE PASSIONATE ENCYCLOPEDIA BRITTANICA READER TO HIS LOVE

As And to Aus, and Aus to Bis,
As Hus to Ita, and Ita to Kys;
As Pay to Pol, and Pol to Ree;
Ah, that is how you are to me!

As Bis to Cal, and Cal to Cha,
As Edw to Eva, and Eva to Fra;
As Ref to Sha, and Sha to Shu;
That is, I hope, how I'm to you.

. . . Father was really pleased with that modest achievement. In fact, he had a respect amounting almost to awe for anyone at all who could write down words and have them publicly printed—at least, he did until he got around to doing the same thing himself, in his two books *Tales of a Wayward Inn* and *Do Not Disturb*. Then he reversed himself in a truly insufferable way. "Why didn't somebody tell me about this writing racket *before?*" he would crow at me, delightedly. "There's nothing to it—I just sit down with a pencil and pad and the pencil fairly flies!" It did, too; he was one of the *easiest* writers I ever saw. Easy to read as well, which is not always the case with facile authors.

However, all that was much later, in 1939 and 1940; in the early days of the Round Table Father was still as starry-eyed about writers as he was about actors. I can see him now, tall, slim, erect and precisely tailored, strolling among the tables in the Rose Room, sitting down here and there for a chat while a busboy scurried

§ 35 §

THE VICIOUS CIRCLE

up with his usual glass of ice water . . . and always, always, with an expectant look on his face as if he were going to a party. It *was* a party for him, every day.

Father never considered himself a wit, and this gave him an enchanting air of surprise whenever he said something really good. He said so many good things that most of them have passed into legend—unfortunately uncredited. The now-famous. "Time wounds all heels" was his; and the comment on a too-talkative woman, "When you ask her a question it's like taking your finger out of the dike." Radio comics have twisted and cheapened his sincere remark one time when he was cautioning a new manager to go easy on dunning actors for their bills because they always paid voluntarily as soon as they could. "I have never been cheated by an actor," Father told the new manager.

"But, Mr. Case, what about *this?*" wailed the new manager, pointing to an entry in the books concerning a seven-year-overdue account run up by a well-known ham who never paid his bills. Father looked at the name.

"I do not consider him an actor," he said gravely, and shut the ledger.

F.P.A. reminded me the other day of his own favorite chance remark of Father's, and at the risk of everyone's having heard it since, in some form or other, I'd like to repeat it here. Adams, coming in to lunch one day at the Round Table, stopped to talk with Father in the lobby and the conversation got around to a certain playwright, detested by all for his miserly habits.

"Haven't seen him around here lately," said F.P.A.,

§ 36 §

A Glance Over the Shoulder

"not since he got engaged to be married to some poor wretch. What's happened to him?"

"Well," said Father, "he had a little accident."

"No!" said Adams.

"Yes," said Father, "he went out to buy the ring for his fiancée, and got his finger crushed between two push-carts."

. . . Was it any wonder that the patrons at the Algonk had as much fun as Father did?

§ 37 §

CHAPTER THREE

Actresses, Attitudes, and Other High Ideals

THE EARLY Nineteen-Twenties were a great time to be alive in New York. The Great War was over, and we had two decades of peace ahead of us. None of the men we knew had been badly hurt in the war—so few, in fact, that Laurence Stallings, who had lost a leg in battle, was pretty much revered as a hero, although he did everything possible to discourage any such reverence. Some days he would come into lunch wearing his artificial leg—in those days a horrific contraption; other days, if he felt like it, he would leave the leg home and breeze in on a crutch. He wasn't interested in how he looked, he was intent only on getting to be a successful playwright. He was getting ready to write *What Price Glory?* His collaborator on that play, the Maxwell Anderson who, alone, was later to write such distinguished successes as *Winterset, Mary of Scotland, Anne of the Thousand Days,* and *Lost in the Stars,* was still writing editorials for the *World.*

The other war veterans at the Round Table were

§ 39 §

THE VICIOUS CIRCLE

equally concentrated on the future. Most of them had come to New York from the West and Middle West; Ross from Colorado by way of San Francisco, Frank Adams from Chicago, the Pembertons from Kansas, and Kaufman and Connelly (a couple of Eastern dudes) from Pittsburgh and McKeesport, Pa., respectively. The war had been a grim interruption to their plans, but it was a war you could forget, and it was over. Its warriors came back impatient to get on to the next thing, and in New York they found a stimulating city.

In 1921, New York had seventy-six legitimate theatres, as against its thirty-two today. The theatre was a live art, undiluted by Hollywood, radio, or television. Producers put their own money into plays and dealt directly with the actors; nowadays, of course, no actor can blow his nose without an agent, and play-producing has become such a high-powered industry that motion picture companies often put on a play just for the prestige of a New York first night before they make the picture. The cost of production in the 'Twenties was a fraction of what it is now, and the stagehands', electricians' and other associated unions were neither so powerful nor so balky. Furthermore, a play could have a fairly long run (200 performances was considered comfortable) at a satisfactory profit without being a "smash" hit—in contrast to the present system, whereby a play is either "terrific" and sold out for six months ahead, or an instantaneous flop.

Some of the plays of the 1921-22 season were *Anna Christie* with Pauline Lord, *The Dover Road* with Win-

§ 40 §

Actresses, Attitudes, and Other High Ideals

ifred Lenihan and Reginald Mason, Maugham's *The Circle* with Mrs. Leslie Carter and John Drew, *Bulldog Drummond* with A. E. Matthews, *Captain Applejack* with Wallace Eddinger and Mary Nash, *Kiki* with Lenore Ulric, *Bluebeard's Eighth Wife* starring Ina Claire, and Katharine Cornell's first big hit, *A Bill of Divorcement*. There were also revivals of *The Chocolate Soldier* with Tessa Kosta and Donald Brian; *Alias Jimmy Valentine* with Otto Kruger and Margalo Gillmore in the roles originally played by H. B. Warner and Laurette Taylor; and *The Squaw Man* with William Faversham himself in his famous part. Over at the 39th Street Theatre, in something called *The Nightcap*, the role of Charles, a butler, was being played by a young Englishman name of Ronald Colman; but it was to be another year before the part of Tyltyl in Maeterlinck's *The Bluebird* was played by a child actor whose voice is now familiar to millions of radio listeners as that of "your announcer, Ben Grauer."

Popular songs, unhackneyed in those days by constant repetition on the air, were allowed to live a little longer, and some of the tunes we hummed in 1921 were so good that they are still with us; "Three O'Clock in the Morning," "April Showers," "Look for the Silver Lining," and "My Man," which Fannie Brice first sang under a street lamp in the *Follies*. The best-selling books of that year were a vigorous assortment, too . . . Sinclair Lewis's *Main Street*, Edith Wharton's *The Age of Innocence*, O'Brien's *White Shadows in the South Seas*, and Wells's *Outline of History* among others. The slick

§ 41 §

THE VICIOUS CIRCLE

magazines included *Vanity Fair, Smart Set, College Humor, Judge,* and *Life,* the old comic weekly, to which Benchley and Sherwood had gone as editors after they quit *Vanity Fair.* A good many of the other boys at the Round Table were then submitting pieces to these magazines, with varying success. Once Marc Connelly, cast down by a crushing series of rejections, fell into black despair and paced up and down the two-room flat he shared with Deems Taylor, solemnly cursing God. At that moment his doorbell rang and the postman handed him an envelope containing an acceptance and a check. Marc raised his eyes heavenward. "I didn't mean it, God," he said.

For Marc those rejections were the darkness before the dawn. For some years F.P.A.'s "Conning Tower" had featured an imaginary character, an engaging featherhead named Dulcinea ("Dulcy" for short) whose bromidic comments Frank quoted from time to time. Dulcy was the forerunner of Gracie Allen and "My Friend Irma," a girl with a heart of gold and a mind of pure meringue, whose conversation consists mainly of clichés. "Live and let live, is my motto . . . All's well that ends well, I always say!" she always says, the while innocently creating chaos around her. In 1921 Marc Connelly and George Kaufman got the idea of writing a play about this character, and George C. Tyler produced it. *Dulcy* ran for almost a year at the Frazee Theatre, and introduced an actress fairly new to Broadway—Miss Lynn Fontanne. In the same year Kaufman and Connelly wrote a second successful comedy, *To the Ladies,*

§ 42 §

Actresses, Attitudes, and Other High Ideals

which featured an actress almost as new—Miss Helen Hayes.

Marc bought a riding habit when the money began to roll in, although he did not as yet own a horse. Kaufman, on the other hand, continuing to toil daily as the *Times's* drama editor, put his play profits in Eastman Kodak Company stock (his wife, Beatrice, came from Rochester, the home of Eastman). Eleven years later, some time after the Kaufman-Connelly partnership had been dissolved, Kaufman and Morris Ryskind wrote the musical show, *Of Thee I Sing*, and found Sam Harris, their producer, a little timid about the cost of putting it on. It was, after all, 1932, and the depth of the Great Depression. "What'll it cost?" Kaufman asked Harris. Eighty-two thousand dollars, Harris told him. Kaufman wrote out a check for the amount and then, as owner of the show, declared Harris, Ryskind, and George Gershwin, who had composed the music, "in" as partners. *Of Thee I Sing* won the Pulitzer Prize that year. Marc Connelly, however, never regretted his riding habit; he had already won his own Pulitzer Prize, in 1930, with *The Green Pastures*.

Romance flourished at the Round Table as well as careers. In 1920 Harold Ross became engaged to marry Jane Grant, a Kansas girl whom he had met overseas when she was working with the Red Cross during the war. Back in New York Jane went to work as a reporter on the *Times*, and Ross was made editor of a publication called *The Home Sector* which later merged with *The American Legion Weekly*. Jane, whose office

§ 43 §

THE VICIOUS CIRCLE

was next to Aleck Woollcott's at the *Times*, had been considerably beaued around by Aleck, and he had even taken her to a dance at his beloved alma mater, Hamilton College, which was about the greatest accolade he could bestow on a woman. Ross and Jane considerately asked Woollcott to meet them for tea one afternoon at the Algonquin, and confided to him the secret of their betrothal. Aleck, after shedding a silent tear over the loss of Jane, instantly took charge of the wedding preparations. It was just as well, since Ross was rushed off his feet by the *Home Sector-American Legion Weekly* merger, already in process; he was to be editor of the combined magazines. The following morning Aleck escorted Jane to Tiffany's to buy the wedding ring.

"I am Alexander Woollcott, and this is Miss Jane Grant," he announced to the salesman, "and we wish to buy a wedding ring."

"Yes, sir," said the salesman, naturally mistaking him for the groom—a pleasing fiction which Woollcott dreamily allowed to continue. "Do you wish both your initials engraved inside?" the salesman asked, after the ring had been chosen.

"No, just the lady's," replied Woollcott. "She might want to use it again."

Jane, therefore, never had Ross's initials in her wedding ring; but she figured she was lucky not to have Woollcott's, at that.

The day of the wedding turned out to be the very day of Ross's magazine merger and Woollcott, who had engaged the minister and the chapel, gloried still further

§ 44 §

Actresses, Attitudes, and Other High Ideals

in his role of impresario as he chased the harried bride-groom from meeting to meeting and finally produced him, breathlessly, at the altar. It is said that most of the few friends present at the ceremony referred to it for some time afterward as "Woollcott's Wedding."

Another romance that flowered at the Round Table resulted in the marriage of Bob Sherwood to Mary Brandon, an actress and a niece of Booth Tarkington's. Miss Brandon was a scant five feet tall, to the groom's six feet seven, but that wedding is chiefly remembered because another well-meaning best man innocently cornered the limelight. This was Douglas Fairbanks, who had come to know Sherwood through the Algonquin, and also because Bob had recently been made motion picture critic of *Life*. Douglas was then married to Mary Pickford, who also attended the wedding at the Little Church Around the Corner, and the crowds both inside and outside the church all but trampled the bride and groom in their mad efforts to get a better look at the King and Queen of Hollywood. Another memento of the Sherwood-Brandon marriage is the telegram Dorothy Parker sent to Mary Sherwood when, in the course of time, their child was born. For nine months Mary had been doing a good deal of public swooning and calling for attention, and it was felt that she had made rather too much of a production of motherhood. "Dear Mary," Mrs. Parker's wire read tersely, "we all knew you had it in you."

Peggy Wood and John V. A. Weaver were both regular members of the Round Table group for some

§ 45 §

THE VICIOUS CIRCLE

time before their marriage. Peggy, a vision of beauty behind footlights, was addicted offstage, in those days, to horn-rimmed glasses, flat heels, and an old raincoat; it was whispered, in fact, that Noel Coward fainted the first time he met her in London, when she came over to sing the leading role in his *Bittersweet* . . . only to swoon with delight later, of course, when he beheld her on the stage. Johnny Weaver was a cricketlike little guy, eternally boyish-looking and amusingly bitter. He was best known for his book of poems, *In American,* but he was dear to Woollcott because he was an alumnus of Hamilton College. The Weaver-Wood marriage led to a Round Table incident very different from the Parker-Brandon barb.

Peggy lost her first baby and was ill for a long time afterward. The first day she returned to lunch at the Round Table, Laurence Stallings, whose own child had been born that morning, bounded in with the news and, with the incredible thoughtlessness of a new father, spent almost the entire lunch-hour describing the new baby, how beautiful she was, how strong and husky and full of beans. Everybody else at the table knew what Peggy must be feeling but there was no stopping Stallings. "I was sitting next to Brock Pemberton," Peggy says, recalling it nowadays, "and just when I thought I couldn't stand any more without bursting into horrible sobs or something, Brock quietly reached over and took my hand under the table, and held it tight. He kept on holding it too, as tight as he could, until somebody finally switched Stallings onto another subject.

§ 46 §

Actresses, Attitudes, and Other High Ideals

"I've never forgotten it," Peggy says simply.

At first, when the ladies began to move in on the Round Table, Aleck Woollcott balked a little. Woman's place was in the home, he announced sternly when George Kaufman brought his wife Beatrice to lunch, and when Ruth Hale took to appearing regularly with or without her husband, Heywood Broun. Whenever Edna Ferber wandered in Woollcott made a point of addressing her peevishly as Fannie Hurst—a popular writer for whose style the Round Tablers felt something less than reverence. However, Mrs. Kaufman, Miss Ferber, Ruth Hale, Jane Grant, and all the other members of the early feminine contingent were his dear friends most of the time, and when their number was increased by young and lovely actresses—to whom Woollcott was ever susceptible—he yielded amiably to the majority and, characteristically, outdid them in the variety of fair guests he entertained there himself.

Margalo Gillmore, who had had her first success in 1919 as the young daughter in *The Famous Mrs. Fair* (starring Blanche Bates and Henry Miller), was known as "the baby of the table" and remembers Woollcott through the years as deadly cutting and marvelously kind. Once, when Margalo was long established in the theatre and was playing with Katharine Cornell in *The Barretts of Wimpole Street,* she brought a young actor from the cast to lunch at the Round Table. He had told her how greatly he admired Woollcott's writing, and how he longed to meet him. When Woollcott arrived he glared at the stranger and, in silence, pointedly took the

§ 47 §

THE VICIOUS CIRCLE

chair farthest away from him. Margalo introduced them, and added, "Aleck, this young man is a great admirer of everything you've written."

"Oh," said Woollcott, not looking up from the menu, "can he read?"

And yet, another time, Margalo mentioned idly at lunch one day that her favorite cartoon was a George Belcher drawing in *Punch* showing two of the famous Belcher charladies in shawls and tipsy hats, having supper at a pub.

" 'Ow's yer tripe, dearie?" one charlady asks the other.

"A bit stringy."

"Try it wiv yer veil off, ducky."

Woollcott said nothing but months later, at Christmas, his present to Margalo was the original Belcher drawing. He had remembered, and had gone to the trouble of getting it from London.

Woollcott's generosity, and the entire Round Table's, overflowed in a backhanded fashion to another young actress, too, in the early days. The actress was Tallulah Bankhead, who, apart from a job understudying Constance Binney in *39 East,* had not yet done much in the theatre and was continuously broke. Tallulah was known as The Great Maw because, lacking cash to buy her own lunches, she would circle the table scooping up a taste of this and that from each plate until she had made a comfortable meal. She had one dress, a black satin number which she wore with an air but wore daily— and black satin is not the most durable material for

§ 48 §

Actresses, Attitudes, and Other High Ideals

constant wear. When it began to turn gray the Round Table voted, to a man, to take up a collection to buy her a new dress. The deal fell through when Tallulah thanked them emotionally but said she would just as soon settle for a penny, because she *had* four cents and needed one more to make up a nickel for carfare.

Not all of the Round Table actresses were beginners. Ina Claire, already a recognized star, was a great favorite, being a fast and funny talker. Miss Claire, however, fell from grace with the Vicious Circle for a time, owing to a somewhat lofty reference she made to a beau of hers, one Prince Frederick of Lichtenstein. The Round Table had an honest loathing for any form of snobbery or pretentiousness, or for what seemed to them to be affectation. For this reason they unitedly disliked a certain producer, Jed Harris, a man of unpredictable and showy gestures. There is a familiar but illuminating story about the time George Kaufman was summoned to Harris's office on business and was received by the producer in the nude. Kaufman regarded him in silence for a moment, then quietly said, "Mr. Harris, your fly is open." It is interesting to record, in this connection, that Ina Claire was restored to favor at the Round Table only when she was able to announce with some pleasure that she had kicked Jed Harris in the stomach.

It seems that she was rehearsing in a Harris production and at one rehearsal Harris had come up on stage before the assembled company and, using her real name, had said, "Miss Fagan, you stink." With Miss Claire, to think is to act. "I grabbed him by the arm,

§ 49 §

THE VICIOUS CIRCLE

like *this*," she related afterward, grabbing a Round Tabler by the arm, "and then I *threw* him onto the floor . . . " By this time her interested listener had to hold on to something to keep standing up. "And then," Miss Claire said dramatically, lifting a dainty shoe, "I *kicked* him. And *good*."

The Round Tablers never tired of this recital— at least not for weeks. When someone appeared who hadn't heard it they would say to Ina, "Tell him what you did to Jed Harris" in much the same way the old vaudeville comedian used to urge his punch-drunk partner to "tell 'em what you did to Philadelphia Jack O'Brien." Ina was always ready to be the other half of the act. "I grabbed him by the arm, like *this*," she'd say, getting a wrestle-hold on the startled newcomer, "and then I *threw* him down on the floor, like *this* . . ." Somebody usually caught the guy somewhere between Miss Claire's blazing blue eyes and the Algonquin's hardwood floor.

One day, while the gag was still fresh, things turned out just right for the boys when Johnny Weaver came in on the heels of Ina Claire. Johnny had a way of being smart to his betters, and the Round Table often felt a need of putting him in his place. "Ina," they urged with one voice, "show Weaver what you did to Jed Harris." Ina got an arm-lock on Johnny. "I grabbed him like *this*," she said, "and then I threw him on the floor like *this* . . . " Johnny weighed about a hundred and twenty pounds, and when Ina threw him on the floor, he lay there. Presently he struggled to a sitting position

§ 50 §

Actresses, Attitudes, and Other High Ideals

and looked up into Miss Claire's triumphant young face. "Listen, Mom," he said, "put on your glasses and let's fight fair!"

That was the end of that gag. And Weaver was the hero of the Table for several days. They always loved the man who had said the latest funny thing, and they loved him more if he had suffered slightly about it in a plain, unaffected way.

Perhaps it is odd that they should have loved anything that was unaffected, even unaffected horseplay, and hated all affectations when, to any onlooker, they must have seemed full of affectations themselves. Ross still sported his inch-and-a-half crew cut—a growth so high and luxuriant that Ina Claire, one Spring day, remarked vibrantly to Father, "Frank, I feel so wonderful I'd like to take off my shoes and stockings and wade in Ross's hair!" Broun's personal untidiness was so startling that a passer-by once handed him a dime outside the Algonquin. Adams looked like a benevolent vulture and habitually greeted bosom friends and acquaintances alike by rearing his head back, dilating his nostrils, and saying exactly nothing—which gave some people the idea that he was not cordial. Sherwood and Kaufman were both so shy that they even delivered wisecracks at lunch with their eyes on their plates, and seldom looked anyone in the eye. Woollcott, of course, was bursting with mannerisms. He wore a scarlet-lined opera cape to opening nights, and he was a revolving luncher. He would poise a good-sized morsel on his fork in mid-air, then rotate rapidly to the right and to the left

§ 51 §

THE VICIOUS CIRCLE

in a series of small bounces, his eyes snapping behind thick lenses as he cased the joint. Somehow the fork always remained stationary until he returned to dead center and bolted the food off it with a birdlike thrust of the head.

As for the girls at the Table . . . aside from the actresses, they were feminists, suffragettes, "career" women, and poets; and one lady member of the group so often tried to do away with herself on account of her complicated affairs of the heart that the sheer number of her attempted suicides amounted to an affectation in itself. The fifth or sixth time this romanticist had been rushed to a 'hospital and returned pale and shaken, Benchley offered her a word of advice. "You want to go easy on this suicide stuff," he said kindly. "First thing you know, you'll ruin your health."

And yet these sometimes comic exteriors and affectations concealed the souls of passionate perfectionists, of crusaders in their own way. The common, unspoken ideal was what bound them together and what made them, in the end, a lasting influence on American writing, American humor, and the American theatre. That influence deserves a chapter to itself, and will get it later. It is enough now, I think, to describe how exacting they were with one another—and also how unselfconscious—in the days before they became an Influence.

The truth is, I think, that the Round Tablers behaved—at least in the beginning—in whatever way came naturally to them, and were unaware of any unusual effect on the beholder. The only reason Woollcott put

§ 52 §

Actresses, Attitudes, and Other High Ideals

on airs from the first was that he was a born poseur, and had happily posed from the age of three. It came natu- rally to him. The Vicious Circle, furthermore, was made up of creative people and therefore pretty intricately constituted, for it is nonsense to say that a person who writes or paints or acts is no different from one who sells hardware; he has to act different because he *feels* dif- ferent, and the reason he feels different is simply that he was born to react to everything in an unusual way. It isn't his fault, any more than it's the hardware salesman's fault for reacting normally and remaining a hardware salesman. Each one is doing what comes naturally.

It's a good bet that whatever eccentricity of manner or appearance the Round Tablers had was unconscious, partly for that reason, and partly because eccentricity in itself did not interest them. What interested each mem- ber of the Vicious Circle was his own work, his friends' work, anybody else's work that was any good, and— always—the common, unspoken standard of perfection.

They had no use for shoddy work of any kind, and no evidence of carelessness was too small to escape their relentless eye. Their weapon was humor, more effective than any amount of noble reproof. When Woollcott noticed that William A. Brady, the producer, was economizing by using the same scenery in successive productions, he wrote a series of hilarious and insulting articles in the *Times* calling Brady a balloon-chested miser and other things and demanding that he loosen up and buy a new stage set. After several weeks of Wooll- cott, Brady *did.* Franklin P. Adams for years waged a

§ 53 §

THE VICIOUS CIRCLE

one-man war against the improper use of "who" and "whom." Whenever he was cut to the quick by this mistake in print somewhere, he would quote the offending passage in "The Conning Tower" with the one-line comment: " 'Whom are you?' said Cyril." Adams's knowledge of Latin and Greek led him to respect the English language, a product of both, and he believed that, as with any other tool, no one should set out to use it without first knowing how.

Accuracy was another thing the Round Table writers demanded of themselves and of other writers, not only in print but in casual conversation. They were quick to pounce on a misquotation or a careless reference from a companion, and Woollcott and Adams once carried on an argument for a whole lunch-hour over the name of a character in a song nobody else had ever heard of. Woollcott, talking away, mentioned "bright Alfaretta" and was instantly transfixed by Adams's slow, accusing stare.

"The name," Adams said, "is *Alfarata*.' It comes from a song called 'The Blue Juniata' that goes like this . . . [Adams warbled a few bars] 'Wild roved an Indian girl, bright Alfarata . . . ' See? Name rhymes with 'Juniata.' "

Woollcott was hard to convince, especially when he was wrong, so a bet was made, five dollars was put up, and the combatants retired to their reference books. Adams was right—it *was* "Alfarata," of course. Adams was seldom wrong.

The Round Table also condemned any over-fond

§ 54 §

Actresses, Attitudes, and Other High Ideals

addiction to a word that resulted in the word becoming trite. They hated "lovely," "sweet," "nice," "terrible," "awful," and all other words that indicated a poverty-stricken vocabulary. One day Heywood Broun arrived for lunch, a great, rumpled, plaintive, and curiously charming man, and leaning his head upon his hand, remarked that he was sick and tired of the way writers everywhere had gone crazy over the word "wistful."

"I keep reading about this 'wistful' actress, this 'wistful' novel, this 'wistful' bit of nostalgia," he complained. "If they have to be 'wistful' why can't they get a book of synonyms and look up a good clean name for it?"

Woollcott listened, fork poised and eyes snapping. As it happened, "wistful" was one of his own pet words. Finally he spoke, his glance raking Broun's engaging bulk.

"Coming from one who, during his entire adult life, has bumped along on the flat wheel of wistfulness," he observed shrewishly, "I find this capsule critique ill-advised."

The Round Table's preoccupation with words, grammar, and accuracy among themselves was the first faint trace of the influence they were to have on American writing as a whole. Such passion is contagious. And since the editors and writers at the Round Table would have nothing to do with any writing that wasn't perfect—or as nearly perfect as possible—a good many even younger writers began trying harder. And writing in general began to get better.

§ 55 §

THE VICIOUS CIRCLE

From my own knowledge I can cite *The New Yorker* magazine as one example of this all-over improvement. Most people agree that the *New Yorker* is a well-written and accurate publication; that is its foundation—the humor and the gags are just the cherry on top, really. Contrary to some rumors, the *New Yorker* is *not* "all written in the office." It is written, and doggedly re-written, by writers who are, every one, trying to come up to the standard of Harold Ross, its editor, and the standard he has trained them to expect of themselves.

Ross has a profound insistence on accuracy, good grammar, and the proper use of a word. Probably he always had it, but I think his instinct was developed and intensified by his association with the Round Table.

I do know, from experience, that Ross's passion for perfection has so infected his writers that a simple "Jesus!" scrawled by the master in the margin of a manuscript is enough to explain fully to any *New Yorker* writer just what is the matter with that word, that line, or possibly that entire paragraph.

A writer doing a piece for the *New Yorker* automatically works more carefully than he does on a piece for any other magazine. (That may be why few free lancers can work for the *New Yorker* steadily—they get comma-conscious.) The writer knows Ross's standards, and his own leap up to meet them. Yet he also knows that, no matter how good the piece seems to him when he submits it, it won't be good enough for Ross. The best he can hope for, if he writes it as well as he possibly

§ 56 §

Actresses, Attitudes, and Other High Ideals

can, is that he will have to rewrite it only once or twice instead of five or six times.

This is hard work, but—as anyone will tell you who has ever had a piece in *The New Yorker*—it is immensely rewarding. Writers worship Ross for the slavish attention he gives to every manuscript. And they respect him, too, as an editor who sees no reason why, if a writer can write a good line spontaneously, he can't write it even better the tenth time he tries.

§ 57 §

CHAPTER FOUR

Crusaders and Infracaninophiles

THE QUESTION that most people of this generation ask about the Round Table is "Why was it important?" and it's a hard question to answer. Almost anybody can explain the Golden Age in Elizabethan England or the Renaissance in Italy; they are far away and history has sharpened the perspective. People can also explain the 1929 stock-market crash and the 1930's depression. They are closer to home and, besides, disasters are always easier to analyze than blessings; everybody has an explanation for a disaster, but nobody can explain a miracle . . . or a renaissance that has taken place under their own eyes.

The Round Table symbolized an American Renaissance, I think, (although any member of it would probably have pulled a knife on me for suggesting anything so highfalutin). Its influence on American literature, drama, and humor was acute, untiring and permament for two reasons. First, the people who sat at the Round Table were interesting people whose doings and

§ 59 §

THE VICIOUS CIRCLE

sayings caught and held public attention; and secondly, they were as brave, mentally, as any dashing medieval cavalier was physically brave. They not only encouraged everything that was shiningly good; they were ready, at the risk of losing jobs, money, or friends, to fight to the death against anything that was, according to their standards, bad.

They had a good deal to fight against, in the early 1920's. The postwar intellectual level was low. People were reading *The Sheik* and crowding in by the thousands to see Miss Ann Nichols's masterpiece, the play called *Abie's Irish Rose.* The Round Tablers shrugged at *The Sheik,* but the theatre was in their hearts and they winced away from *Abie's Irish Rose* in loud bursts of print throughout the play's six-year run. Benchley in particular doggedly ran his own little wailing wall of comment about it every week in *Life's* play directory . . . I quote a few of his weekly remarks down the long years:

1922

Something awful.

Among the season's worst.

Eighty-ton fun.

Made up of jokes from the files of "Puck" when McKinley was running for President the first time.

Showing that people will laugh at anything.

People laugh at this every night, which explains why a democracy can never be a success.

§ 60 §

Crusaders and Infracaninophiles

Just about as low as good, clean fun can get.

Contains everything of the period except a character who says "Skiddoo."

The comic spirit of 1876.

Well, it seems there was a Jew and an Irishman walking down the street . . .

1923

Denounced continuously as cheap by this department since last May, but apparently unconscious of the fact.

The management sent us some pencils for Christmas; so maybe it isn't so bad after all.

We give up.

Where do the people come from who keep this going? You don't see them out in the daytime.

All right if you never went beyond the fourth grade.

The fact that there are enough people in New York to keep this going explains why Hylan is Mayor of New York.

Let's not talk about it.

A year old this week, in spite of all we could do.

Our favorite.

Showing that there is a place for everything in this best of all possible worlds.

Having knocked this show unsuccessfully for over a year, a few weeks ago we tried to kill it by kindness and announced it as "our favorite." Several patrons have written in, having taken us seriously. We will,

THE VICIOUS CIRCLE

therefore, refund the price of two tickets or its equivalent in garden truck to any one whose evening was spoiled by our innocent joke.*

Terrible.

America's favorite comedy, which accounts for the number of shaved necks on the streets.

Judging from the thousands who see and like this play, Henry Ford has a good chance of being our next President.

1924

Happy New Year!

In another two or three years we'll have this play driven out of town.　　·

Probably the finest and most stimulating play ever written by an American. (Now let's see what *that* will do.)

Next week this goes under the heading of "More or Less Serious."

Well, here's the warm weather again.

So we said to him, "George, you can't expect us to do everything in this office, and besides . . ."

And that, my dears, is how Old Doctor Radish came to peep out from under the ground and show his red cheeks to you and me.

The play which made Edwin Booth famous.

For the best comment to go in this space, we will give two tickets to the play.

* To one incensed reader who demanded a showdown, Benchley graciously had delivered a cartload of rutabagas and kale.

§ 62 §

Robert Benchley

Crusaders and Infracaninophiles

And a Merry Christmas to you, Miss Nichols!

1925

Contest for line closes at midnight, or at the latest, quarter past midnight, on Jan. 8. At present Mr. Arthur Marx is leading with "No worse than a bad cold."

We've got those old pains in the back coming on us again. Every spring we have them.

The month this opened (May, 1922) the editor of this department started growing a mustache. He has just shaved it off. Let's see what *that* will do. It's funny we didn't think of that before.

They put an end to the six-day bicycle races by tearing down Madison Square Garden. How about a nice, big office building on the present site of the Republic Theatre?

The oldest profession in the world.

There are 5,280 feet in a mile.

If this runs until May 22 it will have broken the record held by "Lightnin'" for length of run. We are as nervous as a witch. Suppose it should have to close on May 21!

The Phoenicians were among the earliest settlers of Britain.

Aw, shut up!

We will settle for $5000.

The big Michael Arlen hit.

There is no letter "w" in the French language.

Yes, sir, that's my Abie!

§ 65 §

THE VICIOUS CIRCLE

We might as well say it now as later. We don't like this play.

One, two, three, four, five, six, seven, eight, nine, ten.

See Hebrews 13: 8.*

1926

A sincere and thought-provoking handling of inter-racial conflict, shot through with native wit.

Viktusnak most mar nines maradasa otthon. Felt! az 6 Jani urfijat, hogy valami kart tesz magaban.

We see that earthquakes are predicted in these parts some time in the next seven years. Could it be that . . .

Closing soon. (Only fooling.)

And that, my dears, is how I came to marry your grandfather.

Not all of Benchley's crusades were so lighthearted. During the famous Sacco-Vanzetti case he had been one of the witnesses who came forth hotly to testify that he had heard the trial judge, Webster Thayer, speak improperly of the defendants outside of court. "I'll get the bastards good and proper," Judge Thayer declared one day in a Worcester, Massachusetts, golf club, according to Benchley.

The entire Round Table rose up in arms to protest the arrest and conviction of Sacco and Vanzetti, as indeed did thousands of other people in Europe and

* The quotation from Hebrews is: Jesus Christ the same yesterday, and today, and forever.

§ 66 §

Crusaders and Infracaninophiles

America. The case was a cause célèbre of the 'Twenties. As many of us remember, Sacco and Vanzetti were a Boston shoemaker and fishmonger who were tried, sentenced, and—after seven years in jail—finally electrocuted for the killing of a paymaster in a holdup. The two men were members of the anarchist party, and their defenders felt a deep conviction that not only were they innocent and the charge a frame-up, but that they had been convicted for their political beliefs.

The nearest thing to an anarchist at the Round Table was Heywood Broun, who was a Socialist, and what fired the group with a burning sense of injustice was not sympathy with the politics of Sacco and Vanzetti but an unshakable belief in the sacred right of any man to embrace whatever politics he desires. (It was simpler in those days, before the atom and hydrogen bombs.) With one accord the Round Tablers—notably Benchley, Dorothy Parker, Heywood Broun, and his wife, Ruth Hale—shouldered their banners and marched off to Boston to help organize the Sacco-Vanzetti Defense Committee.

Heywood Broun, after several years as sports writer, sports editor, drama critic, and columnist on the *Tribune,* had just gone to the *World,* in 1921, to write his column, "It Seems to Me," on the newly formed page opposite the editorial page—or Page Op. Ed., as it was affectionately called. Page Op. Ed., Herbert Bayard Swope's baby, became the most celebrated feature of the *World,* and carried, besides Broun's, the columns of F.P.A., Deems Taylor, Laurence Stallings, Alexander Woollcott, Frank

§ 67 §

THE VICIOUS CIRCLE

Sullivan, William Bolitho, and Robert Littell. With Rollin Kirby's cartoon and Walter Lippmann's editorial on the facing page, this section of the paper was the first thing every *World* reader turned to, to start his day right. Broun's salary on the *World* was $25,000 a year.

At thirty-three, Broun was a bewildering and bewildered, but peculiarly lovable, mass of contradictions. He was gently bred, slovenly of person, softhearted, steel-minded, evasive and direct, brave and terrified, considerate and tough, gregarious and solitary. His face, under its tangled crown of matted curls, had an intangible beauty of feature, and the soul enclosed in last week's laundry was, of course, the soul of a shining knight. Broun was the greatest of the infracaninophiles, or lovers of the underdog.

Although he weighed close to two hundred and fifty pounds of not-very-flabby flesh and doctors could find nothing wrong with him, he was an ardent hypochondriac. He had claustrophobia so severely that he had been obliged to give up his job as drama critic on the *Tribune* (his assistant, George S. Kaufman, succeeded him) because sitting in theatres suffocated him; trains frightened him for the same reason and he habitually took a taxi home to Stamford, Connecticut, when he lived there . . . the same taxi whose driver, Charlie Horowitz, was more or less permanently subsidized by Broun to drive him everywhere and wait for him outside night clubs, speakeasies, or newspaper offices, sometimes for six or seven hours at a time. Broun was also convinced that he had a bad heart and might drop down

§ 68 §

Crusaders and Infracaninophiles

dead at any minute, and his personal collection of cardiograms was the largest, certainly, of anyone in his set. "Why don't you hold a one-man show of those things some time?" Woollcott callously suggested one day when Broun turned up for lunch with a sheaf of new ones.

Broun had a fatal knack of easing himself into good jobs and fighting his way out of them, and it was to be no different with the *World*. He generally worked at home, in his bedroom in the big, untidy house he had bought on West 85th Street, and nearly always at night, claiming that the toxins of fatigue stimulated his mind. It took him only thirty or forty minutes to write his column because he had always thought it out and, more often than not, tried it out in conversation in his travels around the gin mills and night spots throughout the afternoon and evening. The bedroom which he used as an atelier was furnished with a big double bed in the center with two bridge lamps and a row of ashtrays on each side of it, and Broun worked mostly in or on this bed, refreshing himself now and then from a flask of his favorite gin-and-bitters. Across the room, a large bookcase was crowded with partly opened packages of books from publishers, and there was no other furniture in the room at all. Both Broun and his wife, Ruth Hale, had their minds on higher things than interior decoration, and Murdock Pemberton now insists that there was a long period during which the living room in the 85th Street house had no furniture whatever. Other friends of Broun's recall with some nostalgia that, for a whole year, the bathroom had no door.

§ 69 §

THE VICIOUS CIRCLE

Broun's trouble with the *World* began—and ended —with the Sacco-Vanzetti case. As his interest in it and his passionate rejection of the verdict grew and strengthened, he naturally wrote more columns about it. He had come to know and like the two men, and his arguments were no longer for abstract justice but, more compellingly, for the righting of a wrong done to two innocent victims of a machine. The *World,* trying to take a properly objective view, encouraged its editorial writer, Walter Lippmann, to urge a new trial, but "on the ground of mercy" and with the rather cringing rider, "We do not question and we never have questioned the rectitude of the Governor and his advisory committee." Soon the Broun and Lippmann columns were opposed in other ways than typographically, and before long Broun's column began to be cut by the editors, and sometimes dropped altogether.

Broun now had another cause to champion—the freedom of the press. He felt that he should be free to write as he pleased . . . that all writers should, even Walter Lippmann. But to cut or omit a column of his on Sacco and Vanzetti while leaving intact Lippmann's column on the same subject seemed to him an infringement of one of his dearest ideals—the freedom of the press. He had a few things to say about that too, in his column, and Ralph Pulitzer, the *World's* publisher, began jumping up and down.

When all appeals failed and Sacco and Vanzetti were executed, in 1927, Broun wrote: "They are too bright, we shield our eyes and kill them. We are the

§ 70 §

HEYWOOD BROUN

Crusaders and Infracaninophiles

dead, and in us there is no feeling nor imagination nor the terrible torment of lust for justice. And in the city where we sleep smug gardeners walk to keep the grass above our little houses sleek and cut whatever blade thrusts up a head above its fellows." The *World* printed this column, and a second one the following day, but omitted the next four, explaining in a box on Page Op. Ed. that Broun had ignored instructions to select other topics than Sacco and Vanzetti and that the editors maintained their right of final decision as to what would be published in their columns. Broun sent a telegram from Connecticut saying he was on strike. He stayed away for four and a half months until Herbert Bayard Swope, returning from Europe, patched up a kind of peace and wooed Heywood back onto Page Op. Ed. All might have been well had not Broun, another four months later, written a piece in *The Nation* proclaiming the need for a great liberal newspaper—one that could venture into "the vast territory which lies between the radical press and the New York *World*." He accused the *World* of lacking courage, tenacity, and guts, and of being—along with the rest of the press—terrified of the Catholic Church. "There is not a single New York editor," he wrote, "who does not live in mortal terror of the power of this group. Of course, if anybody dared, nothing in the world would happen. If the church can bluff its way into a preferred position the fault lies not with the Catholic Church but with the editors. . . . Perhaps the first thing needed for a liberal paper is capital, but even more important is courage."

§ 73 §

THE VICIOUS CIRCLE

That did it. Next day, in place of Broun's column on Page Op. Ed., this notice appeared: "The *World* has decided to dispense with the services of Heywood Broun. His disloyalty to this paper makes any further association impossible." As usual with Broun, the knight had tangled with the dragon and got slightly scorched. Broun didn't know he was fired until he saw the announcement.

Another of Broun's crusades eventually proved more successful, and is, in fact, his most enduring monument; this is the American Newspaper Guild (affiliated with the CIO). The story of the Guild has been told elsewhere by Morris L. Ernst and Dale Kramer, among others; it is enough to say here that before it was organized newspaper men were overworked and underpaid and in other ways pretty well exploited by employers who besought them to take comfort in the romance of their calling and the glory of an occasional by-line. The free granting of the by-line in the 'Twenties was actually attributed to the Round Table—by my father, at any rate. "It stands to reason," Father pointed out, "that when editors and publishers began to see the help's wisecracks quoted in rival papers they simply said, 'Look, kids, we'll give you full credit too, if you'll just scatter your pearls closer to home.'" But by-lines and glamour do not buy meat and potatoes, as Broun well knew.

He himself, in spite of his success and big salary, had suffered from the one-sided agreements then prevalent in the newspaper business; his contract with the *World* had stipulated that if he quit he could be re-

§ 74 §

Crusaders and Infracaninophiles

strained from working for any other paper for a period of three years. And he had seen thirty-five-dollar-a-week reporters who had offended the bosses on some matter of policy banished to writing obits at even smaller pay. When Lewis Gannett telephoned him, one day in 1921, and proposed a journalists' union, Broun was ready to do battle for the cause. The Guild was not fully organized, with Broun as national president, until some ten years later, but the seed was sown that day. In the intervening time, Broun made frequent and colorful trips all over the country, making speeches, organizing membership, getting thrown into jail, and marching in another picket line as soon as he got out. For a basically terrified man, he was extraordinarily brave in picket lines. On at least one occasion, when a strikebreaker came out of a newspaper office convoyed by two armed and powerful-looking bodyguards, Broun quietly swept the bodyguards aside, took the scab by the elbow, and said, "Look here, I want to talk to you."

Broun never worked on one crusade at a time—he always had half a dozen going. In his years on the *Tribune,* the *World,* and later the *Telegram* and *World-Telegram,* he was consistently and passionately against censorship, bad manners on the dance floor (to the extent of getting in fist fights on the dance floor with anyone who practiced them), John Roach Straton, Nicholas Murray Butler, badly written books, badly written plays, and using dirty words in the presence of ladies. He was *for* a free press, courteous behavior at all times, Eugene V. Debs, Sacco and Vanzetti, good books,

§ 75 §

THE VICIOUS CIRCLE

good plays, and the use of four-letter words in literature if they improved the quality of the work. Like the rest of the Round Tablers, he would go to bat instantly for anything he thought was good, and he once wrote a review of John Dos Passos' *Three Soldiers* and twisted the arm of the Sunday *Times* Book Supplement (which had already published one review) until they featured it on Page One, because the first review had been unfavorable and Broun thought the book deserved better.

Nobody at the Round Table was ever alone in any crusade, their sympathies were too close and infectious, and Broun was never alone in his. He and Aleck Woollcott, for example, joined up to demand—in their columns and, later, in their radio broadcasts—an audience for Ernest Hemingway, Floyd Dell, John V. A. Weaver, F. Scott Fitzgerald, and many other new writers. Publishers will tell you now that Broun and Woollcott, individually or together, could sell more books than any critic and commentator had ever sold before, or—with the possible exception of Walter Winchell—has ever been able to sell since. There was, of course, no Winchell in the early 'Twenties; Winchell was still hoofing in vaudeville until he went to work for the *Graphic*, in 1924, with a column of lightweight gossip.

Woollcott, too, was a passionate crusader, although not built for it. (It was one of his close friends who likened him, during his intense moments, to a butterfly in heat.) Besides, nobody could ever be sure just what Woollcott would be crusading for next. He could, and did, shout as loud in praise of *Good-Bye, Mr. Chips* as

§ 76 §

Crusaders and Infracaninophiles

in acknowledgment of *The Sun Also Rises.* Often, becoming nostalgic, he wrote so fulsomely in favor of *Little Women* that the Round Table declared, to a man, that by God, he was likely to put that book over sooner or later. Howard Dietz, a frequent member of the group, even took to calling him "Louisa M. Woollcott." But Woollcott's voice was powerful and his intentions honest, and that was true of many other members of the Round Table as well.

F.P.A., for example—whenever he wasn't fussing away at imperfect prose wherever he met it—waged a campaign in his column against illegible or obscure house numbers in New York. Pity the poor delivery man, he wrote again and again. He also inveighed in print against householders who swept their sidewalks with a dry broom, wafting germs to the nose of the passer-by. He pointed out that city ordinances already forbade these evils, and that the city ordinances were ignored. When his frequent reproaches in "The Conning Tower" brought no results from the authorities, Adams started a department in his column headed "Nothing Will Ever Happen." This section was concerned with civic annoyances such as illegible house numbers and dry sweeping, and it also carried a repeated plea which strikes even more poignantly now at the hearts of 1951 New Yorkers . . . that theatre managers and ticket brokers get together and stop gouging the public on the price of theatre tickets. The fact that theatre tickets, in the 'Twenties, cost a fast $3.30 top for most shows, with a broker's fee of fifty cents, was

§ 77 §

THE VICIOUS CIRCLE

not the point; a principle was involved, and Adams's gauntlet was ready.

Adams, today, says that his campaigns got nowhere. "I said nothing would happen, and nothing *did* happen," he reminds you, with the mournful ferocity that is his usual tone. But failure never discouraged a Round Tabler for long.

When the members of the Vicious Circle were not crusading about something outside their particular fields, their own work amounted to a crusade against everything that was phony, pretentious, or untrue, and moreover, it established a standard of excellence that turned out to be enduring. Benchley was probably the first satirist to proclaim, with a kind of comic despair, the fallibility of Twentieth-Century Man; and Donald Ogden Stewart, who often lunched with the group, was among the first to debunk social climbers, in *Mr. and Mrs. Haddock Abroad*. Frank Sullivan, another frequent luncher, loved to prick the balloons of pretentiousness, as he still does in his "Cliché Expert" pieces. Dorothy Parker's poems crisply put love and infatuation where they separately belonged (a thing Mrs. Parker seemed personally unable to do). And Edna Ferber, although no satirist, was also a pioneer; with the able assistance of Jerome Kern and others, *Showboat*, the musical adapted from her novel, surely helped create the modern operetta or *good* play with music which was to banish forever the old-fashioned loosely strung True Story Romance interspersed with songs and dances.

Perhaps these boys and girls accomplished no more

§ 78 §

Crusaders and Infracaninophiles

than any gifted and active individual now accomplishes. The point is that these gifted and active individuals were all members of the same group, and that this group was merely a casual, unorganized gathering of friends who met at the Round Table for no more serious purpose than their enjoyment of one another.

One thing is certain: nothing like the Round Table —for color, interest, and lasting influence—had ever been seen before; and nothing like it has been known since.

§ 79 §

CHAPTER FIVE

Fun and Feuds

THE ROUND TABLE boys and girls were great ones for games of all kinds. They loved word games and quiz games, and would sit up all night in somebody's apartment playing anagrams or Twenty Questions, or inventing questions of fact to toss at one another. This was long before crossword puzzles became popular, or quizzes came to be a paying proposition on the radio, with maid service for a year and a trip to Bermuda for anyone who could pin down by name The Father of His Country.

I never saw an all-Round-Table word game or quiz, but I used to love it when Frank Adams or Bob Benchley came to Sag Harbor, where we lived in the summer, because Father and I were also great ones for this sport and we were sure to have a fine, tough session after dinner, on the veranda looking out over Shelter Island Sound while the moon came up. We called our favorite game "Animal, Vegetable, or Mineral," and we allowed only fifteen questions . . . except when things got hilarious and everybody lost count.

§ 81 §

THE VICIOUS CIRCLE

Our subjects were tough. We liked to get hold of something that was all three—animal, vegetable, *and* mineral—like Donner Pass (the bones of the victims were the animal part); or something that was *none* of the three, like a sense of humor or the soul of the Angel Gabriel; or something that was mineral and possibly also animal and vegetable, like the moon or the planet Mars. Father was a wizard at this game, and one of the few times we stumped him was with a simple subject. We chose the Kaiser's mustache.

In our game one person was challenged to guess the subject, from questions he asked a circle of challengers. The rule (alas, not enforced by radio's Twenty Questions nowadays) was that you had only one direct guess; you could say only *once* "Is it so-and-so" and if you missed on your one guess you were out of the game. The idea was to narrow the thing down by sharp questioning and deductive reasoning until there could be only one possible answer. No guesses.

Father narrowed it down to part of the Kaiser's head in about nine questions, and set out to locate it.

"Is it above his nose?"

"No."

"Is it below his mouth?"

"No."

"It's below his nose."

"Yes."

"*Not* below his mouth."

"No."

Pause, while Pa obviously struggled not to ask "Is

§ 82 §

Fun and Feuds

it his mouth?" To ask the direct question would have put him out of the game if it was wrong. Finally he lost his mind and came out with:

"Is it above his Adam's apple?" (He had already located it on the Kaiser's head.)

We clucked our tongues and gazed sadly at each other.

"I never heard of the Kaiser having an Adam's apple, did you, Margaret?" Frank Adams asked me.

"They just don't mention it, I guess," I said.

"It would make a good subject some time," Frank mused. "Would it be animal, vegetable, or mineral?"

"Oh, I give UP!" Father shouted.

We never let him forget the Kaiser's mustache— not for years, anyway. When he later grew a mustache of his own, a rather weedy affair at first, we would gather around him, staring at it in wonderment, poking it a little, and asking of one another in hushed tones, "Is it animal, vegetable, or mineral?"

Sometimes, in our game, if somebody thought of a good subject and wanted to play it alone, he could challenge the rest of the company with it. One of my happiest memories is of one evening on the porch at Sag Harbor when Bob Benchley challenged the company with his own, secret subject. It was animal, he said, just plain animal.

We narrowed it down to everything possible, and then gave up.

"It's the feeling I get," Benchley said politely to Father, "when I look at your growing daughter."

§ 83 §

THE VICIOUS CIRCLE

The Round Tablers loved poker, and their regular Saturday games, lasting often from Saturday noon till Monday, will have a chapter to themselves later on in this book. They were so addicted to croquet that they played on the public grounds—the Sheep Meadow in Central Park—until they got to know Herbert Bayard Swope and other people rich enough to have country places with croquet grounds, or got so prosperous themselves that they could murder each other under their own wickets. Their croquet games were violent affairs involving trickery, touchiness, and torn feelings. Their croquet was a kind of ferocious golf, with the wrong tools, and no limits. Once, when Woollcott drove Harpo Marx's ball into the woods for the third time, Bea Kaufman found Harpo sobbing his heart out against a tree. Another time, the entire Round Table stopped speaking to Harold Ross for almost a week because he had shoved his ball with his foot. What they objected to was not his cheating at croquet, but his insufferable air of innocence as he looked up, caught in the act, and inquired, "But aren't you supposed to?"

What the Round Tablers liked best of all was Charades, because it gave them an opportunity to act out loud all over the place. All writers are frustrated actors, and all actors and actresses are crazy about acting too, even when they are not getting paid for it. Some geniuses do not recognize this fact. One day, Jascha Heifetz, a guest at the Round Table, complained bitterly to the girl on his left that he was too often asked to play the violin when he was invited out socially. The girl on his

§ 84 §

Fun and Feuds

left was Myra Hampton, a pretty young actress who frequently joined the Vicious Circle.

"How would *you* feel," Heifetz demanded of Myra, "if every time *you* were invited out to dinner, they asked you to get up and *act?*"

Myra gazed at him limpidly.

"I'd love it," she said.

Charades was not a practical game for the Algonquin Rose Room, so it was usually played in the evenings when the group reassembled at somebody's house or apartment, as it often did. The Round Table so often reassembled in the evenings, in fact, that Noel Coward, once meeting the same group of people intact three times in one day in three different places, wonderingly inquired, "But don't they ever see anyone bloody *else?*" Coward became a roving member of the Vicious Circle with his first success, *The Vortex*, in 1927, and at one time—it is said—even fought with Woollcott over the role of an old witch in a charade.

Charades, under the Vicious Circle's lively touch, grew to be much more than the simple acting out of syllables. It became so intense a production, involving so much shouting and argument, that Neysa McMein, the painter and glamour girl of the group, at last crisply wrote down some rules to be adhered to. Her rules are just about the same rules we all use now when we go in for that popular pastime known as The Game.

Sometimes, when the Round Tablers felt a particular need to do some real good acting, their charades developed into Scenes from Great Plays, enacted by the

§ 85 §

THE VICIOUS CIRCLE

group. One such vignette that all of them remember was the balcony scene from *Romeo and Juliet,* staged at Alice Duer Miller's apartment with Peggy Wood as Juliet—a very lovely Juliet—and Alexander Woollcott as perhaps the most remarkable Romeo in the history of the theatre. None of this was a gag, mind you; everybody did his best. And Peggy says that, if you shut your eyes, Woollcott was a very good Romeo.

Woollcott must have had his private tremors, however, because some years later, when he did another scene from *Romeo and Juliet* on his "Town Crier" radio program, with Helen Hayes as his guest star, Woollcott did not play the part of Romeo. Woollcott played the Nurse.

Woollcott's broadcasts remain green in the memory of his guest stars, for a particular reason. It was his habit, they recall with the kind of barbed affection the memory of Woollcott always inspires, to draw relentlessly on his circle of friends for guest artists, give them little or no pay, and never, under any circumstances, give them any billing. He would have Katharine Cornell, Helen Hayes, Lynn Fontanne and Alfred Lunt—all the big names in the world—and they all appeared anonymously as "your Surprise Guest for today, whose name I shall reveal at the end of the program." At the end of the program, with two seconds to go, Woollcott would proclaim, "And now I want you all to know that your Surprise Guest today was . . ." Every time, on the nose, the guest's name would fade into the voice of the announcer saying, "You have been listening to Alexander Woollcott, Your Town Crier." People say that Woollcott's belated timing was

§ 86 §

Fun and Feuds

perfect. One radio technician said recently, "It was Alexander Woollcott's show, and by God, no name was announced on that show but the name of Alexander Woollcott." He thought for a moment and added, "The bastard. God rest his soul."

With all this play acting, professional and otherwise, it was inevitable that the Round Table put on a show of its own, and this it did, in 1922.

One day at lunch J. M. Kerrigan, the actor, smarting over some adverse criticisms of his new play from Benchley, Woollcott, and Broun, said, "You fellows are all so smart—if you don't like the plays you go to see, why don't you put on a show yourselves?" To a stage-struck assembly like that one, the suggestion was straight from heaven. Nearly all of them had unexpected talents. They often held musical evenings at Neysa McMein's studio where, with Deems Taylor (or some upstart like Heifetz or Irving Berlin) at the piano, Benchley would play the mandolin, F.P.A. the flute, piccolo, or harmonica, and Mrs. Parker would perform expertly on the triangle. The rest would sing, and sometimes they allowed their friends Reinald Werrenrath, the baritone, and Paul Robeson to join in too. Bob Sherwood also was quite a singer, although it was not until the arrival of sound pictures that he developed his own theme song. This came about through an occupational hazard of his job as *Life's* movie critic. It seems that, in his rounds of the movie theatres, he kept running into a short featuring Al Jolson singing "When the Red, Red Robin Comes Bob, Bob, Bobbin' Along." After Sherwood had heard

§ 87 §

THE VICIOUS CIRCLE

"The Red, Red Robin" some eight or nine times in one week, the song began to haunt, or madden, him, and one evening at a party with the Marx Brothers he was inspired to render it. The Marx Brothers were so enchanted that they helped him, then and there, work up a little dance to go with it, involving business with a hat and cane. The sight of Sherwood's six-feet-seven Lincolnian frame strutting to this perky little tune is so remarkable that he is still called upon for a performance at all social gatherings.

Not all the Round Table's outside talents were musical. Marc Connelly gave recitations with gestures, two of the favorites being a poem called "You Ask Me About the Crimea" and another, "Barbara Frietchie," which included, when Marc came to the line "Clear in the cool September morn," a gesture depicting the well-known work of art, "September Morn." Bob Benchley, one night at Neysa's, entertained his friends with an imitation of a country-club treasurer making a report of money taken in at a charity bazaar. This, of course, became Benchley's famous "Treasurer's Report" which he later did professionally in *The Music Box Revue of 1926* and in the movies.

The Round Table show was called *No Sirree!*—a pun on *Chauve Souris,* a Russian revue that was popular that season—and had its first and only performance at the 49th Street Theatre on a Sunday night in April, 1922. All the parts were played by the Round Tablers, who also wrote the sketches and lyrics. The program, mostly written by Marc Connelly, is worth reprinting (the footnotes are mine):

§ 88 §

NO SIRREE!

An Anonymous Entertainment by the Vicious Circle
of the
Hotel Algonquin
49th Street Theatre
Sunday Evening, April 30th, 1922
(Theatre by courtesy of the Messrs. Shubert)

Spirit of the American Drama ...... Heywood Broun

OPENING CHORUS *

Alexander Woollcott, John Peter Toohey, Robert C. Benchley, George S. Kaufman, Marc Connelly and Franklin P. Adams

"THE EDITOR REGRETS . . ." **

Mabel Cenci	....	Marc Connelly, '25
George Medici	....	J. M. Kerrigan, '26
A Composer-Author	....	Donald Ogden Stewart, '25
Dante	....	Harold Gould, '28
An Average Male Reader	....	Henry Wise Miller, '22
An Average Female Reader	....	Mary Brandon, '30

Venice at the time of Dante. The editorial offices of "Droll Tales," a popular twice-a-month magazine which flourished at that period

* The "No Sirree!" authors came on in bathrobes and lyrically explained that they had written this show to suit themselves.
** Nobody now remembers what the dates mean, after the names of the players. It seemed a good idea at the time.

§ 89 §

THE FILMLESS MOVIES
Baron Ireland * and F. P. A.

THE GREASY HAG
An O'Neill Play in One Act

CAST
(In the order of appearance)

Elizabeth Inchcape, known as Coal-Barge Bessie, a retired water-front prostitute .... John Peter Toohey

The Murdered Woman .... Ruth Gillmore **

First Agitated Seaman .... George S. Kaufman

Second Agitated Seaman .... Alexander Woollcott

Third Agitated Seaman .... Marc Connelly

Scene

Vote for One

Backroom of Billy the Bishop's saloon, near Coenties Slip, New York
Firemen's forecastle on a freighter bound east from Rio

Time—The present

Incidental music by Arthur Samuels

---

* Nate Salsbury, son of the manager of Buffalo Bill and a frequent contributor to "The Conning Tower."
** Sister of Margalo, also an actress.

§ 90 §

HE WHO GETS FLAPPED *

With Robert E. Sherwood and the following ingenues: June Walker, Winifred Lenihan, Juliet St. John Brenon, Tallulah Bankhead, Mary Kennedy, Ruth Gillmore, Lenore Ulric, Helen Hayes and Mary Brandon

BETWEEN THE ACTS **

The Manager	. . . .	Brock Pemberton
The Manager's Brother	. . . .	Murdock Pemberton

And the following first nighters: Dorothy Parker, Alice Duer Miller, Neysa McMein, Beatrice Kaufman, Jane Grant, Heywood Broun, Alexander Woollcott, Robert C. Benchley, George S. Kaufman, Marc Connelly, Kelcey Allen, Arthur Bachrach

"JOHNNY WEAVER," a Ballad ***
Sung by Reinald Werrenrath

* This act presented Sherwood leaning nonchalantly against the proscenium surrounded by girls and singing Dorothy Parker's lyrics, "The Everlastin' Ingenue Blues":

> We've got the blues, we've got the blues, we believe we said
> before we've got the blues.
> We are little flappers, never growing up,
> And we've all of us been flapping since Belasco was a
> pup . . .

The unfamiliar names among the flappers were all young actresses romantically or intellectually connected with the Round Table. Mary Kennedy, for instance, later married Deems Taylor.

** Scene, a theatre lobby at intermission, with all the first nighters telling the producer how he should have put on his play. Kelcey Allen, drama critic of *Women's Wear,* and Arthur Bachrach, a constant first nighter who was in the wholesale tie business, were included for realism.

*** Parody on "Danny Deever" with the theme (what else?) "For they're hangin' Johnny Weaver in the mo-o-ornin!"

§ 91 §

BIG CASINO IS LITTLE CASINO *

A Samuel Shipman Play

(In Three Acts)

James W. Archibald (a Rich Man)	. . . .	John Peter Toohey
Dregs (a Butler)	. . . .	Alexander Woollcott
Mr. Harper (a Broker)	. . . .	J. M. Kerrigan
John Findlay (a Young Attorney)	. . . .	George S. Kaufman
O'Brien (a Detective)	. . . .	Franklin P. Adams
Margaret (Archibald's Daughter)	. . . .	Mary Kennedy
A Convict	. . . .	Marc Connelly
The Broker's Boy	. . . .	David H. Wallace
The Governor of New York	. . . .	Robert E. Sherwood
Guests	. . . .	Alice Duer Miller, Neysa McMein, Jane Grant

Synopsis of Scenes

ACT I—The Home of James W. Archibald

ACT II—The Same. A week later.

ACT III—A Wall Street Office. Two days later.

Offstage music by J. Heifetz

---

* Samuel Shipman wrote terribly explicit moral melodramas. Offstage music in this bouquet to Mr. Shipman *was* by Jascha Heifetz, and he *was* offstage. A more conspicuous musical contribution was by Irving Berlin, who was allowed to conduct the orchestra in the pit.

§ 92 §

Robert Sherwood, Irving Berlin, Marc Connelly

INTERMISSION

MARC CONNELLY *

"That Somewhat Different Cornettist"

—in—

"A NIGHT AT FRANK CAMPBELL'S"

Scene—Frank Campbell's   Time—Night

ZOWIE **

Or The Curse of an Akins Heart
(A Romanza in One Act)

"Nor all your piety and wit"—From the Persian

CAST

(In the order of appearance)

Marmaduke La Salle (a Stomach Specialist)	....	John Peter Toohey
Lady friend of La Salle's	....	Neysa McMein
Another lady friend of La Salle's	....	Louise Closser Hale
Dindo (a Wandering Busboy)	....	J. M. Kerrigan

* This act cannot be described, even by Marc. "I just gave a recitation," he says.

** Another happy-hearted take-off, this time on Zoë Akins who wrote very successful plays about woeful happenings in high society. Harold Ross, who played the taxi driver, had auditioned for many other parts but was deemed so inadequate an actor that he was finally given the role of Pip, who never appears.

§ 95 §

Zhoolie Venable (a Suppressed De-sire †)	....	Ruth Gillmore
Mortimer Van Loon (a Decayed Gen-tleman)	....	George S. Kauf-man
Archibald Van Al-styne (a Precision-ist)	....	Alexander Wooll-cott
Lemuel Pip (an Old Taxi Driver)	....	Harold Ross

Scene—A Capitol Lunch   Time—Printemps, 1922

† Suppressed in Humansville, Mo., sometime in April, 1908

Offstage music by J. Heifetz

MR. WHIM PASSES BY *
An A. A. Milne Play

Cynthia	....	Helen Hayes
Nigel	....	Sidney Blackmer
Uncle Tertius	....	J. M. Kerrigan

The scene is the morning room at the Acacias, Wipney-cum-Chiselickwick

---

* This needs no comment except one: the inclusion of Sidney Blackmer, the actor, goes to show that the Round Table got to know everyone sooner or later, and the entire cast of the sketch proves that they were not above accepting professional assistance as long as it didn't cost anything.

§ 96 §

SONG: "KAUFMAN AND CONNELLY
FROM THE WEST"

BEATRICE HERFORD
—in—
"The Algonquin Girl"

FINALE
by the entire company

Somehow left out of the printed program of *No Sirree!* was Benchley's "Treasurer's Report"—the only enduring thing in the show, although the Ziegfeld Follies did buy F.P.A.'s "Filmless Movies" in which Adams declaimed movie subtitles to the accompaniment of "mood music" by Baron Ireland at the piano. Baron Ireland, or Nate Salsbury, was a very musical young man, originally beloved by the Round Table as the composer of a ballad entitled "If I Had Of Knew What I'd Ought to Have Knew, I'd Never Have Did What I Done."

In presenting *No Sirree!* the Round Table performed a neat switch by inviting actors and actresses to serve as critics of the show, and the actors and actresses went happily to work. In *The New York Times* of May 1, 1922, Laurette Taylor wrote, in the space usually given to Woollcott:

> Last night at the 49th Street Theatre, the Russians turned the stage over to the critics, office boys, artists and managers and a few complexes.

§ 97 §

THE VICIOUS CIRCLE

They all gathered to show how it should be done, and being a constructive critic I would advise a course of voice culture for Marc Connelly, a new vest and pants that meet for Heywood Broun, a course with Yvette Guilbert for Alexander Woollcott, and I would advise them all to leave the stage before they take it up. A pen in their hands is mightier than God's most majestic word in their mouths.

Heywood Broun, appearing in front of the same curtain that held up Balieff, made me grateful that they had a resemblance at least in size. I had lost my program in the dark, and I couldn't stay for the finish, and I was late arriving. I realize that this conduct would not be tolerated on this particular paper, but I have seen it done on one other. The audience was not too awfully exclusive except in brains, so we had no trouble with the behavior there.

The first beautiful sight that met my eyes was Woollcott, Toohey, Benchley, Kaufman, Connelly and Adams in dishabille [sic] and, believe me, Mabel, it was terrible.

I do think that the performers were "competent," some of them "adequate" and others their usual selves. There was one gorgeous line in a play called *Zowie*—"My Darling, you are like the long-lost laughter of an unfrocked priest."

Everything was made fun of, from O'Neill

§ 98 §

Fun and Feuds

to William Brady's scenery. It really made me rather sad, but I am sure it was sitting in my seat and thinking the way I had always seen the critics look. I suppose there must have been some suppressed indignation in my heart to see the critics maligning my stage, just as there will be at my daring to sit and judge as a critic.

When a lot of people get together to fool or burlesque, there is one thing that is absolutely necessary, and that is a great sincerity. Ruth Gillmore, in a splendid imitation of Ethel Barrymore, made *Zowie* something that was really satire at its best, and the same way in the one-act play, *Mr. Whim Passes By*. Helen Hayes gave a splendid imitation of an English flapper. Neysa McMein was made up as a problem lady with silver stars embracing her brow and waist. Jascha Heifetz played offstage music off-key, and that's how the evening went—making fun of a fine writer, hitting the movie industry right in its middle, Heifetz playing off-key. A night that rather made me wish some people didn't have any sense of humor.

It was also an evening of the perpendicular pronoun, and I think the two who will come out of it the best now will be the ones that would have no nonsense but came downstage and sang, "I'm Kaufman, and that's Connelly." O, Marc, Marc, that you should have been born

§ 99 §

THE VICIOUS CIRCLE

again a Connelly, with a Kaufman instead of a Cleopatra.

Franklin P. Adams gave a humorous impression of an Irish detective called O'Brien. Reinald Werrenrath had a little burlesque of a song to sing, but, unlike Heifetz, he would not get down on all fours and play low. He placed his voice as though he was about to start an aria, sang his little burlesque, and encored with a beautiful song by Deems Taylor. I liked it so much that I am sure it was my night to be sentimental instead of humorous, and for the first time I thought of introducing a bill in Congress so that a critic could say, "It is not my serious night." It must be a comedy, or vice versa, because moods are terrible things to sit with for three hours and watch something that is not at all tuned in the same key or flashed in the same color taking place on the stage.

None of the authors put their names on the playlets, and I don't think there will be any extensive query as to who they were.

Robert Benchley came out and read, as far as I could understand it, the multiplication table, or perhaps it was a time table. It put me in mind of my checkbook the time I accused the bank of being short some $1900, and after many arguments the President, whom I know personally, went over my account and pointed out the fact that I had added in the date. Ever since

§ 100 §

Fun and Feuds

that I have hated figures. So, being a critic for for the moment, I suppose it is all right for me to say I don't like figures, so Benchley's monologue did not interest me. That's what one said about jazz, and I suppose you can say it about figures.

At one stage of the proceedings Heywood Broun said, "We have had a lot of fun, but so far the show has lacked charm." Alexander Woollcott came on with a yellow and red striped tie. Altogether, summing it up briefly, I should say it was a most amusing evening, but it didn't amuse me because I was all dressed up not to be amused.

Thus Laurette Taylor, whose satire became her less on the printed page than it did in person. It was Miss Taylor, you may remember, who gave some pithy advice to George Cukor, the movie director, on the set of *Little Women* when Cukor couldn't get his well-fed actresses to look hungry enough in the scene where they gave away their Christmas breakfast. "Oh God, George, forget the sausages and buns," Miss Taylor advised wearily. "Just tell the girls it's marijuana." It was also Miss Taylor who freely admitted that she went into seclusion with a bottle for some years after the death of her husband, J. Hartley Manners, and who finally emerged to say, in her unforgettable voice, "*Well* now! I sure went on the longest wake in history, didn't I?"

Nobody could be mad at Laurette Taylor, least of

§ 101 §

THE VICIOUS CIRCLE

all the Round Tablers, who admired and loved her. Yet, if you mention her review of *No Sirree!* to any one of them, to this day, he will say, "Oh, that was a *lousy* review—she didn't like it. Whyncha look up some of the *good* notices? I think there was one in the *World*, by some actor who liked the show."

The *World* review, in Heywood Broun's space, was by Wilton Lackaye, an actor and famous wit of the time who was then playing in *The Goldfish*.

Mr. Lackaye wrote:

Last night at the 49th Street Theatre Mr. Frank Case of the Algonquin Hotel gave an entertainment which, at one leap put him in the front rank of New York managers.* Of course it may be said that the members of the cast were habitués of his restaurant, and consequently he had an excellent idea of their capacity.**

It is indeed a labor of love to review this presentation, because it is the first time in our memory that criticism has been carried to its legitimate conclusion—that the critics may be criticized.

I was instructed, as a tyro, to follow the critical habit, to come late and leave before the performance was over. The best numbers on the program were those I didn't see.***

* Father had nothing to do, with it, of course: this was Lackaye humor, Mr. L. being an old friend of Pa's.
** Well, Wilton Lackaye was *so* a wit!
*** Catch on?

§ 102 §

Fun and Feuds

The names of the authors were not given, a thing to be regretted, because the burlesques were admirably written—the acting, well, however.

I thought *Big Casino* unduly flattered Mr. Samuel Shipman, and *Zowie* was not as good as Miss Akins's best work.

Mr. Heywood Broun was the Joe Humphreys * of the occasion. His patter was more consciously funny than Mr. Humphreys's, his elocution not so good. However, this was atoned for by his personal charm, which not only captured the audience but aroused such enthusiam in Miss Ruth Hale, who sat in front, that she was almost willing to acknowledge herself Mrs. Broun.** Mr. Walter Kingsley,*** who permeated the lobby, will be able to report to Mr. Albee **** his discovery of several vaudeville specialties, the introduction of which would be the crowning effort of the Keith Memorial Week:

Baron Ireland and F.P.A., who made a wonderful act; Messrs. Kaufman and Connelly, who established that the Middle West's loss was New York's gain, and Mr. Robert Benchley

* Famous tough-talking fight announcer at Madison Square Garden.
** President of the Lucy Stone League, women who insisted on keeping their maiden names. They are dealt with in a later chapter.
*** An executive of the Keith-Albee vaudeville circuit.
**** The boss.

§ 103 §

THE VICIOUS CIRCLE

who, in an exceedingly witty speech, gave an explanation for the publication of *Life* which was almost satisfactory.*

I liked the acting of J. M. Kerrigan and Ruth Gillmore, but I will not be able to tell how good they are until I read some of their stuff. The audience was a real gathering of the cognoscenti, far superior to the numerous much-touted gatherings of societies for the uplift of the Russian drama, if you get what I mean. There were a good many professionals in the audience. I sincerely wished there had been more. I do not think that it is the intention of artists to ignore the critics. Most of them sincerely wish to please the faculty. They have been somewhat handicapped by not knowing what kind of acting the critics want. Now that the critics have shown them, I look for an enormous improvement in local performances.

Certainly, as most of these gentlemen would have said before they came to New York, a good time was had by all. The authorship was admirable; the acting—well, it was something like an actor writing criticism. If I may be allowed to quote from a little thing I once did at the Lambs Club:

* *Nobody* knows what this means. And I'm getting pretty good and sick of these asterisks, aren't you?

§ 104 §

Fun and Feuds

"The moral of this playlet is the trite and trench-
  ant fact
That the actor shouldn't author and the author
  shouldn't act."

Possibly these reserved panegyrics convinced the
Round Table that actors shouldn't author, but nothing
could persuade them that authors shouldn't act. The
following November they put on another show, *The
Forty-Niners,* with somewhat less success. Woollcott
stayed out of the cast this time and reviewed it for the
World:

An expectant audience packed the little
Punch and Judy Theatre last evening for the
pre-release showing of *The Forty-Niners,* due
to hold their first public revels here tonight.
Here, we said, would be fine fooling. Here were
some of the most gifted and most fantastic humorists of their time, summoned for once in a
way to write their prankful whimsies under the
thrall of no dull commercial manager and without a thought for that huge, threatening, hydra-
headed half wit—the public. Here were Ring
Lardner, Franklin P. Adams, George Kaufman, Marc Connelly, Heywood Broun, Robert
C. Benchley, Dorothy Parker and Montague
Glass, turned loose in a little theatre and bidden
to cut loose. My, what fun! And then it wasn't.
It wasn't fun. Not at all.

It is not any too easy to say just why. It is

§ 105 §

THE VICIOUS CIRCLE

true that there was hit-or-miss showmanship about it. It is true that, like the precious *Zuleika Dobson,* of which any twenty pages was always enough for us, it ran too much in the single vein—rather like a dinner consisting of five courses of perfectly splendid lemon meringue pie. . . .

After this melancholy admission that *The Forty-Niners* plunged us into a very abyss of boredom, it should immediately be admitted that there were gleams of engulfed and enshrouded gaiety on which we stumbled from time to time.

There was one patch of delightful nonsense by Benchley *—tolerably well delivered by one Denman Maley. Also a moment or two of mad humor in a languid adventure in nonsense by Ring Lardner **. . . . And a bright morsel of a sketch by Kaufman. Also a fair-to-middling travesty on all the musical comedies of the last twenty-five years—this last by Franklin P. Adams. . . . We carried away this as our most definite impression—a lot of extremely clever people being given too much rope, a lot

* Treasurer's Report.
** Lardner's short play, *The Tridget of Greva*—companion piece to *Cora*—or *Fun at a Spa, Clemo Uti*—*The Water Lilies,* and *I Gaspiri (The Upholsterers).* One of these—I forget which—contains the celebrated exchange: First Stranger: Where was you born? Second Stranger: Out of wedlock. First Stranger: That's mighty pretty country around there.

§ 106 §

Fun and Feuds

of celebrated comedians of the printed page
under orders to romp around in an elfin manner
and not presenting a too edifying spectacle.

In spite of the failure of *The Forty-Niners,* all this
outside activity cast an additional glow over the Round
Table, and it was no passing glory, either. Columnists
referred to *No Sirree!* frequently for many months, and
the show's own authors and stars were naturally not
above giving it a pleased mention from time to time. It
is no wonder that certain people who had not been asked
to join the Vicious Circle began, on viewing these phe-
nomena, to get a little fidgety. This feeling presently led
to the first big feud, known as the Ryskind Rift because
it mainly involved a man named Morris Ryskind.

Ryskind was a friend of most of the Round Table,
and in fact later collaborated with George Kaufman on
the book of the Pulitzer Prize musical comedy, *Of Thee
I Sing.* He often lunched with the group, where his presence was received calmly, without undue rejoicing or
displeasure. However, when he took to bringing too
many friends of his own—a noisy but colorless crew who
were strangers to most of the Circle—they took him aside
and firmly discouraged this practice. Ryskind retorted
that the Round Table wasn't so much anyway, and that
if they didn't like his friends, he and his friends would
form their own Round Table, right in the same dining
room and under the noses of the original group. This
they did—or rather, they tried to do it.

Any attempt at duplication is unfortunate, and Rys-

§ 107 §

THE VICIOUS CIRCLE

kind's Round Table was a particularly daft gesture. Nobody now remembers exactly who attended it, but they were pale copies of the original group. I myself recall them as a kind of blurred assortment of men with loud voices and big cigars who had a habit of table-hopping in their overcoats, and I know that this used to distress Father a good deal. Nothing makes a dining room look tackier than a lot of men standing around in camel's hair ulsters. Besides, they demanded an unreasonable amount of service, made more noise than any other four tables combined, and were a pretty unkempt-looking set . . . not with Broun's noble carelessness, just mussy-looking. My father was a patient man, but one day he went over to the imitation Round Table and said, "Boys, it's fine that you like to lunch here and all that, but I do wish you'd shave once in a while before you come in."

He might just as well have set fire to the tablecloth. Ryskind jumped up, rushed out to a telephone booth, called Herbert Bayard Swope, the editor of the *World*, and poured out his story of the gross insult received from the Algonquin proprietor. "Frank Case is anti-Semitic!" he yelled. The Algonquin was news, and so was the Round Table. Swope, ever the newshound, unfortunately printed Ryskind's whole story, along with his charge of Father's anti-Semitism. Father, who was about as anti-Semitic as a Raphael cherub, was terribly unhappy over the incident, even though the *World* later printed a retraction and people who knew how absurd the whole thing was tried to laugh him out of it. The only thing

§ 108 §

Fun and Feuds

that cheered him faintly was the memory of Ryskind's parting shot as he and his cronies left the hotel that day.

"We'll never darken this door again!" they promised.

That was the only feud that ever involved Father or the Algonquin, but the Round Table had its own intramural tiffs now and then, sometimes reaching heroic proportions. Some of the liveliest occurred between Woollcott and Edna Ferber, each of whom was something of a firebrand. Once, when the Vicious Circle were playing a game at Miss Ferber's apartment which involved turning out the lights, Woollcott, riled by something or other, departed in the darkness without saying good night. Miss Ferber practically never got over it. "I am weary of the tyranny of this New Jersey Nero," she remarked to one and all. Irksome as Woollcott's regal mannerisms were, Miss Ferber herself, on at least one occasion, brought about a serious rift. It happened when Woollcott was acting in *The Dark Tower,* a play he had written with George Kaufman.

One of Aleck's more admirable passions was his insistence on people's arriving at a play on time. He himself was always punctiliously prompt and he expected other people to be the same. Naturally, he felt even more deeply about this when it concerned his own play in which he was personally appearing.

Miss Ferber attended the opening night of *The Dark Tower* with Stanton Griffis, the industrialist and diplomat on whose yacht the Vicious Circle had enjoyed many an excursion. Unfortunately they arrived late,

§ 109 §

THE VICIOUS CIRCLE

and since their seats were well down in front, Woollcott, from the stage, saw them come in after the curtain was up. His first word as he left the stage when the act was over was a vow that he would never again speak to Edna Ferber. Perhaps he kept it, or perhaps Miss Ferber was true to some later vow of her own. In any case, they were not speaking when Woollcott died in 1943.

Against Mr. Griffis, that evening, Woollcott proclaimed an even darker and more terrible threat.

"I'll never go on Stanton Griffis's yacht again!" he announced.

§ 110 §

CHAPTER SIX

Abide with Me

ALTHOUGH THE Vicious Circle made the Round Table its focal point, its members obviously had to have somewhere to live and work. They solved their housing problems simply, by offering a boundless hospitality to one another. Anybody who lacked a place to lay his head was welcome to stay with anybody who had a roof over *his*, and this led to a pretty colorful floating population.

None of these visitors could be set down as the ordinary, run-of-the-mill, humdrum house guest. When Franklin P. Adams went to stay with friends he took along his fife, piccolo, mouth organ and penny whistle, and played on them as the fancy seized him. Dorothy Parker, coming to visit, usually brought one or two dachshunds or poodles which appeared to have been rigorously trained to do their duties only on bedroom or living-room carpets. Brock Pemberton, otherwise a quiet fellow, had a whistling clothesbrush, a gadget he had picked up in a joke shop which, when wielded, gave forth whistles, shrieks, and alarums; *he* just kept chasing people

THE VICIOUS CIRCLE

into corners and brushing them. He brushed people in the City Club, where he shared quarters with Woollcott for a while, and later when he went to stay with F.P.A. at a house Adams had taken, he brushed everybody there too, until Adams, pretending a fascination with his hideous toy, begged it as a gift and threw it in the ashcan.

One of the most generous as well as the most solvent of the Round Tablers was Alice Duer Miller, the novelist. Mrs. Miller, the author of *The Charm School, Manslaughter, Forsaking All Others* and other light fiction, was admittedly no great shakes of a writer, at least until she wrote *The White Cliffs* in 1940, two years before her death. But she was a woman of extraordinary personal charm and mental toughness—the hobby with which she whiled away her leisure hours was higher mathematics—and the Vicious Circle adored her. "At the Round Table," one of them recalled not long ago, "they treated her as though she were Henry James. Not, of course, that she ever *exacted* such respect." Where their affections were involved the Round Tablers could sometimes forget their passion for literary perfection.

(I should like to inject here a remark my father once made, somewhat in this connection. Father's taste in reading was fairly catholic, but he could not abide the grimy horrors of William Faulkner's books. Meeting Faulkner in the lobby one day, he said, "Hello, how are you?" and Faulkner replied that he wasn't feeling so well, he'd had kind of an upset stomach lately. "Ah," said Father, "something you wrote, no doubt?")

§ 112 §

Abide with Me

Back to Mrs. Miller. Running into Harold Ross one time during his bachelor days and noting his furrowed brow, she learned that he was fretting about his mother back in Aspen, Colorado. It seems that he had idly been mentioning his New York friends in his letters home, and Mrs. Ross had become alarmed at the thought of her son adrift among a galaxy of people whose names she had never before heard. "You mention a Miss Edna Ferber," she wrote him once, rather tensely, "and I have looked her up. A mother's interest, you know." Now, Ross told Mrs. Miller, his mother had announced that she was coming to New York to visit him and find out just what he was up to. This was fine with Ross, except that he was living in one room somewhere and had no place to put her. Mrs. Miller at once turned over her handsome East River apartment to Ross and his mother for the length of her visit, and further saw to it that Mrs. Ross was welcomed with orchids and a great reception to introduce all of her son's new friends.

At this affair, Woollcott, Benchley, Dorothy Parker, Broun, Adams, the much-considered Miss Edna Ferber, and the others passed down the receiving line and Mrs. Ross greeted them politely but blankly. Not until Ethel Barrymore appeared before her did her face light for the first time with a smile of recognition. "Of *course* I know Ethel Barrymore!" she cried warmly. "I used to see her on the stage when I was a little girl!"

With a large residence at his disposal Ross naturally gave parties every night, and his mother, retiring early, would sometimes hover around a bit in the hall, worry-

§ 113 §

THE VICIOUS CIRCLE

ing about her son's late hours. One night, a feminine guest who had arrived late went to powder her nose and returned to the living room looking nervous.

"You got any ghosts in this apartment?" she asked Ross.

Ross said certainly not, nobody ever had ghosts in an apartment.

"Well, you got one here now," said the lady. "It's in the bathroom, wearing a grey wrapper and kind of moaning."

Not all of the shared rooftrees started off on a casual basis—although most of them ended that way. Sometimes three or four Round Tablers would set up housekeeping together, sharing expenses in a communal scheme of living. The most vividly remembered ménage of this kind was the house in Hell's Kitchen which was shared by Harold Ross and his wife, Jane Grant, Aleck Woollcott, and Hawley Truax, a former classmate of Aleck's at Hamilton and now an executive of the *New Yorker* magazine. They referred to this dwelling as "the Gash-House" and the neighborhood as "the Gash-House District."

The four of them had bought two brownstone houses on West 47th Street between Ninth and Tenth Avenues, and thrown them into one. Here they prepared to live together on a co-operative plan—if the word "co-operative" can be applied to any arrangement including A. Woollcott.

It wasn't that he lacked his usual enthusiasm or his usual charm—he was brimming with both. But Wooll-

§ 114 §

Abide with Me

cott's emotions, like the waves of the sea, always returned gift-laden to their original source, which was Woollcott. He had the knack of continually enriching his own life, sometimes at the cost of impoverishing others. At 412 West 47th Street, he happened to live with three immensely polite people who nevertheless declined to be impoverished.

"We adored Aleck, you know," Jane Grant says now, "all of us always adored him. And he was perfectly *fine* in almost every way. He didn't drink, to speak of, and he was meticulous about money matters, and God knows he was entertaining. I don't know *why* there always came a time with Aleck when you couldn't *stand* it any more. . . ." At this point Jane looks faintly shocked at herself. Like Woollcott's other fellow tenants at No. 412, she looks back on their life with him with the mixed emotions of an animal-lover whose pet waltzing rat has suddenly turned on him and bitten off a finger.

Ross and his wife, Jane, Truax, and Woollcott each had their own apartments at 412, but shared the kitchen and the dining room. Jane did the housekeeping with the help of a colored couple, Marie and Arthur Treadwell (whose son, young Arthur, later became Woollcott's famous "Junior" when he set up his own ménage at "Wit's End" and, still later, at Lake Bomoseen). Ordering meals for the three men residing at 412 was a task to stagger any woman. Ross already had the beginnings of the stomach ulcer that has since obliged him to tote his own bottle of milk to cocktail parties; (his many skepticisms include an iron disbelief that the average

§ 115 §

THE VICIOUS CIRCLE

host's refrigerator has any milk in it). Hawley Truax
also had a delicate stomach. For these two, Jane had to
order clear broth, lean meat, plain-cooked vegetables
and, usually, cooked fruit for dessert. Woollcott, on the
other hand, ate like a horse and liked rich food; cream
soups, a fish or lobster course, meat with curry and other
fancy sauces, vegetables drowned in butter and herbs,
elaborate salads, and always and ever a huge dessert with
frosting or whipped cream or rum sauce.

That Jane managed to feed such contrasting in-
teriors at all is a miracle, and she didn't always achieve
it without offending Aleck. If she had two kinds of soup
—clear and cream—Woollcott would claim that the clear
soup was green turtle with sherry and that his own cream
soup came out of a can, and he would flounce out of the
dining room, passionately announcing that he was being
starved. If she had a fruit soufflé for dessert, with whipped
cream to be taken or declined, Woollcott would demand to know where the pudding was, or the pie, and
flounce out anyway.

The quartet planned to celebrate their installment
at 412 with a housewarming, to be given in the Ross
apartment which had the biggest living room. Woollcott produced his list of the people he wished invited
and instantly blue-penciled any amendments or sug-
gestions from Ross, Jane, or Truax. When they in turn
objected to this highhandedness, Woollcott withdrew
from the plans altogether and went off in a huff to his
family retreat at Phalanx, New Jersey. His co-tenants
sighed and went ahead with the party, which was a

§ 116 §

Abide with Me

rousing success until, at nine-thirty in the evening, Woollcott unexpectedly returned from Phalanx, strode into the Ross living room, scooped up his own buddies among the guests, and took them upstairs to his own apartment. The hilarity that drifted down the stairs then attracted the other guests, who gradually followed. When Ross, Jane, and Truax finally went up to see what had become of their housewarming, they found that Woollcott had locked his door.

Such childishness was something to indulge and ignore as far as possible, but Woollcott was not always ignorable. The Ross apartment was in the front of the house, its bedroom windows facing the street. When Aleck, then drama critic of the *Times,* came home from a first night he would get out of his taxi and glance at the Ross windows to see if there was a light. If there was, no matter what the hour, he would push open their bedroom door and bustle in, ready for several hours of good talk. Both Ross and Jane worked daytimes and needed their sleep, and anyway this nightly invasion began to make them nervous. It got so that they would hastily switch off the light when they heard a taxi pull up outside, but sometimes they were not quick enough. In a minute or so Woollcott would be rapping on their door with his stick and caroling, "You can't fool *me,* you fawn's behinds! *I* saw your light go off just a second ago!" If they didn't answer, he would fling open the door and bounce in. Nobody at 412 ever had any keys—except Woollcott.

The household in 47th Street lasted about five

§ 117 §

THE VICIOUS CIRCLE

years, and they were happy years for everyone on the whole, even though occasionally ticklish. The house became a great rendezvous for the Vicious Circle and their friends, and there were so many parties that the urchins of that tough neighborhood took to gathering on the doorstep almost every evening to comment and stare. "Geez, lookit! Gold slippers!" they would roar, hilariously pointing. Woollcott's top hat and opera cloak had already long since affected them strongly, sometimes producing an awed silence, at other times snowballs and tin cans. Inside the house Aleck was scarcely safer. He was, understandably enough, the butt of most antics and gags because he objected to them so violently.

One of his dearest possessions was a portrait of himself in his Army private's uniform, painted by C. Leroy Baldridge and entitled "Soldier with Book." He was holding a book in the picture. This likeness hung proudly on one wall of his apartment. While Aleck was away on a trip, the Rosses had Baldridge paint a copy of the portrait which they inserted neatly in the frame over the original. The copy was identical except that the drawing was about an eighth of an inch out of line, so that it looked just faintly askew, as though someone had mysteriously been able to reach into the canvas and give the Soldier with Book a slight shove. When Woollcott returned, Ross, Jane, and Truax all took to glancing quizzically at the portrait now and then, as if puzzled. Finally they asked him, "What's happening to your picture, Aleck? It's *moving*, or something."

§ 118 §

Abide with Me

Woollcott nearly went crazy for two months, squinting and lying on his stomach to get perspective, calling up Baldridge to come and squint and lie on *his* stomach, and loudly demanding to know why *his* portrait should so promptly suffer from the ravages of time when the Sistine frescoes were still intact. Next time he was called out of town the Rosses quietly removed the copy from the frame, and Aleck, coming home to find his picture perfect once more, announced that everybody was crazy. As far as anyone knows, that was the nearest he ever came to finding out the truth.

A simpler gag was a Christmas prank sprung on him once, after he had earnestly proclaimed all year that what he wanted to find in his stocking was a set of the *Oxford Dictionary* in twelve volumes. Half a dozen of his friends got together and, on Christmas Day, each one gravely presented him with a copy of Volume A.

A man who enjoyed that gesture was Hawley Truax, who had already been the victim of a book gag, a year or so before. Woollcott had originally introduced his Hamilton classmate as one of the world's Great Scholars, and had in fact made so much of Hawley's tremendous erudition that Ross and Jane felt bound to acknowledge it suitably.

For Christmas, that year, they gave Truax a book printed in the original Estonian.

The household at No. 412 broke up gradually. Woollcott was the first to go, at the reluctant suggestion of Ross and Jane who, worn down by sleeplessness, had sadly decided that it was the only solution. Aleck con-

§ 119 §

THE VICIOUS CIRCLE

sented sunnily to terminate his co-operative agreement
with them, and with Hawley Truax, and departed with
no hard feelings. Then, with one of his waltzing-rat
reversals, he suddenly wrote Ross a letter so vitriolic that
Crosby Gaige, the theatrical producer and curio collector,
later paid Ross twenty dollars for it.

The letter was written after some mix-up about a
dinner engagement to wind up the details of Woollcott's
withdrawal from 47th Street:

Monday

Dear Ross,

I agree with you that the fewer dealings
one has with you and the fewer debts one per-
mits you to incur, the less chance there is to be
subjected to your discourtesy. I have enjoyed
your company so much that I have been one of
the last to make this simple discovery. The rem-
edy is even simpler.

It seems hard to believe that you really
think I objected to your breaking a dinner engagement with me. As I was sound asleep upstairs, I didn't even know you hadn't come. I
was a trifle revolted that you should have
thought your casual imposition on the amiable
Junior so richly comic. And your subsequent
paroxysms of mirth made me a little sick. Any
tyro in psychology recognizes that urchin defense mechanism, but the person who jeers at
me when there is a good audience and waits for

§ 120 §

Abide with Me

privacy to apologize is manifesting a kind of poltroonery I find hard to deal with.

Hawley tells me that the money for my fourth of the house equipment is due from you. You will remember that we agreed to leave the fixing of the amount to him. He has, I believe, figured this out. Then you were to take over, I believe, some proportion of the $325 I spent on my apartment. Will you send me a check for this or your note for three months? I should be reluctant to burden you with more favorable terms. You can, if need be, borrow the money from some innocent who does not suspect how deeply he will thereby be incurring your antipathy.

I think your slogan "Liberty or Death" is splendid and whichever one you finally decide upon will be all right with me.

A.W.

When Ross sold this missive to Crosby Gaige he appended this footnote for the purchaser:

The author of this letter is the gentleman who left for France last Spring failing, despite urging, to sign a check for losses at cribbage. He had to catch the boat. It sailed at 10 o'clock in the morning, and it was then 2 a.m.

Such skirmishes were frequent between Woollcott and his friends and they bruised, but did not shatter,

§ 121 §

THE VICIOUS CIRCLE

the texture of friendship. People knew that the Woollcott who flew out at them with bared fangs was the same inwardly lonely man who longed to be loved, who lavished himself in affection and attentions and loyalty upon the friends he himself loved; and was so incurably unsure of their affection toward him that the slightest casualness on their part sent him into a wounded rage. The Woollcott who wrote vituperations to his good friend Ross was the same Woollcott who, after his sister Julie's death, wrote to Lucie Christie Drage (a friend of Julie's) a letter that might well stand as a classic in simple feeling:

> . . . So one by one the lights go out. I have had to write you about them. It is because Julie loved you with a surpassing loyalty and tenderness. The miles and the years between made no difference to her at all—none at all. I think you knew that there was always that lamp in her window for you, always that loving kindness in her heart.
>
> Something stops me from trying to say anything of the impoverishment I feel. What a world this would be—what a morning light would shine across it—if all people were like her. I think of that and of many things and I send you her love and mine. I wish I could stand beside you at some window today and look out into the twilight and say nothing.
>
> Aleck.

§ 122 §

ALEXANDER WOOLLCOTT

Abide with Me

This letter was no single exercise in prose such as almost anyone can, and almost automatically does, write when he loses someone dear to him. Aleck kept up a correspondence with Julie's friend, who lived in Kansas City, all his life. His last letter to her, giving a lively account of his summer at Antibes with "Bernard Shaw and Elsa Maxwell . . . Mary Garden and Grace Moore . . . Somerset Maugham and Irene Castle . . . Lady Mendl . . . Frank Harris . . ." (all the famous and gossipy names calculated to delight a lady in Kansas City) was dated September 14th, 1942; fourteen years after Julie died, and four months before his own death.

It was no wonder that, to a man as sentimental and loyal as Woollcott, his friends were able to forgive much.

Besides, Woollcott was valuable. When Ross started the *New Yorker,* and for many years afterward, no contributor was more popular with readers than Aleck. None was more enthusiastic, either, or faithful, in his fashion. And certainly no contributor was ever more trouble to his editors.

But all that came later. In the meantime there was another slight encounter in the Woollcott-Ross duello over the affairs of 412 West 47th Street.

The Rosses were the next to depart from 412, after Woollcott, leaving Hawley Truax, who lived there until a few years ago. Ross and Jane were later divorced and eventually remarried to other people; Jane to William B. Harris, a senior editor of *Fortune,* and Ross to a young lady of French extraction somehow named Frances

§ 125 §

THE VICIOUS CIRCLE

Clark. (His second marriage was also dissolved and he is now married to Ariane, a beautiful blonde.)

In the interval after his divorce from Jane, Ross went to live with Edward MacNamara, "the Singing Cop." Ed MacNamara was a big, easy-going Irish ex-policeman who had successfully turned to the stage and was a great favorite with everybody at the Round Table, where Broun had originally introduced him. He had a fine singing voice (a boon to the musical evenings) and a vast repertory of drinking songs which he and J. M. Kerrigan performed together and taught to the rest of the group. One ballad they treasured went, in part:

> The mist on the glass is congealing,
> 'Tis the hurricane's icy breath
> And it shows how the warmth of friendship
> Grows cold in the clasp of death.
> Stand, stand to your glasses steady
> And drink to your sweetheart's eyes . . .

To Ross and MacNamara as dinner guest one night came A. Woollcott returned from foreign shores, his anger forgotten as usual. Ross's wrath had, of course, died down too, and dinner went swimmingly until Woollcott happened to admire the table silver and asked his hosts how they had come by it. When neither one was certain which of them it belonged to, Aleck sprang triumphantly to his feet brandishing a spoon and pointed out a "B" engraved on the handle. "I knew it! I knew it!" he shouted. Sure enough, the silver belonged to the Bucklin family (a branch of Woollcott's family)

§ 126 §

Abide with Me

and had been mistakenly turned over to Ross when the household at No. 412 disbanded.

Woollcott roared out of the apartment and made the rest of the night hideous with telegrams to Ross accusing him of larceny and loose living, and promising lawsuits and a jail sentence if his family silver were not returned forthwith. The next morning, even before the Western Union wires could cool off, he sent his valet, Junior, around with more threats and a basket. Ross happily handed over the silver, and MacNamara peacefully went out and bought new knives and forks at the Five and Ten.

The various rooftrees that sheltered the shifting population of the Algonquin Round Table when they were away from the Algonquin are hard to keep track of, and nobody now remembers when the Ross-MacNamara household broke up. Probably it was when Ross remarried. Sometime later, at any rate, Ed Mac-Namara went to live with Broun and his wife, Ruth Hale, in their house on West 85th Street. Ruth Hale was the president of the Lucy Stone League, the organization of women who kept their maiden names although married, and Jane Grant was its secretary-treasurer— which is the reason I have had to speak of "Ross and his wife, Jane Grant" and "Broun and his wife, Ruth Hale" throughout this chapter. There will be more about the Lucy Stoners in the next chapter, and there is a great deal to be said for their aims and accomplishments. But I bet the girls never knew how much trouble they were cooking up for me when I came to write this book.

§ 127 §

THE VICIOUS CIRCLE

Ruth Hale was a thin, intense, forceful young woman from Tennessee who was very successful as the Selwyns' press agent. She had first met Broun in 1914, when Alice Duer Miller (a baseball fan) took her to a game and Broun, then sports writer for the *Tribune,* invited them both into the press box. On that afternoon Miss Hale scared him half to death by remarking that she found his baseball stories inaccurate. She also pointed out to him just what his errors were. This was stimulating to Broun, and he made a date to see her again. He was at that time recovering from a broken love affair with someone as little like Ruth Hale as could be imagined—Lydia Lopokova, the ballet dancer. Lopokova, after tenderly encouraging him for a spell, had eloped to Europe with one Randolfo Barocini, Diaghilev's secretary and manager. She later divorced him and married the English economist, John Maynard Keynes . . . again a man as different as possible from Broun, whose system of bookkeeping was to put his bankroll in one pants pocket and his winnings in the other so that, when both pockets were empty, he could know he had broken even.

Broun and Ruth Hale were married in 1917 and went to France, where Ruth worked with the Red Cross and Broun on the *Stars and Stripes.* After the war they came home and bought the house on West 85th Street. They had been given a choice between that house and another at 51st Street and the East River but after one look at the East River house they concluded, rightly, that the neighborhood was a slum, and chose the West Side

§ 128 §

Abide with Me

place. In the next two or three years 51st Street on the East River became Beekman Terrace where Katharine Cornell, Margalo Gillmore, and even flossier citizens began to reside and where houses and land suddenly sold for a thousand dollars an inch or thereabouts. Broun and Ruth didn't care particularly. They settled down in their West Side dwelling with no furniture in the living room and no door on the bathroom, and eventually bought a country place too, in Connecticut. Here, at Sabine Farm, there was not only no door on the bathroom, there was no bathroom. You washed in the pond, shoving away scum, or in a tin basin on the back porch. My father spent one weekend there and came home grey with horror at the sanitary arrangements.

"I give you my word, Margaret," he confided to me, "there is *one* towel, hanging on a nail on the back porch, for *everybody* to use." He thought for a minute, and added, "And *that* towel must have come with the house."

The Broun household was always interesting, though, and especially so while MacNamara lived with them . . . the two men were so huge and placid, and Ruth Hale was so mettlesome and thin, darting around and between them like a dragonfly in a bears' cage. MacNamara had a beautiful speaking voice, while Broun's was high and rather breathless. One evening, during one of their long and amiable discussions about life, literature, politics and other topics of concern, Mac-Namara grew eloquent and, pounding the arm of his chair (they had acquired a few chairs by that time),

§ 129 §

THE VICIOUS CIRCLE

·inveighed at some length against the Very Rich. Broun listened pensively. "Mac," he said at length, "it's a shame that with a voice like yours you don't ever know what the hell you're talking about."

Although MacNamara was a big man, Broun was even bigger, and so notoriously careless in his dress, even in uniform during World War I, that General Pershing once paused before him in astonishment during an inspection.

"Did you fall down?" the General inquired.

During MacNamara's residence in 85th Street Broun was invited to a great dinner at Mrs. William Randolph Hearst's one night and borrowed a tail coat and dress waistcoat from Mac to wear with his own trousers. Due to his greater height and bulk there was a gap of several inches between the waistband of his trousers and the bottom of Mac's waistcoat—too much for even Broun to carry off with ease. He had to spend the evening bent over, in order to keep the edges together, and this gave him the appearance of bowing so often and so deeply that Mrs. Norman de R. Whitehouse commented on it to Frank Adams.

"Mr. Broun has the *courtliest* old-world manners!" she said. "I can't understand how he ever got that reputation as such a great rude bumpkin!"

MacNamara's stay with the Brouns ended abruptly one night when he came home to 85th Street from work at the old Famous Players Studio uptown, where he had been making a picture, and found his trunk in the hall with a note asking him to call Broun at a new telephone

§ 130 §

Abide with Me

number. "I forgot to tell you, I sold the house," said Broun on the telephone.

Heywood and Ruth moved more or less permanently to Sabine Farm, where Broun wrote, fished, painted pictures, and did spasmodic odd jobs around the house. One of these was to put a screen on the back door. There were no screens on the front door or in any of the windows. "Not necessary," Broun explained to inquiring visitors. "Flies are dumb, haven't you noticed? They all congregate in one place, usually the place they can't get in. And when they can't get in there, they haven't got brains enough to try anywhere else."

It was after the trek from 85th Street that Broun was presented with a large bill from the moving men for hauling and cartage which seemed unreasonable to him, since he and Ruth owned positively nothing that they couldn't get along without. On his next trip to New York he delivered an ultimatum about it at the Round Table.

"Cartage delenda est," he said.

§ 131 §

CHAPTER SEVEN

Manners, Maneuvers, and Married Maidens

MANNERS AT the Round Table were always casual, and sometimes a little less than that. Woollcott, once catching Stanton Griffis's eye on him as he was inhaling a wedge of lemon meringue pie, remarked with his mouth full, "I am interested to observe the mixture of hero-worship and genuine nausea with which our friend Mr. Griffis regards me."

No man ever stood up when any woman came to the Round Table, or left it. There were two good reasons for that, one practical and one intellectual. The practical reason was that the coming and going was so constant that any man who rose for each lady would have been bobbing up and down all the time. The intellectual explanation was that the Vicious Circle received women on a more truly equal footing than any other group in the Nineteen-Twenties. The Woman Suffrage Amendment had been ratified only in 1920, and equality for women was a fairly new thing, but at the Round Table

§ 133 §

THE VICIOUS CIRCLE

it was taken for granted. Most of the girls in the group were self-supporting—actresses, writers, press agents and painters—and even the most prettily feminine of them all, Dorothy Parker, would have been alarmed by any undue cosseting from the boys. The Vicious Circle operated, on the whole, under the steady glow of good-fellowship between the sexes, high-lighted by sparks from two firebrands—Ruth Hale and Jane Grant.

Ruth, the press agent, and Jane, the newspaper-woman, were both militant feminists and had marched and made speeches and chained themselves to railings with the rest of the suffragettes in their time. Almost singlehanded, Ruth Hale had founded the Lucy Stone League, an outgrowth of the feminist movement, which claimed that—among other equal rights—a woman had a right to be known by her own name after she married. When skeptics suggested that, in any case, a woman's name is that of her father (just another man, God forbid), Miss Hale snapped back, "*That* is the fault of our mothers, who were not enlightened." Jane Grant, who became interested in the Lucy Stone League through Ruth Hale, had the same driving spirit and soon became the League's secretary-treasurer.

Ruth Hale and Jane Grant would as soon have been called anathema maranatha * as be called Mrs. Broun and Mrs. Ross. When it was necessary to join themselves with their husbands in holy print on announcements or invitations they were "Ruth Hale and Heywood Broun" and "Jane Grant and Harold Ross." Ruth Hale died in

* A mighty pretty name, too.

§ 134 §

RUTH HALE, JANE GRANT

Manners, Maneuvers, and Married Maidens

1934, but Jane still keeps the Lucy Stone banner flying. Now happily married to Bill Harris, she gives marvelous parties to which the invitations always read, "Jane Grant and William B. Harris," and this seems entirely natural to her friends. Jane's is the reward of persistence. She has become so well-known as Jane Grant simply by fighting to *remain* Jane Grant that, if anyone spoke of her as "Mrs. Harris" even to her closest friends, the automatic reply would be, "Who?"

This insistence on retaining a maiden name may seem a tiny cause nowadays; but it must be remembered that the Lucy Stone League came into being at a time when women were just beginning to have equal rights with men as citizens. To a Lucy Stoner, her maiden name was a symbol of her individuality and her personal rights, not as a woman but as a citizen. The maiden-name crusade was sincere, and it was also a flare touched off to light the way for women to become doctors, lawyers, judges, senators, and congresswomen. Ironically enough, not one woman who has since become famous in any of those professions, from Mrs. Anna Rosenberg to Ma Ferguson and Clare Boothe Luce, has ever been a Lucy Stoner.

"That's true," Jane Grant says, when reminded of this, and adds thoughtfully, "Very few men who design airplanes actually fly them, have you noticed?"

Lucy Stone, for whom the League was named, was a New England feminist who lived in the early part of the nineteenth century. She was married to a man named Henry Browne Blackwell, a hardware merchant whose

§ 137 §

THE VICIOUS CIRCLE

sister, Elizabeth Blackwell, was the first woman ever to receive a medical degree. Elizabeth and Lucy were friends, and together they campaigned up a storm on behalf of antislavery, women's rights and other progressive causes. (One cannot help but think of Henry, coming home from a tough day with the hardware to an even brisker evening with the girls.)

In Lucy's day, women were chattels. In many of the United States a man had the legal right to beat his wife and could not be arrested or even reprimanded for it. Moreover, whatever property she inherited, or otherwise acquired, automatically belonged to him; this included the clothes she wore, and there was more than one case of a husband teaching his wife not to gad about by locking up her clothes and pocketing the key. A woman, in most states, could not own property, engage in business, or sign documents. And certainly, she had no say in her country's government.

Lucy Stone succeeded in partially correcting these ills by instituting various test cases, one of which she won with the sympathetic aid of Chief Justice Salmon P. Chase. President Lincoln was on her side too, but was assassinated before he could do anything constructive.

When Ruth Hale married Heywood Broun in 1917 one of the witnesses rushed up to her after the ceremony and said, "Best wishes for your happiness, Mrs. Broun." Ruth later described the incident to Doris Fleischman, a member of the Lucy Stone League.

"I was furious," Ruth told Doris. "I looked at this creature and I said, 'I am *not* Missis Broun! I am Ruth

§ 138 §

Manners, Maneuvers, and Married Maidens

Hale!' . . . I was so upset" added this pioneer in women's rights "that I rushed home and had hysterics."

Although Jane Grant was equally interested in feminism and woman suffrage, she was less emotional about it and, at first, indifferent about preserving her identity by means of her maiden name. Once, she was even careless enough to refer to Ruth and Heywood in their presence as "the Brouns"—a bit of absent-mindedness that won her a sharp reproof from Miss Hale. However, when Jane married Harold Ross and the rector's secretary called *her* "Mrs. Ross," she was just as startled as Ruth had been, and so, for that matter, was Ross. He gave her a strange look and said "Gee, I've known you all this time as Jane Grant, I don't think I can get used to this 'Mrs. Ross' stuff." It was actually Ross who suggested, one night when the two girls were discussing the subject at a party, that they form an organization. His exact words were, "Aw, why don't you two hire a hall?"

Some of the charter members of the League were Theresa Helburn and several other women among the Washington Square Players, Lucy Huffaker, Doris Stevens (feminist and wife of Dudley Field Malone), Doris Fleischman (ditto and wife of Edward L. Bernays), Ruth Pickering (ditto and wife of Amos Pinchot), and Fola La Follette (ditto and wife of George Middleton).

Aside from Ruth and Jane, most of the Round Table women were cool toward the Lucy Stone League. Dorothy Parker (née Rothschild) was making her husband's surname so famous that she never thought of joining, nor did Neysa McMein after she married John

§ 139 §

THE VICIOUS CIRCLE

Baragwanath; Alice Duer Miller had long since established her combined maiden- and married-names as her professional signature. Actresses were automatically known by their stage names and saw no sense in making any further fuss about it. "I don't have to put up a battle to keep *my* name—I already *got* it," said one. Another argued that a Lucy Stoner might do better to accomplish something big and impress her name on people, rather than cram the name itself down the public throat, and she illustrated her feeling with the story about John Drew and the club bore. This man kept coming up to Mr. Drew at the Lambs Club and saying "You don't remember me, do you?" Finally, in desperation, Mr. Drew replied, "No. But say something wonderful now, so that I'll never forget you."

Unabashed by adverse comment, the Lucy Stone League went into action. Some of the evils of Lucy Stone's day still prevailed in many states in spite of the 19th Amendment, and the Lucy Stoners set up test cases all over the country like Roman candles. Before long, with the help of Senator La Follette (Fola's father), they won the decision in a case involving the right of a woman in Wisconsin to own property in her own name. But it was not until the big Passport Dilemma that the League really made news. The League claimed that a married woman could, and should, obtain a passport under her maiden name if that was the name she was commonly known by, and cited the legal fact that there is no law compelling a woman to assume her husband's name. The Passport Bureau said No Passport under those con-

§ 140 §

Manners, Maneuvers, and Married Maidens

ditions, and was backed up by the State Department. The League resorted to its favorite device, the test case.

In 1925, Doris Fleischman applied at the New York Bureau for a passport, wrote "married" in the married-or-single space on the application, wrote "Edward L. Bernays" under name-of-husband, signed her maiden name, and was refused a passport. When she protested, the clerk ironically suggested that she write to the Secretary of State about it.

"Certainly," said Miss Fleischman, and added the following note to her application:

> Mr. Secretary:
>
> Will you kindly have issued to me a passport under my own name. There is no law compelling a woman to use any but her own name, and I have never done so. Since it is apparent that the purpose of a passport is to establish identity, I assume you will not wish me to travel under a false name.
>
> (Signed) Doris Fleischman

In Miss Fleischman's own words, "That did it. In a few weeks the historic passport was launched . . . and ship-news photographers clicked their shutters at the newsworthy sailing of the first American married woman to travel abroad under her own name. Newspapers next day actually ran the story and pictures of this event."

The State Department seems to have been a little bruised by this encounter. In the summer of 1948 Jane

§ 141 §

THE VICIOUS CIRCLE

Grant applied for a passport in the name of Jane Grant and was refused. Jane went to Washington about it, and got the passport. "There is no law that says you *cannot* get a passport under your own name," Jane points out, operating obliquely from the negative in her truly feminine way.

The New York Passport Bureau is a mite touchy about the whole thing, these days. Queried recently as to the possibility of a married woman's obtaining a passport under her maiden name, the Bureau's spokesman gave a short answer.

"Uh-uh," he said.

Under pressure, he qualified that. A married woman *can* obtain a passport under her maiden name if she (a) signs an affidavit to the effect that her maiden name is the one she is commonly known by, and (b) follows her maiden signature with the words, in parentheses, (Wife of John Doe). Questioned further about how long this ruling has prevailed in the New York office, he said "Since the summer of 1948. Some dame raised the roof in Washington."

If there were some people who rather felt that in crusading so violently for the right to keep their maiden names the Lucy Stoners had more or less fastened their banner to a twig, the girls' husbands were not among them. Willingly and even enthusiastically Broun, Ross, Bernays, and all the other partners in these independent marriages went through the wedding ceremony without the wedding ring (since the ring was denounced as a symbol of bondage), baffled hotel clerks by inscribing

§ 142 §

Manners, Maneuvers, and Married Maidens

guest registers "Heywood Broun and wife, Ruth Hale" or "Harold Ross and wife, Jane Grant," and patiently corrected the fatheads who ignorantly addressed their wives as "Mrs." When children were born to these couples the expectant mother went into the hospital as "Miss" Whoever, to the curiosity and confusion of the hospital staff. The fashionable Miss Lippincott on Madison Avenue was so unstrung, in fact, when a daughter was born to Miss Doris Fleischman in her sanitarium that she presented the birth certificate with the anguished query, "Do I have to put in 'illegitimate'?"

After the death of Ruth Hale the Lucy Stone League simmered down to a state of inactivity, although there is now talk of reviving it. No president was appointed to succeed Miss Hale, and, with the exception of Jane Grant, the girls pretty well subsided. A woman's rights as a citizen and an individual are taken for granted these days, and no longer present the flaming problem they did in the 'Twenties, nor is the burden of a husband's name considered the ruinous shackle it appeared to be then. One Lucy Stoner, Doris Fleischman, came out in print in a magazine not long ago with the wistful revelation that she would now like to be known as Mrs. Edward L. Bernays and was having a tough time training people to stop calling her Miss Fleischman. She has now changed her mind again, however, and is one of the group's active reorganizers.

Throughout the rise and fall of Lucy Stonerism, the relations of the sexes at the Round Table remained amiable and mutually respectful. Sometimes theirs was a

§ 143 §

THE VICIOUS CIRCLE

working companionship, and it was one of these that produced an incident that was always a favorite of my father's. When Edna Ferber and George S. Kaufman collaborated on their play, *The Royal Family*, in 1927, they wrote a good part of it in Miss Ferber's suite at the Algonquin, often working through the day and into the night. One midnight a new and over-zealous clerk telephoned the apartment and inquired "I beg your pardon, Miss Ferber, but is there a gentleman in your room?"

"I don't know," Miss Ferber replied. "Wait a minute and I'll ask him."

Career women the Round Table girls might be, and two of them militant feminists, but they never looked like the popular conception of the strong-minded female. Granted that Ruth Hale was no clotheshorse, she liked to go dancing in silks and satins, and the rest of the girls were as fond of pretty things to wear as any unenlightened belle. Jane Grant—who for a short interlude had been a professional ballroom dancer at Shanley's Restaurant in New York—had an eye for the right clothes to enhance her slim figure and lively face. Dorothy Parker was all frills and enormous picture hats loaded with flowers, fruit, *and* vegetables from beneath which her gamin face with its dark bangs looked out irresistibly. Neysa McMein seldom came to lunch but when she did, although a bit disheveled and paint-stained, she was charming to look at. Beatrice Kaufman, a tall, handsome woman, went in for tailored effects and was one of the best-dressed women in the Algonquin (which is saying quite a lot). Edna Ferber—another infrequent

§ 144 §

Manners, Maneuvers, and Married Maidens

luncher, since she liked to work through the noon hour
—also wore tailored things mostly and was always beautifully groomed, if a trifle crisp. Miss Ferber, never known
for honeyed talk, clashed slightly with Noel Coward one
day when they both turned up at the Round Table
sporting new double-breasted suits.

"You look almost like a man," Mr. Coward told
Miss Ferber.

"So," Miss Edna replied lightly, "do you."

The Round Table girls were a good-looking crew,
although there wasn't a classic beauty among them—with
the exception, perhaps, of Margaret Leech, a newcomer
in the 'Twenties who had written two novels, *The Back
of the Book* and *Tin Wedding,* and later, in collaboration with Heywood Broun, wrote *Anthony Comstock:
Roundsman of the Lord.* Miss Leech subsequently married Ralph Pulitzer and is most recently known for her
book, *Reveille in Washington.* Peggy, as everyone called
her, had blonde hair, a roseleaf complexion, and a mind
like a steel trap. She could be as devastating in her way
as Dottie Parker, although she didn't work at it as much.
It was Peggy who, when F.P.A. once came in to lunch
after a morning of tennis with his sport shirt open at the
throat revealing tufts of curly black hair, glanced up
and remarked:

"Well, Frank, I see your fly is open higher than
usual today."

Adams had a pet name for Peggy for a long time
after that. He called her, indulgently, "Vinegar Nell."

F. P. A. was a great admirer of Peggy's earthy wit

§ 145 §

THE VICIOUS CIRCLE

and good looks. "So to H. Broun's, where a great party and merry as can be. . . ." he wrote in his *Diary of Our Own Samuel Pepys;* "Miss M. Leech there too and Mistress Pinna Cruger, one prettier than the other. . . ."

And, speaking of good looks, it was Adams, too, who, emerging haggardly from the Algonquin with Broun one noontime after an all-night poker party, met a little boy coming in. Adams gazed in astonishment after the tot.

"Gad," he marveled to Heywood, "how can they keep a child like that up all night and have him look so wonderful?"

No matter what pains the girls of the Vicious Circle took with their wardrobes, their appearance never quite satisfied Woollcott, who fancied himself as an expert in haute couture. After some months of grumbling he announced impatiently that *he* would design some decent clothes for all of them, something truly expressive of each one's personality; and this he did, going into furious consultation with Muriel King, a young designer who had just started in business in New York. Naturally, the whole thing threatened several times to break up in a row, when Muriel, who was not in business for her health, refused to give Aleck a big enough professional discount on the dresses. However, matters were smoothed over and the gowns at last finished, to Woollcott's exact specifications. He then presented them to the girls and, with their somewhat startled assistance, staged a fashion show for invited guests in Neysa McMein's studio.

"The dresses were really frightening," Jane Grant,

§ 146 §

George S. Kaufman, Edna Ferber

Manners, Maneuvers, and Married Maidens

Peggy Leech and Margalo Gillmore now agree, "all covered with great fringes and sashes and huge bands of fur. But we had fun, sweeping around like mannequins, and of course Aleck had the time of his life as entrepreneur. He had christened each creation, just like the French couturiers, and there was one black number called 'Last Will and Testament of Simon P. Entwhistle,' and another—all rabbit fur to the armpits—that he called 'Fawn's Behind.' "

Mercifully, after a time, Woollcott forgot his career as the Christian Dior of his day, and his creations were allowed to languish in their reluctant owners' closets.

Oddly enough, the woman who came into the Algonquin looking most like a pioneer in women's rights was probably the most fancifully minded woman who ever came in there. She was Gertrude Stein, the author of *Tender Buttons, Lucy Church, Amiably, Four Saints in Three Acts* and many other works written in her unique prose. (Best-known quotation: "Rose is a rose is a rose." Most sensible quotation: "In the United States there is more space where nobody is than where anybody is. This is what makes America what it is.")

Miss Stein, whose style was appreciated in the 'Twenties by few people except Carl Van Vechten, was arresting enough in appearance to make even the Round Table look at her. She was almost completely square; and she wore her hair in a way that was less than a crew cut and a fraction more than a complete shave. Her all-over effect was grey—grey tweeds, grey head, square greyish face—

§ 149 §

THE VICIOUS CIRCLE

and it was a granite grey, not a cloudy one. She looked like a rock that a sea gull might perch on.

Yet, under this stony exterior there lurked a heart of innocent merriment. At least, Father told me so, after he got to know her. And trust Father to find a merry heart if one was there.

He told one story about her in his book, which I would like to elaborate a little, as he told it to me.

Gertrude Stein and Louis Bromfield, who had been old friends and neighbors in France, happened to register at the Algonk a day apart, neither knowing that the other was there. Father, who always had his finger on the social pulse of his hotel, and unconsciously ran it like a salon (he certainly couldn't say *that* in his own book!), telephoned Miss Stein and said that Louis was again a neighbor of hers, and would she like to see him?

"*Would* I!" said Miss Stein, who talked like anybody else in ordinary conversation. So Pa called Louis, and a date was made for Miss Stein and Father to have cocktails in the Bromfield rooms that day. They arrived, and were introduced to Bromfield's father, an honest Ohio farmer, slightly deaf, who was rather belligerently visiting his son in the big city. The elder Bromfield stared a moment at Miss Stein's sheared head and tweed-squared shoulders, and clammed up. But the little party went along well until Miss Stein, with her impeccable manners, leaned forward and asked old Mr. Bromfield how he liked New York.

The elder Bromfield cupped his ear and shook his head.

§ 150 §

Manners, Maneuvers, and Married Maidens

"Louis!" he shouted.

His son hurried across the room and Father Bromfield hooked a horny thumb in Miss Stein's direction. "What did the gentleman say?" he asked.

. . . Out in the corridor after the party, Father caught Gertrude Stein's eye. Once they touched glances they both dissolved in laughter, and Father came home to the 10th floor still smiling.

"You know, Margaret," he said, sitting down in his own wing chair and reaching for the crossword-puzzle book that was his before-dinner stimulus instead of cocktails, "I am a very lucky man."

He opened the puzzle book and took a Blackwing pencil No. 602 (he would use no other) from the ruby-glass jar that was kept filled for him at his elbow.

"What now?" I asked.

Father looked at me absently over the top of the puzzle book. Then, realizing that I had asked a question, he closed the book and put the pencil back in the jar. He was the most meticulous man I have ever known; I never saw him leave a book open or a pencil out of place. He now gave me his courteous attention.

"I get a thousand laughs a day," he explained, sitting back and marveling to himself. "Do you understand that, Margaret? A thousand laughs a day!"

I must have given him a kind of look. I was newly embarked on a reporter's career and I was death on stark facts, so I must have given him a kind of look. I'm sorry about it now, just as I was sorry about not finding dragons

§ 151 §

THE VICIOUS CIRCLE

for Mr. Fairbanks, because Father suddenly said, very loud, "All right, make it a *hundred* laughs a day!"

He picked up his newly sharpened Blackwing from the ruby-glass jar and opened the crossword-puzzle book.

"Let's just say," he said, grinning to himself, "that Gertrude Stein and I got one laugh apiece today."

CHAPTER EIGHT

Onward and Upward

ONE OF the reasons that Marc Connelly gives for the existence and growth of the Algonquin Round Table is the magical timing that brought success almost simultaneously to all of its members. "We all hit at the same time," is the way Marc describes it. And certainly, as the 'Twenties progressed, so did the Round Tablers.

Kaufman and Connelly followed their first two hits, *Dulcy* and *To the Ladies!* with two more, *Merton of the Movies* and *Helen of Troy, N.Y.,* and with a less successful but charming fantasy called *Beggar on Horseback,* starring Roland Young. *Beggar on Horseback,* for which Deems Taylor composed the ballet, "A Kiss in Xanadu," was the first American play to feature audience participation; at intermission ushers ran up and down the aisles distributing copies of a four-page newspaper called

THE MORNING-EVENING
With Which Has Been Combined
THE EVENING-MORNING
Retaining the Best Features of Each

§ 153 §

THE VICIOUS CIRCLE

The *Morning-Evening* carried news stories about a murder which took place in the play, photographs of the killer, Roland Young, interviews with celebrities (" 'What this country needs,' said Senator Gabrilowitch, 'I've got.' "), Letters to the Editor ("I dare you to print this. (Signed) DISGUSTED"), Bright Sayings of Little Ones ("The cat was playing with a ball of yarn underneath the dining room table. 'Glubub wook projem' said Donald, who is only five. The bishop left rather hurriedly.—J. J. Meck, 2162 Oakdale Avenue."), and some advertisements ("The Nouveau Clothing Shop, in the Woolworth Tower. 'Climb Sixty Flights and save Three Hundred Dollars.' ") This somewhat different gazette was written and edited by those somewhat different playwrights, Messrs. Kaufman and Connelly.

The *Morning-Evening* also offered a burlesque play review gently ribbing the on-the-fence attitude of certain critics which was even then driving playwrights crazy. The review read, in part, as follows:

NEW PLAY MAKES HIT OR DOES NOT
By Rashwyn Bramott
"The Ribifch Dorley" by Bharve Vegring, which these tired eyes looked at last night may be amusing to several million citizens but hardly entertaining or amusing in any way. . . . We or I may be wrong, but if "Rogklyup" is not the greatest play in spite of its frightful writing that has ever been written in the Nordic era, we or I may be quite wrong . . .

§ 154 §

Onward and Upward

It is interesting to note that, twenty-six years later, a recent review of a new play in *the New Yorker* (written by Douglas Watt, not by the magazine's usual critic, Wolcott Gibbs) reads in part as follows:

> "The Consul," the musical drama that came to the Ethel Barrymore Theatre last week is a history-making accomplishment. Although, as I see it, neither the book nor the music—both the work of Gian-Carlo Menotti, who also staged the piece—is of a very high order, they combine to give Broadway its first successful all-out opera. . . . The libretto, though serviceable, is coarse in texture, and so is the music, but they have been synthesized into an exciting work of art instead of merely an unsophisticated and slightly patronizing theatrical production. . . . Menotti is a new kind of man around the theatre. It's probably too bad that he's not a more original thinker, but still there's nobody else quite like him.

After a quarter of a century the critics, it seems, are still waiting for that cat to jump.

Around 1925 the Kaufman-Connelly team amicably separated, each to write a play alone; George wrote *The Butter-and-Egg Man* and Marc wrote *The Wisdom Tooth*. After that, Kaufman collaborated with Morris Ryskind on *Animal Crackers* for the Marx Brothers, with Ring Lardner on *June Moon*, with Edna Ferber on *Old Man Minick*, *The Royal Family*, and *Dinner at Eight*,

§ 155 §

THE VICIOUS CIRCLE

and with Alexander Woollcott on *The Channel Road*—until 1930, when *Once in a Lifetime* began his profitable partnership with Moss Hart. In the same year Connelly, after various rather unsatisfactory collaborations, wrote and produced *The Green Pastures,* which won him the Pulitzer Prize.

Robert Sherwood's first play, *The Road to Rome,* was presented in New York in 1926, with Jane Cowl and Philip Merivale as Amytis and Hannibal. In the next five years he turned out a play a year: *The Love Nest, The Queen's Husband* (with Roland Young), *Waterloo Bridge, This Is New York,* and his first starring vehicle for Alfred Lunt and Lynn Fontanne, *Idiot's Delight.* Theatregoers will fondly recall this as the play in which Lunt, as the vaudeville hoofer, did a song-and-dance number to "Puttin' on the Ritz" and also sang a "patter" to the tune of "Swanee River." This patter-song was especially written for the occasion by Irving Berlin, who, upon meeting Sherwood for the first time in Neysa McMein's studio in 1930, liked his familiarity with popular music. Although "The Red, Red Robin" is the only number he performs in public, Sherwood knows not only the tune, but the lyrics of just about every popular song ever written.

By the mid-'Twenties Brock Pemberton was securely established as a producer with *Enter Madame,* starring Gilda Varesi, *Miss Lulu Bett,* starring Carroll McComas, *Rita Coventry* with Dorothy Francis, and Pirandello's *Six Characters in Search of an Author* with an impressive cast: Florence Eldridge, Moffat Johnston, Margaret

§ 156 §

Onward and Upward

Wycherly, Ernest Cossart, and Dwight Frye. Brock was so successful, in fact, that when he produced a talky flop called *Swords* the Vicious Circle pounced on it gleefully. The scene of one of the sketches in *No, Sirree!* was the front of the theatre where *Swords* was playing. On all of the lobby signs the authors had removed the first letter of the play's title, so that the announcements proclaimed simply, "*Words*—produced by Brock Pemberton."

In 1922, F.P.A. and "The Conning Tower" moved from the *Tribune* to the *World's* famous "page-opposite-editorial" where they remained, along with Broun, Woollcott, Deems Taylor, Frank Sullivan and the other brilliant contributors to that page, until the *World* closed down in 1931. It was a bright decade for all of the Vicious Circle, the writers writing, the producers producing, and the actresses acting like mad. Dorothy Parker was putting out her best poems and short stories, including "Big Blonde" which has since been in perhaps more anthologies than Gelett Burgess's "Purple Cow." Edna Ferber was writing *The Girls, So Big, Show Boat* and *Cimarron* —to name a few of her novels during that time. Margalo Gillmore had begun to play leading roles in Eugene O'Neill plays, and in *He Who Gets Slapped, Outward Bound, The Green Hat* and *Ned McCobb's Daughter*— again to mention only a few. Peggy Wood starred in *The Clinging Vine* and other musicals in New York, and in the London production of *Bittersweet,* and also played Portia in *The Merchant of Venice* and the title role in *Candida.*

§ 157 §

THE VICIOUS CIRCLE

The Round Table's minnesinger was coming right along, too. In 1927, Deems Taylor composed the opera *The King's Henchman,* with libretto by Edna St. Vincent Millay, and a few years later he wrote *Peter Ibbetson.* Both operas were performed at the Metropolitan Opera House in New York. The fact that Deems Taylor has since become best known as a critic and a radio commentator is partly explained by his old friends from the Round Table, who call him Joe. "Joe has too much humor and is too nice a guy to be just a great composer," they say, adding, "You got to trip up old ladies and beat little children to be Wagner." Taylor greets these affectionate comments with a smile and goes on hammering at a chair, a table, or a new wing he is building for his house in the country. "I don't claim to be a great composer, or a great critic, or a great commentator," he admits through a mouthful of nails; then he takes the nails out and ringingly announces, "But, by God, I *am* a great carpenter!"

Great or not, Taylor has had a staggering success in popularizing good music throughout the country by means of the Deems Taylor Concerts, and his personality on the air is unique. He is probably the only long-haired musician in the world who would dream of announcing, as he recently did to his millions of listeners, "The next number is Paganini's 'Perpetuum Mobile,' whose function is to prove how many notes the violinist can play within a certain time without dropping dead."

Throughout the Nineteen-Twenties, which were famed for their loose living, mad spending, and general

§ 158 §

Onward and Upward

carelessness, the Algonquin Round Table stood like a rock as a symbol of hard work and devoted aims.

Everybody at the Round Table worked hard and continuously, and the work that most of them had chosen was the kind that demands steady and lonely toil. A writer has to shut himself up alone with a piece of blank paper until he produces something. An actress has to shut herself up alone with a part and pace back and forth with it until she learns it by heart. A composer has a piano for company, but not much else. Creative art is a lonely business to get into. Perhaps that is why the Round Table was so important to the boys and girls who lunched there; it was not only a sort of clearing house of news and ideas, it was the place where they could count on relaxing once a day among good company and plenty of laughs.

There was never any drinking at the Round Table —partly, of course, because Prohibition was in force and my father was a law-abiding man. He had, in fact, closed the Algonquin bar in 1917, three years before Prohibition went into effect, because (as he has told in his book, *Tales of a Wayward Inn*) it worried him to see young actors and writers sitting around drinking away their talents and not getting anywhere. These young people antedated the Round Table by several years, however. The main reason the Vicious Circle didn't drink (at lunch, anyway) was because they didn't feel the need of it. They were working too hard to give any real time to drinking, and they were having too much fun to give it any thought.

§ 159 §

THE VICIOUS CIRCLE

Sometimes in the evenings, when they gathered at Neysa's or at the Ross-Woollcott house in 47th Street, they saw nothing against a few Scotch-and-sodas; but even in convivial moments the tastes of at least two of them were not epicurean. Broun seldom drank anything but gin. As for Woollcott, he would touch nothing except potions sugary enough to blot out the taste of the liquor; his only cocktail was the whipped-cream concoction known as the Alexander, his favorite wine the sweet Chateau Yquem, and his pet liqueur an apricot or peach brandy.

"No wonder Aleck is so gay at lunch, with no liquor at all," Brock Pemberton once remarked. "Those drinks of his are the kind it must be perfect ecstasy to miss!"

The gags that flew about the Round Table ranged from the simplest throwaway quips to the most elaborate pranks. John Peter Toohey, being a large, sedate, and dignified gent, was a favorite butt. Toohey was also a careful man who did a good deal of worrying and consulting with Georges the headwaiter about the prices on the menu. At that time the Algonquin printed its own menus on a press in the basement, so the boys got Father to print up some special menus for the Round Table one day, and Georges presented them without comment. Toohey took a look at his and hit the ceiling. "Ham and eggs . . . $2.50" it read; "French fried potatoes . . . $1.75. Apple pie . . . $1.00. Coffee . . . .90."

"That does it!" roared Toohey, and flinging down his napkin he strode from the hotel. He was back pretty soon with a menu from Henri's, the restaurant next door,

§ 160 §

Onward and Upward

and collaring Father in the lobby, he confronted him with the two menus and the contrasting prices.

"What is the meaning of this?" he demanded.

"I'm sorry, John," Father said gently, "it's just economics. It costs me more to buy food, so I've got to charge more for it. I have to make a living, you know."

"I fail to see the necessity!" Toohey exploded. "Anyway, you can make it out of somebody else—not me!" And again he departed violently. He managed to stay away about a week, then, returning unobtrusively to lunch one day, observed with satisfaction that prices were back to normal.

"Well," he said, "I'm certainly glad that Frank Case has finally seen the light!"

Father himself had a lot of fun with his printing press and his menu. When wholesale prices did go up so, far that he was obliged to charge two dollars for a steak, the menu announced simply, "Sirloin steak . . . $2.00, and it's not worth it." When a certain critic (not at the Round Table) grew overly inclined to nag the waiters and find fault with the food, Father, in a burst of candor, named a dish after him and featured it large among the entrées: "Stewed Tripe à la Burton Rascoe."

Woollcott gradually, through sheer persistence, became the arbiter of the Round Table. He was a master performer in the Cult of Rudeness which had developed among the Vicious Circle, in which insult was the accepted coin of conversational exchange. Adams, Kaufman, and Connelly were not far behind him, but Woollcott's vocabulary of abuse was a flexible and glittering

§ 161 §

THE VICIOUS CIRCLE

weapon and he used it brilliantly and, more often than not, in great good humor.

"Hello, Frank, you greasy mass of Gentile self-pity," he once greeted Frank Sullivan in the Algonquin.

Sullivan, that mild-mannered Hibernian, looked startled. "Why 'Gentile'?" he asked wonderingly.

To Noel Coward, of whom he was genuinely fond, Aleck would begin a letter by paraphrasing one of Coward's lines in *Private Lives:* "Dear Noel," Aleck wrote, "there isn't a particle of you that I know, remember, or want." His liking for Coward dated from their first meeting, at the opening night of somebody else's ill-favored play, when Woollcott asked Coward what he thought of the show.

"Very vexing," Coward replied.

Woollcott's word-arrangements were not always abusive, but they were always felicitous. One night, Neysa McMein turned up at a party in a new gown glittering with spangles. "Why, Neysa," Aleck exclaimed, "you're scrofulous with mica!"

I myself was twice on the receiving end of Woollcott's milder poisoned darts. Once I was lunching with Father at the Algonquin, during the time Eugenie Leontovich was playing in *Grand Hotel,* and we got into a discussion about the pronunciation of the actress's name. Father said that, in New York, it was pronounced "Ewgeeny Lee-ON-tovich." I, recently from France and rather uppish about it, maintained that I had met many Russians in Paris, and that the name should be pronounced "Euhgzhay-NEE Layon-TO-vich."

§ 162 §

Onward and Upward

"Why don't you go over and ask Marc? He'd probably know," Father said.

Marc was an old friend (and had given me a volume of Austin Dobson's poems, romantically inscribed), so I skimmed over to the Round Table, leaned over Marc's shoulder, and said "How do you pronounce the name of the actress in *Grand Hotel*—the one who plays the ballet dancer?"

Before Marc could answer Woollcott looked up from his plate, his glasses glittering. "Any moron knows it's Ewgeeny Lee-ON-tovich," he said.

Taken aback, I murmured "Yes, but I'm not just *any* moron." It was feeble but the best I could do, and it seemed to please Woollcott faintly, for he addressed me as "Repulsive" thereafter—which, coming from him, amounted to the accolade. He even asked me, once, to an Easter prom at his cherished alma mater, Hamilton College, but I, with the fatuousness of youth, declined, having a previous engagement at the University of Virginia which seemed to me very pressing at the time. I have often since regretted that hasty refusal; it would have been something, indeed, to prom-trot with Alexander Woollcott.

My other slight brush with Mr. Woollcott occurred several years later, when I once telephoned him to ask some minor point of information for a Profile I was writing for the *New Yorker*.

"Why should I give you that information for your loathesome hack work? I might want to use it in a piece myself," he said charmingly, and hung up.

§ 163 §

THE VICIOUS CIRCLE

Woollcott's favorite weapon was belittlement, and for some reason it always seemed particularly delicious to him to establish anyone as having come from a small town. (He himself was born in Phalanx, New Jersey.) "Ah, the fair Miss Leech of Newburgh, N.Y." he would greet Peggy; or, to Frank Sullivan, "Well, well, the scintillating Sullivan of Saratoga Springs!" Russel Crouse, later co-author with Howard Lindsay of *Life with Father,* but then a columnist on the New York *Evening Post,* was addicted to wearing dark blue shirts—the kind actors call "thousand-mile shirts" because they can be worn forever without showing the strain. "Touching, isn't it," Woollcott would remark pensively, "how ever-faithful Buck Crouse is to that little old general store at the crossroads, back home in Saugerties, N.Y.?" The fact that Crouse came from Findlay, Ohio, made no difference to Aleck; Saugerties sounded better.

All this was gentle spoofing but it could become a little wearing, and the laughter was never more general than on the day Aleck, looking across the Round Table at Henry Wise Miller (husband of Alice) and visibly planning to put that polished gentleman in his place, softly inquired "And where were *you* born, Harry?"

"I?" said Mr. Miller, looking a little surprised. "I was born in Nice." Then he wondered why everybody roared and regarded him so affectionately. Not even Woollcott could do anything with "Henry Wise Miller of Nice." It just didn't come out right.

Aleck enjoyed his own comeuppances as much as anybody did. He once waylaid his friends for days to

§ 164 §

Onward and Upward

tell them what Frank Sullivan had said to him after he (Woollcott) returned triumphantly from a long lecture tour.

"I spoke to ten thousand women in St. Paul," Aleck told Frank complacently.

"What did you tell 'em? No?" Frank inquired.

In spite of this genial camaraderie, Woollcott liked to boss the Round Table to such a degree that he often found himself pinked by the Vicious Circle's own weapon of casual mockery. One time, after Aleck had been laying down the law daily for several weeks, Harold Ross found a place on Sixth Avenue that sold lapel buttons and imitation postage stamps engraved with any desired photograph, and he ordered a supply of each bearing Woollcott's likeness. Next day the entire Round Table, except Woollcott, turned up wearing Woollcott buttons and prattling excitedly of the new philatelic find, the Woollcott Stamp. For some time they continued to wear the buttons and to plaster their letters with Woollcott stamps until at last Ross said disgustedly, "We might as well give up. That guy *never* gets sick of the sight of his own face."

There was always a kind of edginess between Ross and Woollcott, as indeed there was between Woollcott and many people. Marc Connelly now explains Woollcott's combativeness in a pensive sentence-and-a-half.

"Rancor was Aleck's only form of exercise," says Marc. "Oh, sure, he did a few physical reflexes over croquet, but . . . "

Some people, including Marc, think that the Ross-

THE VICIOUS CIRCLE

Woollcott feud which everlastingly waxed and waned between these two true friends stemmed, partly at least, from Ross's happy indifference to time in those days as contrasted with Aleck's almost violent punctuality. One broken appointment between them was clearly Ross's fault, and it led to a lively evening.

Aleck had invited Ross to dinner at his apartment— this was after the 47th Street household broke up—and to a first night afterward. Woollcott had long made it plain to his friends that an invitation from him was a command, and most of them indulged this whim— partly because of his compelling personality and real charm as a host, and partly because they preferred to obey his slightest wish whenever convenient rather than suffer the abuse that would follow if they didn't.

Early in the evening Ross ran into Marc Connelly, who also asked him to dine, at the Algonquin.

"Can't do it," said Ross. "I'm having dinner with Aleck and he's taking me to an opening."

Marc can look horrified better than anybody else in the world, and he did it then. "*Tonight's* opening?" he exclaimed. "But that's the worst play in history! Nothing like it has ever been seen for sheer *nothing!* Haven't you read the out-of-town notices? Look here, Ross, Aleck can't *do* that to you!"

Ross stood still in his tracks. "Why, that God damn son of a bitch," he said sincerely, "this is the *second* time he's taken me to a lousy play. Lead on, Connelly."

Ross and Connelly were dining pleasantly when Woollcott, lacking his guest, bounced into the Algon-

§ 166 §

Onward and Upward

quin in search of somebody to take to the play. "He was wearing his opera cape and he looked just like a Sandeman Port ad, blown up for posters," Marc remembers. After a tour of the lobby Aleck glanced into the dining room and, naturally, the first thing his eye lit on was his expected guest, Ross, comfortably having dinner with Marc. Aleck marched up to the table and delivered himself of a six-word diatribe that Ross still cherishes.

"You," he said to Ross, "are *a fourth-rate person*."

After Aleck had bustled out, cape flowing and sparks flying, Ross worried a little. He *had* been rude in standing up his host, and the Round Tablers were never rude to each other , except conversationally. They weren't even rude to Woollcott, unless in self-defense. Ross was unhappy about the whole thing until Marc solved it by sending for a telegraph blank and wiring the following message to Woollcott:

> Dear Aleck,
>
> I find myself in a bit of a jam. If anybody asks you where I was tonight would you mind saying that I was with you?
>
> Yours
Ross

Woollcott's rancor, in his worst moments, did not always have to have as reasonable a source as it had that night. Sometimes, if he got it into his head to work up an anger against women writers, say, or Catholics, or Protestants, or Jews, or people with six fingers, he would attack personally anyone who happened to be a woman

THE VICIOUS CIRCLE

writer, a Catholic, a Protestant, a Jew, or (this seldom occurred) who happened to have six fingers. He liked to attack in public, with an audience, and at such times his language was shocking, his raging mind darted everywhere to produce the wounding word, and his reckless tongue flared out like an arsonist's senseless fire. It was not a pretty spectacle. Much as we all admired Woollcott for his brilliance, his hidden (often too well-hidden) tenderness, and his talents as a storyteller, a good many of us in New York think that the people who managed to get along with him at the Round Table, in one way or another, for more than a decade deserve some kind of award. Perhaps a Woollcott Button.

Except for Woollcott's occasional spasms, the Round Table was a perfect miniature democracy. Its members included Gentiles and Jews, Catholics and Protestants, Republicans, Democrats, and Socialists. They were all friends, all working in pretty much the same field, and although they had many stimulating quarrels about this and that, it never occurred to any of them to question another's religious or political beliefs. They were all for one, and one for all, and the individual was the important thing—not what God he believed in, or how he voted.

Not even Woollcott's habit of sudden abuse could destroy the texture of the Round Table. But it could strain it, and sometimes did.

One day Aleck found himself seated, at lunch, between his two dear friends, George Kaufman and Dorothy Parker. Kaufman is a Jew, and perfectly content with

§ 168 §

Onward and Upward

it. Dorothy Parker, née Rothschild, is the daughter of a Gentile mother and a Jewish father, and has never seen fit to boast of either in the way that Woollcott always bragged about the Bucklins and his other forebears— although she could justifiably point with pride to her mother's Scottish ancestors and the fact that her father was a distinguished Talmudic scholar.

It just never occurred to Kaufman or Mrs. Parker that their ancestry could possibly be as interesting as they, themselves, might one day be.

On this day at the Round Table, Kaufman said something Woollcott disagreed with, and Woollcott— for no reason anyone will ever know—suddenly spurted venom.

"Shut up, you Christ-killer," he said.

There was a moment of shocked silence. Then Kaufman rose and spoke calmly to the Round Table.

"This is the last time," he told them, "that I will tolerate any slur upon my race at this table. I have had enough from Mr. Woollcott. I am now walking away from this table, out of this dining room, and out of this hotel."

He threw down his napkin, pushed back his chair, and looked at Dottie Parker.

"And I hope," he added, "that Mrs. Parker will walk out with me—half way."

§ 169 §

CHAPTER NINE

The Birth of The New Yorker

"I THINK I shall discover electricity," said F.P.A. to Harold Ross and George Kaufman one May day in 1924 when they were lying under a tree in Connecticut.

Ross nodded gravely. "It would revolutionize everything," he agreed.

For a moment there was silence, except for the humming of the bees, the nodding of the wildflowers. (Wildflowers creak in Connecticut.)

An apple blossom fell on Ross's forehead. "I think I would rather discover the law of gravitation," he said presently. "Then people would no longer have to walk upstairs, because it would lead to the invention of the elevator."

Kaufman stirred languidly. "I have already discovered the law of gravitation," he informed the other two. "I was lying in a fig orchard the other day and a fig hit me on the head. From that it was only a step," he added, "to the invention of Fig Newtons."

§ 171 §

THE VICIOUS CIRCLE

. . . In 1924, Harold Ross's personal law of gravitation was swinging him rapidly toward his own center, which was to be *The New Yorker* Magazine. His career up to that time had included newspaper jobs from Salt Lake City to San Francisco, a couple of editorial stints in New York, and a hitch in the A.E.F. during which he was managing editor of the Army magazine, *Stars and Stripes.*

Immediately after the end of World War I, Mrs. William Brown Meloney, who was then editor of *Delineator,* sent an emissary to Paris looking for the genius, or geniuses, who had made such a brilliant success of *Stars and Stripes. Delineator,* a fashion magazine, was owned by the Butterick Publishing Company and Butterick wanted to get the men who had put out *Stars and Stripes* to start a new magazine in the United States. It was to be a magazine for ex-soldiers, called *The Home Sector,* and Butterick hoped that, like the ex-soldiers, it would gradually gentle down into a civilian career.

Mrs. Meloney's emissary found that the *Stars and Stripes* was gotten out by Ross, John T. Winterich, Aleck Woollcott, Hudson Hawley, C. Leroy Baldridge, A.A. Wallgren, and—for a time—Franklin P. Adams and Stephen Early. Adams thankfully accepted a transfer after a few uncomfortable weeks, since he was the only man on the staff with the rank of Captain and the nominal, or military, editor was also a Captain . . . one Captain Visniski (now deceased) of whom Ross still speaks as "our maniac commanding officer." With all that rank around the office, there was naturally friction.

§ 172 §

The Birth of The New Yorker

Stephen Early is, of course, the same Early who later became White House Secretary under Franklin D. Roosevelt.

Of the *Stars and Stripes* staff Ross now says, "I was the so-called managing editor . . . and I was that in name only. The true facts are that it was really a collaboration—one of 'the few successful ones of such intensity I've ever seen in my life—and that all the writers, and to a certain extent the artists, too, were editors. Hudson Hawley and Woollcott were more writers than editors, though, and Winterich and I did the desk work. Winterich was as much a managing editor as I was and it is my impression that he was carried as such officially, I believe."

Winterich now writes for the *Saturday Review of Literature* and *The New Yorker,* and is a sort of roving editor of both. Hudson Hawley, who was known to his comrades as The Saluting Demon of the A.E.F. because he was so shortsighted that he saluted everybody for fear of missing a superior officer, became a foreign correspondent for INS after the war and went to live in Rome. C. Leroy Baldridge, an artist who specialized in painting the Orient (and occasionally that flower of the Occident, Alexander Woollcott) has published three books about the Orient which are now collectors' items, and is a commercial artist, book illustrator, and typography consultant. A.A. Wallgren, another painter, died in 1948.

After a few conferences with Mrs. Meloney's representative this staff—or most of them—sailed for America,

§ 173 §

THE VICIOUS CIRCLE

full of steam and ready to put out the greatest American weekly magazine the nation had ever seen.

The Home Sector lasted for four issues. It was as well-written and as well-edited as the *Stars and Stripes*, which is saying a good deal, but it retained a certain flavor of the war, and people wanted to forget the war. A general printers' strike gave *The Home Sector* its final kick in the teeth, and in 1919 it merged with the new-born *American Legion Weekly*, with Ross going along as editor of the combined magazines.

Ross stayed with the *American Legion Weekly* until 1924, and then became editor of *Judge*, the old comic weekly, but he was restless and unhappy. He now avers that the *Judge* outfit never had one idea of its own all the time he was there; furthermore, *Judge* had the reputation, justly earned, of being the slowest pay in the publishing business—they practically never paid contributors until threatened with lawsuits, and Ross, though anguished by such conduct, found himself powerless to do anything about it. Besides, he was bothered by certain ideas of his own that had long been churning in his mind. One was the notion of starting a tabloid newspaper that would be free of the sensationalism of the then-current *Graphic* and other tabloid sheets. Ross never carried out this idea, but it proved so contagious to Ralph Ingersoll when he was *The New Yorker's* first managing editor, that he later went off and started the tabloid, *P.M.* Another project even dearer to Ross was a plan for a purely local humorous weekly based on his theory that the more local humor is, the better it is

§ 174 §

The Birth of The New Yorker

within its limited circle. He explains, these days, that the reason he went to *Judge* in the first place was to get a toe hold in the humorous magazine business.

On Sundays Ross and his wife, Jane Grant, would take long walks all over New York, along the river front and often as far as Chinatown or the Bronx. Ross had lived and worked in cities, but he was still the boy from Aspen, Colorado, with a capacity for being astonished by the big town—although he now denies this with some heat. "I may well have been the boy from Aspen, all right," he wrote me crisply in a recent note, "but I point out that I left at the age of six and thereafter lived in cities—Salt Lake City, Denver, San Francisco, Panama, New Orleans, New York, and Paris, more or less in the order named. I was really just the petted darling of world capitals." At any rate, during these walks around New York, he and Jane lengthily discussed the idea that was crystallizing in his mind: a humorous weekly magazine strictly about New York, and written for New Yorkers.

The original staff of *The Home Sector* (and *Stars and Stripes*) welcomed the project, and so did other friends of theirs: Hawley Truax, Henry Wise Miller, Ralph Barton, Lloyd Stryker, Katharine Angell (now Mrs. E. B. White), and Rea Irvin. Soon the Ross house on 47th Street and the Algonquin Round Table buzzed with plans. John Peter Toohey suggested *The New Yorker* as a title and received $1,500 in stock for it, thus becoming one of that envied little band of pioneers, the original stockholders. Ross thought that $50,000 would be enough

§ 175 §

THE VICIOUS CIRCLE

at least to try out the idea, and he and Jane raised half of that amount. The other half came from Raoul Fleischmann of the baking family, whom Ross had first met at the weekly poker games held by the Thanatopsis Literary and Inside Straight Club in the Algonquin. There was also a fairly definite prospect of more money later from Fleischmann's very wealthy cousin, Julius Fleischmann.

Ross himself wrote the prospectus for the new publication, and this document has since become a classic in publishing circles because of its simplicity and sincerity, and because *The New Yorker* today reflects its principles as completely as it did in its first issue. For anyone who is interested in what other editors and publishers still speak of as "the best goddam prospectus ever written" the Ross document is quoted herewith, in full:

ANNOUNCING A NEW WEEKLY MAGAZINE

The New Yorker will be a reflection in word and picture of metropolitan life. It will be human. Its general tenor will be one of gaiety, wit and satire, but it will be more than a jester. It will not be what is commonly called radical or highbrow. It will be what is commonly called sophisticated, in that it will assume a reasonable degree of enlightenment on the part of its readers. It will hate bunk.

As compared to the newspaper, The New Yorker will be interpretative rather than sten-

§ 176 §

The Birth of The New Yorker

ographic. It will print facts that it will have to go behind the scenes to get, but it will not deal in scandal for the sake of scandal nor sensation for the sake of sensation. Its integrity will be above suspicion. It hopes to be so entertaining and informative as to be a necessity for the person who knows his way about or wants to.

The New Yorker will devote several pages a week to the covering of contemporary events and people of interest. This will be done by writers capable of appreciating the elements of a situation and, in setting them down, of indicating their importance and significance. The New Yorker will present the truth and the whole truth without fear and without favor, but will not be iconoclastic.

Amusements and the arts will be thoroughly covered by departments which will present, in addition to criticism, the personality, the anecdote, the color and chat of the various subdivisions of this sphere. The New Yorker's conscientious guide will list each week all current amusement offerings worth-while—theatres, motion pictures, musical events, art exhibitions, sport and miscellaneous entertainment —providing an ever-ready answer to the prevalent query, "What shall we do with this evening?" Through The New Yorker's Mr. Van Bibber III, readers will be kept apprised of what is going on in the public and semi-public smart

§ 177 §

THE VICIOUS CIRCLE

gathering places—the clubs, hotels, cafés, supper clubs, cabarets and other resorts.

Judgment will be passed upon new books of consequence, and The New Yorker will carry a list of the season's books which it considers worth reading.

There will be a page of editorial paragraphs, commenting on the week's events in a manner not too serious.

There will be a personal mention column —a jotting down in the small-town newspaper style of the comings, goings, and doings in the village of New York. This will contain some josh and some news value.

The New Yorker will carry each week several pages of prose and verse, short and long, humorous, satirical and miscellaneous.

The New Yorker expects to be distinguished for its illustrations, which will include caricatures, sketches, cartoons and humorous and satirical drawings in keeping with its purpose.

The New Yorker will be the magazine which is not edited for the old lady in Dubuque. It will not be concerned with what she is thinking about. This is not meant in disrespect, but The New Yorker is a magazine avowedly published for a metropolitan audience and thereby will escape an influence which hampers most national publications. It expects a considerable

§ 178 §

The Birth of The New Yorker

national circulation, but this will come from persons who have a metropolitan interest.

The New Yorker will appear early in February.

The price will be: Five dollars a year
Fifteen cents a copy

ADVISORY EDITORS

Ralph Barton	George S. Kaufman
Heywood Broun	Alice Duer Miller
Marc Connelly	Dorothy Parker
Edna Ferber	Laurence Stallings
Rea Irvin	Alexander Woollcott

H. W. Ross, Editor

The story behind the impressive list of Advisory Editors has its own piquancy. As *The New Yorker's* first issue was going to press (*without* any list of Advisory Editors), Raoul Fleischmann came to Ross, looking worried.

"I've been talking to this friend of mine," he said, "and I'm afraid he's got a point. *He* says that *The New Yorker* will never work out because your idea of not having any famous contributors, or not even signing their names if you *do* have them, is all wrong. He says people buy magazines for the famous and familiar names in 'em, and that nobody will read a magazine that hasn't got any famous names."

To Ross, Fleischmann looked like a man on the verge of backing out. Ross made a quick decision.

§ 179 §

THE VICIOUS CIRCLE

"If it's names you want," he said, "names you'll get."

In a series of fast telephone calls, after Fleischmann had gone, he rounded up ten of his own friends; then he invented a title for them and quickly sent the list through, along with the first issue. "Some of them didn't really work on the magazine, and others I had no expectation of getting actual help from," Ross admits now, adding, "It was one of the shoddiest things I have ever done. I have been ashamed of it ever since."

Any magazine that wholly lived up to Ross's prospectus in its very first issue would have had to be bound in angels' feathers. The first issue of *The New Yorker*, on February 21st, 1925, did not entirely fulfill the promise of the prospectus; but it didn't betray it, either. In a gay and open-faced way it carried out Ross's conviction that New York is just a village. The Personal Mention column, for instance—a parody of rural style by metropolitan wise guys—offered such items as, "Miss Kate Sproehnle, fair equestrienne, was seen riding in the Park on Sunday"; and "A prominent dramatic critic walking along Park Row was hailed by Robert C. Benchley. 'Hello, George,' said Benchley. He thought that it was Murdock Pemberton." To anyone who knew the people concerned these items were either interesting or funny, but the department was soon dropped as being too intramural. It is the only department mentioned in the prospectus that has ever been dropped.

For the first cover Ross had considered an idea suggested by an artist sent to him by Elmer Adler, who was

§ 180 §

The Birth of The New Yorker

Beatrice Kaufman's cousin . . . it was to picture a great curtain going up on New York. None of the drawings of this scene quite came off, however, and meantime Rea Irvin thought up, and drew, the Regency gent with the top hat, monocle, and butterfly who has come to symbolize *The New Yorker* and whose portrait still appears on every anniversary issue. This character was nameless until Corey Ford, using him in a series of *New Yorker* ads he wrote sometime later, christened him Eustace Tilley.

At first *The New Yorker* was written largely by members of the Round Table and their friends, anonymously or under pen names like "Golly-wog," "Quid," and "Ambrose Glutz." This was in keeping with Ross's belief, which he still maintains, that it is the text that matters and not the signature. "Ambrose Glutz," also a frequent contributor to "The Conning Tower," was actually the Mayor of Saratoga, N.Y., but nobody on *The New Yorker* staff remembers exactly who "Golly-wog" and "Quid" were. Even dramatic criticism was, for a time, signed "Last Night"—although the critics themselves were not unknown. Herman J. Mankiewicz, Charles Brackett, and Gilbert W. Gabriel were among the early ones. About the only *New Yorker* sobriquet that ever became famous, however, was that of Lois Long, who signed her night-club column "Lipstick" and soon became better known by that name than she was known by her own. Lois also merely initialed *The New Yorker's* fashion department, "On and Off the Avenue," which she made illustrious, not only as a darn good fashion department

§ 181 §

THE VICIOUS CIRCLE

written in colloquial English instead of coy clichés, but also, with Ross's encouragement and support, as the first fashion department in the business that was positively not afraid of advertisers. If a firm that advertised in *The New Yorker* produced dresses that stank, "L.L." said so, and the hell with it; let the firm withdraw its advertising if it wanted to—or produce better dresses. This stand created grey hairs in *The New Yorker's* advertising department (and still does), but it established, too, a lasting respect in the fashion trade for *The New Yorker's* opinion. To any designer or retailer, a good notice in *The New Yorker* amounts to the laurel wreath. They know it can't be bought.

This kind of honest independence was, of course, not limited to the fashion department. It pervaded the whole magazine, and was possibly one of the reasons for its success. (The other reason is that it's a good magazine.) Years after its first issue, I wrote a Profile for *The New Yorker*, about Elizabeth Arden, in which I quoted *Consumer's Research* as saying that a bottle of Arden Skin Tonic which sold at retail for eighty-five cents, cost her three cents a bottle to manufacture. The Profile came out, and Miss Arden got on the phone, tooth and claw, to a *New Yorker* editor.

"Your Profile writer is a big liar!" she shouted. "That Skin Tonic costs me *twelve* cents a bottle to manufacture!"

She then stormily canceled her advertising in *The New Yorker*—quite a blow, since this was in the 'Thirties when business was not good. She put it back after six

§ 182 §

HAROLD ROSS

The Birth of The New Yorker

weeks, of course; but the thing that always enchants me about this story is that I never even *heard* it until it was all over. To *The New Yorker* editors it was so open-and-shut that it wasn't even worth mentioning next time I saw them.

I perceive that I have digressed some at this point from the day-by-day inception of *The New Yorker,* so let me digress a little more . . .

Lois Long and I were both working on *Vanity Fair* as some kind of assistant editors in 1924, when the news of a new magazine called *The New Yorker* began to circulate. Lois quit *Vanity Fair* almost immediately, and went to work for the new magazine. I am told now that I could have had a job on it too, at that time, but I am a slower thinker than Lois and anyway, I was very happy where I was. I was making a fast $40 a week for doing absolutely nothing but make up the theatre pages, escort actors and actresses to Steichen's studio to be photographed, write all theatre captions and all captions for humorous drawings, interview new writers, make free translations of all the French stories *Vanity Fair* bought cheap in the original, think up ideas for picture pages aside from the theatre and assemble photographs for same (with humorous captions), and write a fiction story a month. For the fiction story—always a glittering slice of life on Park Avenue, where I had never lived—I got an extra $100 a month. Why should I leave this cushy job for a new outfit, just starting out? It never even occurred to me to think of it.

Besides, we had a lot of fun at *Vanity Fair.* Frank

§ 185 §

THE VICIOUS CIRCLE

Crowninshield, the editor, was always stopping all work to show us a new trick with a pack of cards or a vanishing handkerchief or a glass of water and a coin. Crowny was a passionate amateur magician, and his friends John Mulholland and Keating, the master wizards, often materialized in the office too, and pulled live canaries out of my hat, or love notes out of the water cooler from me to Johnny McMullin. Johnny McMullin, with whom I shared an office, was "Him"—the men's fashion editor of *Vanity Fair*—and his manner to me could only be described as queenly.

In addition to all this we had, for a time, the Keene Twins. The Keene Twins were a pair of musical comedy dancing sisters, temporarily working as file clerks because one of them had had an appendectomy and couldn't dance for a while. They practiced around the office a good deal, however, going into their act at the slightest notice, and they also did stretching and limbering exercises by pulling all the top drawers of the files almost all the way out and then, dancing along the cabinets, kicking the drawers the rest of the way out. It took four new girls six weeks to get the files back in order after the Keene Twins returned to their art.

The day the first issue of *The New Yorker* came out, Crowny came through my cubbyhole with a copy of it and beckoned me into his own office. I sat beside him at his desk while he took one of those square mints he was always nibbling, offered me one, and then, in his habitually neat way, opened the new magazine and spread it flat on the desk. Crowny had a meticulous way of using

§ 186 §

The Birth of The New Yorker

his hands . . . he always reminded me of Father that way.

We went through *The New Yorker* together, page by page, and when we had finished Crowny leaned back and took off his pince-nez.

"Well, Margaret," he said, "I think we have nothing to fear."

Dear Crowny. All *The New Yorker* eventually did was put *Vanity Fair* out of business.

Nobody, it is true, could have guessed that that would happen from reading *The New Yorker's* first issue. Compared to *Vanity Fair's* rich Steichen photographs, imposing array of names, and handsome make-up, it was pretty flimsy-looking. But its humor was, from the beginning, fresh and unexpected—the humor of understatement—and in its first issue it declared war ringingly against the old comic-weekly he-and-she type of joke by publishing the now-famous "optimist" gag which appeared in every anniversary issue until about five years ago:

"A man who thinks he can make it in par."
Johnny: "What is an optimist, Pop?"

Profiles were another protest against conventional journalism, being utterly different from the accepted rags-to-riches success story popular with magazines of the period. The early Profiles (Gatti-Casazza and Jimmy Walker were among the first subjects) occupied only a page or two, and were simply what the name implies— an impression of a character. Nowadays, Profiles some-

§ 187 §

THE VICIOUS CIRCLE

times run to three or four installments and can take a writer anywhere from six weeks to six months to complete. About half of this time is spent in getting material and writing the piece, and the other half in rewriting and polishing according to editorial suggestion and in answering marginal queries from editors and checkers. These queries range from Ross's harassed "Wording. What mean, for Christ's sake?" to the checkers' courteous "Guess this was in 1938, not 1939." The finished product is as perfect as combined human effort can make it, and Profiles, along with Notes and Comment and Talk of the Town, are now pondered over and analyzed in many journalism classes as examples of good factual writing.

Three weeks after *The New Yorker's* first issue came out, Julius Fleischmann died suddenly while playing polo. The loss of his potential support was a bitter blow to Ross, particularly since Raoul Fleischmann showed signs of weakening about the whole thing after his cousin's death. Things got so tough in the Spring of 1925 that Ross had practically decided to suspend publication while he looked around for a new backer. The magazine was saved, then, by a kind of mad minor miracle. Its date of publication had just been changed by advancing it three days, thus making a ten-day week, or a ten-day interval between issues. During the extra three days Raoul Fleischmann decided to go along with the project . . . and *The New Yorker* survived.

It lost money for three years, and finally turned the corner largely because of another whimsical trick of

§ 188 §

The Birth of The New Yorker

timing. Alice Duer Miller sent a young cousin of hers around to see Ross, a girl who wanted to be a writer, and Ross told her to go ahead and write. When she sent in her first piece, about débutante parties, it seemed to him more suited to *Vogue* or *Vanity Fair,* but it was good and he published it. It was called "The Stag Line" and its author was Ellin Mackay. Ellin Mackay was news, not only as the daughter of Clarence Mackay but as the brand-new bride of Irving Berlin, and Ross was not above a little canny advance promotion about her story coming out in his magazine. The day after it appeared every newspaper in town carried quotes from it under such headings as "Daughter of Clarence Mackay Raps Social Conventions" and "Socialite Deb Goes to Town in New Yorker Magazine." Not even this hullabaloo could have saved a magazine that did not have the seed of permanence in it, but it did provide a turning point, and from that moment *The New Yorker* has gone steadily (to use its own phrase) onward and upward.

. . . Another digression here, saving your presence. One evening in 1926, when I was newly married myself and living on, of all places, Park Avenue, we had Elsie Janis and her mother and Irving Berlin to dinner. Mrs. Janis had always been not too secretly in favor of a marriage between Elsie and Irving, who were devoted friends although not matrimonially inclined toward each other, and throughout dinner she kept pointedly remarking on the virtues of married life. "Just look at Margaret and Morgan!" she would exclaim, feeding a

§ 189 §

THE VICIOUS CIRCLE

portion of soufflé to the small dog in her lap. After
dinner Elsie and Mrs. Janis had to hurry down to the
Palace Theatre where Elsie was playing, and after a
while Irving left too, saying he had a date. The date the
little rascal had was to get married to Ellin Mackay.
They were married that very night, and found shelter
from reporters in the Ross house on 47th Street until it
was time for their ship to sail.

I have always liked this small anecdote because it
proves so cosily what Ross has always said—that New
York is just a village. . . .

In its first two or three years *The New Yorker* staff
was enriched by four people who, although they have
never held any titles in the organization (there are no
formal titles at *The New Yorker*) have become, next to
Ross, the main factors of its success. They are Katharine
White, E. B. White, James Thurber, and Wolcott
Gibbs. Katharine White, a Barnard graduate, was the
magazine's first fiction editor and brought all her literacy
and good taste to the selection of short stories, or
"casuals" as the staff calls them. She was, and remains,
the "refining" influence, although she will probably
hit me on the head for saying so, if she ever reads this.
Her husband, E. B. ("Andy") White, was the first writer
of Notes and Comments and Talk of the Town, and
set a style for those departments so distinctive that
various squads of other writers have been able to carry
it on since. Andy White is also eligible to fame as the
man who pulled Thurber's pensive doodlings about

The Birth of The New Yorker

dogs and people out of a wastebasket and insisted that *The New Yorker* publish them. Thurber worked only at writing in those days, and would still rather be considered a writer than an artist. Gibbs, now the magazine's drama critic and author of some of its best Profiles and "casuals," and of the hit play "Season in the Sun," was another cousin of Alice Duer Miller's whom she sent around to see Ross about a job as copyreader in 1927, after he had spent a lively year or so as a railroad switchman. "I don't give a damn what else you do," said Ross, hiring him, "but for God's sake, don't seduce the contributors."

According to Ross no magazine is better than its desk men, and he is scrupulous about giving credit to these otherwise anonymous toilers. "Shawn on factual pieces," he points out, "Lobrano on fiction, Geraghty on drawings, Peppe on make-up, Whitaker in the checking department . . . where would the magazine be without them? Where would I be, for that matter?" It is his mournful plaint that Wolcott Gibbs, busy with being drama critic and playwright, no longer has time to be a desk man. "He was one of the best goddam editors in the world" is Ross's salute to Gibbs.

About nine months after *The New Yorker* started, a young bandleader recently out of Yale, and traveling around playing dance dates with his orchestra, sent in a couple of spot-drawings (those vignettes in the middle of a page) which the editors bought, and followed them up with the first of the famous Whoops Sisters cartoons. This was, of course, Peter Arno, whose real name was

§ 191 §

THE VICIOUS CIRCLE

Curtis Arnoux Peters, and who soon became not only a *New Yorker* tradition but, for a time, the husband of Lois Long.

Many of the Round Table people were too occupied with their own jobs during *The New Yorker's* early years to contribute much, if anything, although off and on from 1927 to 1931 its book-reviewer was Dorothy Parker, signing herself "Constant Reader." Mrs. Parker, it may be recalled, made her most notable pronouncement in this department when, reviewing one of A. A. Milne's sugary works, she remarked, "At this point, Tonstant Weader fwowed up." Aleck Woollcott had early made it plain that he took little or no interest in the magazine; his time was too valuable, he stated, to waste on any non-paying proposition. However, his personal skirmishings with Ross—for which he seemed to have all the time in the world—had become so conspicuous that, in 1926, when the staff put out a privately circulated issue in honor of Ross's birthday, Rea Irvin was inspired to draw a special cover. It represented Ross as Eustace Tilley, with top hat, high stock, and cowlick, gazing through his monocle and sticking out his tongue at a pudgy hovering spider. The spider's face was the face of A. Woollcott.*

* The birthday issue, very intramural and now a collector's item, also carried this paragraph in Talk of the Town—it may amuse readers who have read Chapter Seven: "The Lucy Stone League is making progress, although nobody knows it except possibly ourselves—and we only through the accident of our acquaintance with Harold Grant, the founder. 'How are things getting on?' we asked, seeing him in a passing taxicab. 'Fine,' he called as the traffic swallowed him, 'I'm calling myself Ross now, you know.'"

§ 192 §

The Birth of The New Yorker

Aleck did not like to be left out of a going concern any more than he liked being associated with a losing one, and three or four years later he began his *New Yorker* page of anecdote and comment entitled "Shouts and Murmurs." His relationship with the magazine turned out to be a kind of Seven Years' War, punctuated throughout by battle cries and frequent and stormy resignations. It got to be so that any unusually loud ring of the telephone in *The New Yorker* offices would draw from some tired editor the weary conjecture, "It's probably just Woollcott resigning again." He carried on running hostilities with copyreaders and checkers over questions of fact, spelling, and even punctuation, and on one occasion triumphed gloriously over them— a victory that so enraptured him that he behaved like an angel for almost a month afterward.

Woollcott's assistant in the drama department of the *World* was a quiet young Englishman named Jeffrey Holmesdale who had started work on the paper as a ships' news reporter—one of the toughest and most thankless jobs on any newspaper, involving, as it does, hurtling out of the harbor in a tug to meet incoming ships of a cold winter's dawn. Holmesdale handled this assignment calmly and well, and was promoted to the drama department where he assisted Woollcott capably for about a year before explaining apologetically one day that his father was ill and he would have to go home to England for a time. Some weeks later Aleck, unfolding his paper one morning, came upon a picture of his assistant, clad in ermine, over a press dispatch announcing

§ 193 §

THE VICIOUS CIRCLE

the death, in England, of the fourth Earl Amherst and the sucession of his son, Viscount Holmesdale, who had recently been pursuing a literary career in New York.

Pretty soon the fifth earl was back at his job in the drama department, and Woollcott was in transports. Having had a real Viscount as his assistant was exciting enough, but having a belted earl working for him was heaven. Beaming, he sat down and wrote the whole story for his "Shouts and Murmurs" page in *The New Yorker,* and so unconsciously brought upon himself even greater laurels as just about the only writer who ever got the best of a *New Yorker* checker. (New Yorker checkers are infallible and, like any group of infallible people, are feared and hated to a man by *New Yorker* writers.) In his manuscript Woollcott wrote Holmesdale's title—correctly—as "Earl Amherst." The *New Yorker* checkers, through some surprising lapse, changed this to read *"the* Earl *of* Amherst," and it came out in the magazine that way—which was wrong. Woollcott's emotions, on viewing this error in print, were shock and anger—soon giving place, however, to a wild, demoniacal joy.*

Aleck and *The New Yorker* parted company for good in the late Nineteen-Thirties, when Ross flatly declined to publish the smoking-car stories Woollcott had grown increasingly fond of featuring in "Shouts and

* I once scored a mild victory over *The New Yorker* checkers myself. Writing about Mrs. Cole Porter's jewels, I mentioned her collection of aquamarines, and a checker's query read: "Does she buy these or paint them herself?" Wish I had had the presence of mind to reply "She paints them" and let it go at that.

§ 194 §

The Birth of The New Yorker

Murmurs." Ross is a fearless puritan ("He's real un-inhibited that way," a female contributor from the South once remarked admiringly), and no smutty or even questionable line gets into his magazine if he can help it—and Ross is the boy who can help it. The one vulgarity that ever sneaked in was the drawing of a man and a girl on a country road at night, carrying the back seat of an automobile between them and saying to the local constable, "We want to report a stolen car." Ross's friends maintain that the reason that one got by was simply that Ross didn't understand it, but he protests this notion with some fire. "I knew what it was about, all right—why else would I have run it?" he says, adding thoughtfully, "My theory was, they'd just been sitting on it."

A great deal has been said and written about Ross's naïveté, and this is a delusion that he does nothing to correct, being a man who often looks puzzled and has a habit of rubbing his hand over his face in a gesture of seeming bewilderment. Actually, he is about as naïve and bewildered as Machiavelli, Winston Churchill, Gypsy Rose Lee, or the President of Standard Oil. Perhaps his truest quality is a sort of tired but unconquerable enthusiasm. After twenty-five years of editing *The New Yorker* his viewpoint still is always fresh and unfailingly interested. He reads every word of every piece that goes into the magazine and, in most cases, makes careful marginal notes to the author. Ross's marginal queries—treasured by all who have received them—are a wonderful combination of his own wish

§ 195 §

THE VICIOUS CIRCLE

to "assume a reasonable degree of enlightenment" on the part of New Yorker readers, and the general belief of editors everywhere that the reading public don't know from nothing.

"Who he?" Ross queries briskly whenever he comes on an unfamiliar name in a manuscript which is not explained at once. Occasionally his thirst for explicit information becomes a little startling to his contributors; S. J. Perelman, in a humorous manuscript for *The New Yorker*, once referred to "the woman taken in adultery."

"What woman?" Ross inquired.

Another time, Perelman referred in manuscript to "the dark and bloody ground," and Ross's comment was equally crisp.

"Locate," he directed.

He is, however, the most helpful editor in the world. If an anecdote (those rare and precious nuggets that writers grow gray digging for) occurs to him while he is reading a manuscript, he will call up the writer and tell it to him then and there. He is the world's worst anecdote-teller; laughs all the way through, and says "See?" at the end of every sentence. But his anecdotes are always just exactly right. He has an ear for an effective story just as he has an eye for a right or wrong word. A few years ago, *New Yorker* staff writers— especially those who write Talk of the Town—became so at ease in the chatty, colloquial style they had perfected that two of their pet locutions began cropping up in the text like dandelions on a lawn. One was "pretty" ("Seemed pretty funny to us . . . ", or "pretty

§ 196 §

The Birth of The New Yorker

grim" or "pretty obvious" . . .) and the other was "a little"; ("She was a little bewildered . . . " or "It was a little as though . . . "). Ross detected these echoes before anyone else did, and an almost complete ban was placed on the two expressions. "I try to ration one 'a little' to a piece," he says. "I mean a *long* piece."

Ross's searchlight gaze is equally busy on the drawings that go into the magazine. At art meetings he will stare gloomily at a drawing and mutter, "Who's talking?" This means that the picture goes back to the artist to have the speaker's mouth opened wider. Or he will twist his long body around to peer at the perspective of another cartoon from every angle, and then inquire plaintively, "Where am *I* supposed to be?" No detail of *The New Yorker* is too minute to escape his deep attention, and any flaw personally afflicts him, because his standard is perfection. As Russel Maloney once wrote of him, "perfection, in the mind of Harold Ross, is not a goal or an ideal, but something that belongs to him, like his watch or his hat."

A good many things afflict Ross, including the fact that nobody will call him by his first name. However, he doesn't like his first name and winces if anybody *does* address him by it. "I like my last name," he admits. "My grouse is that in my office I am almost totally surrounded by people who call me *Mr.* Ross. This makes a man feel old. . . . My God, some of the younger fellows call me Sir!"

Ross is a lean and meditative man to look at, with a furrowed brow and a skeptical, harried air. "He looks

§ 197 §

THE VICIOUS CIRCLE

like a dishonest Abe Lincoln," Woollcott remarked during one of his fonder moments. Beset by candor from his friends, Ross will sometimes defend himself stubbornly.

"One thing I'll say for myself, I never struck a woman but once," he stated during a poker game at the Algonquin.

"And even then unfavorably, I'll be bound," said F.P.A., raking in the pot.

§ 198 §

CHAPTER TEN

The Sophisticates and the Logrollers

AS EARLY as 1923, the Algonquin Round Table had become sufficiently famous to be called names by persons of equal or greater renown, and in *Black Oxen,* a best-selling novel of that year, Gertrude Atherton took a dim view of the group. Mrs. Atherton was a long-time patron of the Algonquin—a wonderful woman who, it was rumored, had taken the Steinach rejuvenation treatment in Vienna (she didn't admit it until some years later), and who pinned up her long blonde hair with jeweled shamrocks when she dressed for dinner. The shamrocks appeared to be just a gesture, because Mrs. Atherton's coiffure was the most precarious in the world, and the most unpremeditated. Taffy-colored tresses, shaken loose by the elevator trip from her rooms to the dining room (although nobody else in the elevator had suffered so much as a nosebleed), would wave behind her as she sailed in to dinner, and sometimes one of her women guests would instinctively put out a corrective hand. Nobody ever quite dared correct Mrs.

THE VICIOUS CIRCLE

Atherton's coiffure, though. For one thing, she *liked* her hair that way; for another, although she looked forty in 1923, she was actually a rather grand old lady aged sixty-six.

"I like to think that I discovered the Algonquin for myself before it became famous," Mrs. Atherton wrote to my father in a letter dated 1938. ". . . When I returned late from a party the lift boy unhooked me in the back. . . . And one evening when I was going out to dinner and felt very tired I went downstairs and confided in the headwaiter and he mixed me the only cocktail I ever was able to drink, a Bronx.

"Although at that time the Sophisticates had not discovered the Algonquin—nor themselves for that matter—[Mrs. Atherton's letter continues] the hotel was interesting for another reason. John Drew, and, I think, Ethel Barrymore, had made it a fashionable resort for the aristocracy of the stage, and while I was there, at least, it seemed to me that it was the headquarters of every pretty girl in the United States who aspired to act, or had already obtained a small part. As they were all very young and unchaperoned, it is probable they had been directed to a hotel so distinguished in its patronage as to give them a certain semblance of protection.

"Great changes since then," Mrs. Atherton

§ 200 §

The Sophisticates and the Logrollers

sighed, toward the end of her letter. ". . .
When friends from other cities are in New York
and expect something really interesting in the
way of entertainment I call up Georges and
ask him to reserve a table; and it is invariably
one against the wall where we can sit side by
side and command a view of the entire room.
Sometimes there are only one or two authentic
celebrities present, but I wave my hand and
murmur: 'They all do things,' and that [the
lady concludes crisply] is quite satisfactory."

From her table against the wall Mrs. Atherton
focused a lorgnette as powerful as Eustace Tilley's upon
the Round Table, and rather coldly reported on it
in *Black Oxen*. Calling the group The Sophisticates,
she described them meeting "at the Sign of the Indian
Chief where the cleverest of them—and those who were
so excitedly sure of their cleverness that for the moment
they convinced others as well as themselves—fore-
gathered daily. There was a great deal of scintillating
talk in this group on the significant books and tenden-
cies of the day. . . . It was an excellent forcing house
for ideas and vocabularies. . . . They appraised, de-
bated, rejected, finally placed the seal of their august
approval upon a favored few."

Mrs. Atherton was not alone in her feeling of dis-
trust and even distaste toward the group. Many of the
older writers genuinely considered it a collection of
brash and self-important upstarts. More than once

THE VICIOUS CIRCLE

Irvin S. Cobb spoke ironically of "the famous Round Table where sits in splendor Gotham's favorite wag—and his own." And the great reporter, Frank Ward O'-Malley of *The Sun*, lunching one day with Father, glanced over at the Round Table and said, "Frank, the boilers in the engine room are right under the Round Table, aren't they?"

The boilers are out under the sidewalk, but Father was always one to go along with a gag. "Yes," he said. "Why?"

"If those boilers exploded today and obliterated every person sitting at that table," O'Malley intoned earnestly, "do you know what the headlines in tomorrow's papers would be? 'Yesterday the boilers exploded at the Algonquin.' That's all."

Nobody, I think, can explain exactly why the Round Table was able to ignore its detractors, or why it survived so many of them. It had the bloom of youth and success on it, to be sure, but so did another table at the Algonquin, occasionally occupied by certain young people who were just beginning to be successful in the 'Twenties. These were Theresa Helburn, Lawrence Langner, Philip Moeller, Helen Westley, Maurice Wertheim, Rollo Peters, and Lee Simonson. What *they* were doing was starting the Theatre Guild. But few people ever gave them a single glance. And *everybody* stared at the Round Table.

I have a simple explanation for the Rose Room's indifference toward the Theatre Guild pioneers. First

§ 202 §

The Sophisticates and the Logrollers

of all, they lunched there seldom—generally they grabbed the hamburger nearest to the Provincetown Theatre on MacDougal Street, or the Garrick Theatre when they moved uptown, or the Guild Theatre when they finally established it on 52nd Street. Second, they seldom lunched together; they were too busy lunching with somebody or other who might give them money for the Guild. And third, they were intense people, lacking the casual gaiety of the Round Table. Nobody wants to look at intense people, and except for the customers who knew and appreciated their aims, the Guild crowd went fairly unnoticed in the Algonquin dining room.

By 1923, with three seasons under its belt, the Guild had sold its first block of stock, and was preparing to produce George Bernard Shaw's *Saint Joan* with Winifred Lenihan in the title role. On opening night, the play ran until midnight and the Guild cabled Shaw for permission to cut, explaining that people who lived in the suburbs had to catch trains. The master's reply was characteristic. "Begin at eight or run later trains," he suggested. However, he did come through with his own shorter revision. Later in the play's run Theresa Helburn wrote Shaw that the Guild was using the French pronunciation of "Rheims" and "Dauphin." Shaw replied:

Terry dear, you know but little of the world.

The population of New York City is 5,620,-048. The odd 48 know that the French call

§ 203 §

THE VICIOUS CIRCLE

Rheims Rah'ce, and themselves call it variously
Rance, Ranks, Rangs, Wrongs, Rass or Rams.
The other 5,620,000 wonder what the 48 are
trying to say, and call it Reems.

The 48 also call the Dauphin the Dough-
fang or the Doo-fong.

The public laughs, and writes to me about
it.

The 48 call Agincourt (an English word
unknown in France) Adj Ann Coor.

You had better do what I tell you every
time, because I am older than you—at least my
fancy pictures you younger, and very beautiful.

The Guild had learned to handle these skirmishes
ever since the original one, over *Heartbreak House,*
their first Shaw production in 1920. They had announced the opening for October when a cable came
from Shaw forbidding them to open until after the
Presidential election. The Guild protested that if they
waited that long they would lose all the fine actors they
had engaged. Shaw cabled "Inexorable," and followed
the cable with a letter saying "Better to produce *Heartbreak House* with the first cast you could pick out of the
gutter on Nov. 15, than to produce it on Oct. 15 with
Sarah Bernhardt, the two Guitrys, Edwin Booth, John
Drew, Maude Adams, Mary Pickford and Charlie
Chaplin."

§ 204 §

The Sophisticates and the Logrollers

The Guild crowd took incidents like these in their stride, and did not hoard them up for anecdotes at lunch as the Round Tablers would have done. They saved their showmanship for the theatre. In spite of their dissimilarities, however, the Vicious Circle and the Guild were bound by a common love for the theatre and were friendly, though not effusively so. Later, of course, the Guild had business dealings with several Round Tablers, notably Robert Sherwood, several of whose plays they produced, and Margalo Gillmore, who acted in many Guild productions. Toward the critics at the Round Table—Broun, Woollcott, and Benchley—the Guild directors socially maintained a pleasant aloofness, much as a girl wearing a new picture hat stays out of a high wind.

Since the Round Table included critics, columnists and other writers who were truly interested in the work of their colleagues and liked to say so in print, and since that work was consistently good, the Vicious Circle naturally came to be accused of undue mutual back-patting, or logrolling. This accusation was as unfair as the other one—that all writers and actors not invited to join the group were ridden with envy and wounded feelings. The Round Tablers candidly found themselves and one another more interesting than anyone else in the world, and not without reason. But they were not the kind of people given to false praise for sweet friendship's sake; for one thing, their standards were too

THE VICIOUS CIRCLE

strict, and for another, nobody at the Round Table particularly needed any such blatant helping over stiles.

In her autobiography, *A Peculiar Treasure,* Edna Ferber writes of the group:

> Far from boosting one another they actually were merciless if they disapproved. I never have encountered a more hard-bitten crew. But if they liked what you had done they did say so, publicly and whole-heartedly. Their standards were high, their vocabulary fluent, fresh, astringent and very, very tough. Theirs was a tonic influence, one on the other, and all on the world of American letters. The people they could not and would not stand were the bores, hypocrites, sentimentalists and the socially pretentious. They were ruthless toward charlatans, toward the pompous and the mentally and artistically dishonest. Casual, incisive, they had a terrible integrity about their work and a boundless ambition.

The Round Table on the whole took the charge of logrolling lightly, although on occasion they rose in self-defense. In his *Diary of Our Own Samuel Pepys* in the *Tribune,* F.P.A. wrote, after the opening of Kaufman and Connelly's *To the Ladies!* in February, 1922, "So to an inn, and met G. Kaufman and M. Connelly, and I said, You boys are good playwrights and are doing what Mr. Ade should have done, and I said, Let us set at rest this talk of Log-Rolling, so I shall say,

§ 206 §

The Sophisticates and the Logrollers

Your play is rotten, and to show how fair you are, you say in your paper I am a prince.

"But about Log-Rolling," Mr. Pepys concluded, "there is this to be said: that friendships are first formed through admiration of work, rather than the other way about."

Three years later, in 1925, the Round Table was still being accused of logrolling (as indeed it was throughout its career, by this or that tenacious belittler) and an early issue of *The New Yorker* carried a full-page burlesque of the Inquiring Reporter—a type of newspaperman who had just begun to show his ears and nostrils in certain tabloids. *The New Yorker's* question was:

> Do the critics and writers who lunch at the Algonquin Hotel log-roll for each other, or is that just another lie of the interests?

The answers, written and illustrated by Ralph Barton, were:

Alexander Woollcott   "Stuff and nonsense! There is no such thing as an Algonquin group, and if there were, they would never have a kind word for each other. . . ."

Heywood Broun   "I don't know anything about log-rolling, but I know what I like. . . ."

§ 207 §

THE VICIOUS CIRCLE

Franklin P. Adams   "Whom are you to ask me
                     such a question like you sus-
                     pected me of log-rolling? . . .

Georges   "I am only a headwaiter,
                     but. . . ."

Ross does not like to be reminded of this faintly collegiate jest, and excepting Miss Ferber's forthright remarks and F.P.A.'s pungent statement, no member of the Round Table ever bothered much to deliver any riposte to its defamers. This airy indifference probably won as few friends for the group as anything else they did.

The Vicious Circle had its own gods, and when H. G. Wells, or Arnold Bennett, or Mrs. Fiske, or John Drinkwater, or H. L. Mencken lunched at the Round Table as guests, as they often did, the group welcomed them with respectful, though not slavish, attention. Yet not one of them except Woollcott would have gushed in public or in print about anyone he admired, and even Woollcott had his moments of reserve. With Aleck, it was sometimes hard to tell when he was being reserved and when he was being just ornery. One day Father, knowing that Richard Harding Davis had always been one of Aleck's idols, leaned over his chair and said quietly, "In case you're interested, that young girl sitting just back of you is Richard Harding Davis's daughter."

Woollcott spun round in his chair and treated Miss Davis to a long stare. "Nothing could interest me less," he said loudly, and turned back to his lunch.

Unpredictable was, however, the word for Wooll-

§ 208 §

The Sophisticates and the Logrollers

cott. When he got home that afternoon and (in the words of Margalo Gillmore, who recalls this tale) "his editorial juices got to working," he sat down and wrote a drenchingly sentimental magazine piece about this fair young girl, the tender fruit of a union between the stalwart and dashing war correspondent, Richard Harding Davis, and Bessie McCoy, the beloved "Yama-Yama Girl" of haunting memory, and how his old eyes, dwelling upon her, had been stung to unaccustomed tears. . . .

Webster defines a sophisticate as one who is deprived of original simplicity and made wordly-wise, and in a sense the boys and girls at the Round Table were precisely that—with one exception. The exception was Neysa McMein. Miss McMein was no country bumpkin, certainly, but she was a warmhearted and unaffected hero-worshiper with a quality of wide-eyed wonder that was conspicuously lacking in the rest of the group. Like the soundboard in a violin, she supplied the sympathetic surface against which the complicated noises of the Vicious Circle resounded best. She genuinely believed that they were all geniuses—a very soothing belief to geniuses who never quite dare admit it to themselves. And while she never actually said that George Kaufman was a better dramatist than Shakespeare, or Woollcott a greater wit than Voltaire, she gently and steadily implied that, given the choice, she would take Kaufman and Woollcott every time.

She was no stooge, however. The very simplicity of her character made her something of a personage, and besides, she was brimming with that ineluctable quality

§ 209 §

THE VICIOUS CIRCLE

called charm. She was an extremely successful painter—
of magazine covers, mostly—who had arrived in New
York from Quincy, Illinois, by way of a Chicago art school
sometime just before the 'Twenties . . . a tall, tawny,
impressionable blonde named Marjorie McMein. (She
changed her first name on the advice of a numerologist.)
Her talent was little more than a knack plus a sense of
color, and she never pretended to be a great artist; people
interested her more, and she had a way with them that
amounted to a kind of genius in itself. One of her first
gestures in New York was so charmingly naïve and yet
so canny that people still wonder just how artless it was;
she went to call on F.P.A. at the *Tribune* to tell him
how much she admired his column, and brought him a
great bunch of sweet peas. Adams, enchanted, put it in
the paper and took her to lunch at the Round Table,
where she bloomed quietly all over the Vicious Circle.
It was probably the first real womanly homage the boys
had known, and from that moment they were enslaved.

Neysa seldom lunched at the Round Table, being a
homebody at heart, but when the Vicious Circle met outside of the Algonquin it was generally at her studio. Most
of the rehearsals for the Round Table show, *No Sirree!*
took place there; charades, which Neysa developed into
The Game, began there; and there was usually a musical
group around the piano, and a table of anagrams or cribbage going on in another corner. Amid this swirl of
people Neysa worked happily away at her easel, wearing
a paint-smattered smock and, occasionally, a streak of
scarlet or emerald across her brow as she swept a lock of

§ 210 §

The Sophisticates and the Logrollers

molasses-colored hair out of her eyes. Her studio was one of the last intellectual salons in New York, and Neysa herself was the perfect realization of a glamorous lady-painter. She was the last romantic.

Many more people than the Round Table regulars filled her studio. George Gershwin and Bill Daly played Gershwin's *Rhapsody in Blue* and *Concerto in F* there, before either was performed in public. Irving Berlin or Jascha Heifetz often dropped in and sat contentedly strumming at the piano and talking to Neysa, who was painting away. (Musicians always make straight for the piano in anybody's house, unlike writers, who can ignore a typewriter in the same room *forever*.) One day Heifetz, striking chords, noticed something odd about the piano's tone and, lifting the top to peer inside, was only mildly surprised to find that half a dozen caramels had melted on the strings. Neysa, though glamorous, was well-known to be a little careless in her housekeeping.

It was at her studio that Charles MacArthur, possibly affected by the glamour of it all, once made a remark so utterly winsome that it haunted him down the years and he looked a little pinched when anybody mentioned it. At a party there, in 1925, MacArthur met young Helen Hayes, who was still an ingenue actress and socially rather shy, and offered her some peanuts out of a paper bag. "Ooh, peanuts!" exclaimed Miss Hayes, taking a handful. "I wish they were emeralds," said Charlie. He and Miss Hayes were married three years later, with Aleck Woollcott as best man. A year or so ago, Mac-Arthur was able to bury his winsome remark for good

§ 211 §

THE VICIOUS CIRCLE

and all. He brought his wife a necklace of cabochon emeralds and dropped it in her lap, saying airily, "I wish they were peanuts."

The charm of Neysa McMein was more intangible even than most charm; people invariably remember her as beautiful and glamorous, and yet she was probably the most untidy woman in the world. The perfect grooming which, so the fashion magazines tell us, is a necessary ingredient of charm meant nothing to Neysa. Safety pins held her together, and at least once she received callers with the elastic broken in one leg of her bloomers so that one pink silk bloomer-leg hung below her smock almost to her ankles. She met such accidents as debonairly as she handled her housekeeping, which featured wonderful food served in a fairly haphazard fashion. One evening, when her dinner guests had been kept waiting half an hour beyond the usual dinnertime, she called her maid in and asked the reason for the delay. "It's the soup plates, ma'am," the girl stammered. "The people downstairs that we've been borrowing them from for seven years moved out today."

With all of her disorderly ways Neysa—unlike most of the Vicious Circle—was not at all emotionally or psychologically disorganized. The rest of the group bristled with complexes, phobias, psychoses, and other inner compulsions and frustrations. Neysa, tranquil, steady, and sunny-natured, blossomed like a rose among the neuroses. The Round Table cherished her lack of complications and strove, by a system of gentle ribbing, to keep her that way. "And so to Jane Grant's and played a bit of

§ 212 §

The Sophisticates and the Logrollers

vingt-et-un," F.P.A. once wrote in his *Pepys' Diary*, "[we all] carrying on our conversation in French, Italian and Spanish, much to Neysa's discomfiture, she understanding only a fraction of English, and the postage stamp flirtation, and the language of flowers."

Women liked Neysa as well as men did—which is a tribute rarely won by any glamour girl. In a letter to another friend Janet Flanner, who is "Genêt" on the *New Yorker,* wrote about her:

> It must be of some importance about her that her old friends are, in so many cases, completely devoted to her; it's a description of her. It isn't that they don't see through her few bad qualities, but rather they see into her; this comes more from the illumination she gives out than from illuminating minds on their part. She must know several hundred thousand people. . . .

And Alice-Leone Moats, another crystal-surfaced sophisticate who doesn't think much of women in general, wrote to me, shortly before Neysa's death in 1949:

> She had qualities all the others of the Round Table group lacked; earthiness, real loyalty, no nerves, a kindly sense of humor, no brilliant wit (in that group, it was a quality because she was someone who could appreciate a mot without trying to cap it), wide-eyed wonder, and a genuine admiration for the talents of

§ 213 §

THE VICIOUS CIRCLE

the others with no exaggerated ideas as to her own. . . . She was the fire at which they could warm their hands, with no risk of getting burnt."

Neysa's only feud with any member of the Round Table was with Woollcott. (Who else?) Woollcott had often contemplated marriage, somewhat in the same way that Hitler later contemplated the conquest of the next country—that is, without serious thoughts of rejection. This was surely part bravado, for Woollcott had had a real tragedy in his early life; an attack of mumps in his twenties had left him impotent. He found himself, in his thirties and forties, a man tormented by emotions about women which he could not fulfill and, as he usually did when thwarted about anything, he set about him with large gestures. He harangued the Round Table often and at length about the blessed state of wedlock and his own determination to join the ranks of the blessed. His friends greeted these discourses without excitement. "Aleck just wants somebody to talk to in bed," one of them opined.

Woollcott's other outlet was matchmaking, and he was the greatest little matchmaker in his set. He had encouraged and presided over Jane Grant's marriage to Harold Ross (after sportingly giving up the idea of marrying Jane himself), Helen Hayes's marriage to Charles MacArthur, and that of C. Leroy Baldridge, the painter, to Caroline Mundell, a San Francisco newspaper-

§ 214 §

The Sophisticates and the Logrollers

woman. The Baldridges rather lost touch with him in later years, and they have an explanation for that . . . "We were too happily married," they say. "Aleck liked it better if a marriage he had fostered went on the rocks, so that he could preside over the break-up as well as over the union." Although the MacArthurs' happy married life did not ruffle his friendship for them, it was true that Woollcott enjoyed m.c.-ing a disaster and usually became bored with other people's humdrum contentment. The more complications there were for him to straighten out (or, on occasion, more deeply entangle) the better he liked it. When Madeline Hurlock, a beautiful Hollywood actress, married Marc Connelly, and later divorced him and married his good friend, Robert Sherwood, Aleck fairly popped with the deliciousness of it all.

Woollcott's own contemplated wedding, with Jane Grant as the bride and himself as groom, had been harshly interrupted by Jane's marriage to Ross. Recovering from that setback, he dreamed of marrying Neysa McMein. It must be said, in fairness to Woollcott, that he truly loved these women; Neysa perhaps more than Jane, because Jane was a crisp, self-sufficient young woman, but Neysa represented all that was warm, tender, and sheltering, and Aleck needed that. He set about his wooing of Neysa with unusual secretiveness. He told only Jane and Harold, with whom he was living at the time, that he had arranged to sail on the same ship that was taking Neysa to Europe, that she didn't know he was

§ 215 §

THE VICIOUS CIRCLE

to be among the passengers, and that his plan was to pop up in mid-ocean beside her, a cribbage board in one hand and his heart in the other, and propose marriage.

He did exactly that. And Neysa's own warm heart nearly broke when she had to tell him that his proposal was out of the question, since she had secretly married John Baragwanath, a mining engineer, a month earlier.

Woollcott, the extrovert, couldn't be crushed even by two almost identical turndowns. He proceeded to London and Paris where he frolicked with the best hostesses, with no hard feelings toward Neysa. When they both returned to America they remained good friends, even throughout the necessary interlude required for Woollcott's inspection of Neysa's new husband. It was a one-sided decision. Woollcott would telephone Neysa and say, "How is that moneygrubber, your husband?" or "It would be nice to have you with us tonight, we're playing anagrams. But I presume Mister Baragwanath cannot spell out words?" or "Woollcott speaking. Since, my proud bride, your helpmate is illiterate, *who* spells his name for him?"

Once more, Woollcott had chosen the wrong person to hate, just as he always chose the wrong person to love. John Baragwanath had turned out to be a completely charming and humorous young man with an amused tolerance for the Round Table, and everybody at the Round Table had liked him on sight. It was pretty shattering to Woollcott to find that the Round Table had approved of a stranger in his absence, particularly the stranger who had stolen Neysa from him, and espe-

§ 216 §

The Sophisticates and the Logrollers

cially a stranger who never came to lunch at the Round Table. Woollcott muttered about him for several weeks until, one night, Neysa asked him to dinner. The next day he turned up at lunch, beaming.

"I don't know why you've all been criticizing Jack Baragwanath," he said. "I *like* Jack Baragwanath!"

Informed of Woollcott's proclamation, Mr. Baragwanath is said to have stated modestly, "It is the accolade. I kneel. I will not fight against it."

Even Aleck was not proof against such steadfast good humor, and he rapidly made one of his re-friendships with the Baragwanaths. It lasted until shortly before his death in 1943. The year before, Neysa, getting up at night for a drink of water, had fallen down a flight of stairs in her apartment and broken her back. Woollcott, who was already seriously ill, rallied sufficiently to install himself with nurse and attendant physicians in the Baragwanath apartment, where the two fabulous invalids held a double salon, receiving as many as twenty-seven visitors in one day. In the autumn, when Neysa could be moved, they both went to Woollcott's island on Lake Bomoseen in Vermont to recuperate from the rigors of convalescence, and it was there that their only grave quarrel occurred. It was their first, and last.

Woollcott took Neysa for an automobile drive one afternoon, to admire the autumn foliage, and kept her out for several hours in spite of her protests that her back was causing her agony. When they finally bumped home over the rough roads, toward evening, she was almost in a state of collapse, and Aleck was petulant. She

§ 217 §

THE VICIOUS CIRCLE

had ruined his day, he complained to his other guests; he had never thought she could be such a spoilsport. Neysa, shocked by his cruel selfishness and not realizing that he was a desperately sick man, left Bomoseen that night, and wrote to Aleck later that, although she would always be fond of him, they had better not see each other for a while.

They never saw each other again. Woollcott died in January, during a radio broadcast of "The People's Platform."

CHAPTER ELEVEN

How To Be a Wit

MOST OF the Round Table group worked in offices (or living quarters) near the Algonquin, and one o'clock every day would find them converging briskly on foot toward the common watering hole. Those who came from the north often took a short cut through the Seymour Hotel, a few doors east of the Algonquin, which had a long corridor leading directly from 45th Street to 44th. The Round Tablers found this very convenient, especially in bad weather, and they would scurry through the corridor, muddying up the carpet, and naturally never pausing to give the Seymour any trade—not even so much as buying a paper at the Seymour newsstand. One snowy day Marc Connelly limped indignantly into the Algonquin and, meeting Father, said with some heat: "Wouldn't you think those Seymour people would have the decency to clean their sidewalk? I just slipped on a piece of ice outside their door and damn near broke my ankle!"

"My, my," Father murmured sympathetically. "If I

§ 219 §

THE VICIOUS CIRCLE

were you, Marc, I'd march right back in there and tell
'em you'll never walk through their old hotel again!"

Marc visibly enjoyed this—when he laughs, his
shoulders come up around his ears and he shakes all
over—and after lunch, he rewarded Father with a laugh
of his own. He came out of the dining room brushing
violently at some lint a new napkin had left on his dark
blue trousers.

"You know what?" he said. "I'm going to have a
suit made of lint and see if I can pick me up a blue serge."

Possibly Marc had already sprung this line at the
table a moment before, but the Vicious Circle were always refreshingly candid about repeating a good crack.
They never said, as bores do, "Did I tell you what I said
to so-and-so last Friday?"; their quips were too fast and
frequent to be resurrected and rehashed. But when one
of them did say something good, and a little later ran
into a friend who hadn't heard it, no false modesty re-
strained him from generously sharing it again.

Because they were all so full of drolleries and retorts,
and wished none to be lost in the general conversation,
they developed a miraculous sense of timing. A Round
Tabler might treasure for half an hour a remark he had
thought up, chatting amiably meanwhile, and then, in
the space of an indrawn breath, expel it into precisely
the right moment of silence.

Round Tablers had a sense of rhythm, a sense of
the dramatic . . . and, besides, they were all born hams,
in the most lovable sense of that word.

Oddly enough, the writers were better at this trick

§ 220 §

How To Be a Wit

than the theatre people, whose profession demanded split-second timing. Even so expert an actress as Peggy Wood at least once muffed a line at the Round Table.

"Well, back to the mimes," she said one day, rising to return to rehearsal. Peggy has since freely admitted that she thought of this japery the night before, and could hardly *wait* to get to the Round Table to utter it casually.

Nobody heard her except George Kaufman, sitting next to her, and he merely threw her a brief approving glance over the top of his glasses. It would have been against the rules for George to say, "Hey, did you hear what Peggy just said?" or for Peggy to repeat it. The Round Table knew the code of true comedy and the danger of anticlimax. With them, a joke had one chance, and one only. Operating by this creed (with which every right-minded writer, storyteller, or comedian must agree) it is hardly any wonder that they were often accused of sitting around the table waiting for a lull like vultures hovering and waiting for a man to die.

Rugged as they were with one another, they were even more severe toward any outsider who even inadvertently repeated a Round Table crack without giving credit to its originator. Grim-lipped, they would track the offender down and make him eat his words. One time, they were discussing a charity affair to be given for the benefit of the A.S.P.C.A. A guest at the Round Table that day was Kate Sproehnle, a young writer from Chicago who was distantly related to Franklin P. Adams.

"You know what?" somebody said. "The tickets to

§ 221 §

THE VICIOUS CIRCLE

this damn show are going to cost fifteen dollars apiece!"

"Goodness," Kate exclaimed innocently, "it would be cheaper to buy a horse and just be kind to it."

Kate's line got around, and soon reached Neysa McMein, who told it to Douglas Fairbanks. A few nights later Fairbanks, called on suddenly for a speech somewhere, repeated the line without mentioning Miss Sproehnle—whose name he had genuinely forgotten, or, perhaps, never heard. The next morning F.P.A.'s "Conning Tower" took him to task, none too gently, for his oversight. If Adams thought Douglas would feel rebuked by his paragraph, he simply didn't know Fairbanks.

Douglas Fairbanks was a man who never read *anything*. Even his method of deciding on scripts was to glance over them rapidly and then hand them to someone more fond of reading than he. Sometimes it would be his wife, Mary Pickford (always a great and studious reader of practically everything), sometimes it was his director, sometimes his trainer, often his butler, and most often his stooges . . . people like Bull Montana and Benny Zeidman. Douglas would do *anything* to get out of reading the printed word. It was not lack of intelligence or intellectual curiosity that prevented him—simply the fact that he couldn't bear to sit still long enough. Father once said to me, in a bewildered kind of way, "I don't know how I can be so fond of a man who has never read a book."

Douglas seldom read even a newspaper, so he naturally missed F.P.A.'s reference to him in "The Conning Tower." The next day he breezed into the Algonquin

§ 222 §

How To Be a Wit

in his usual bonhomous way, greeting friends left and right, and pausing for a cheerful' word at the Round Table. He was met by cool stares, and the crisp demand to know what the hell he meant by using Kate Sproehnle's line without giving her credit.

"Well, I just couldn't remember her name on the spur of the moment," Douglas explained. "Anyway, I didn't know she was a special pal of you people."

"Special pal or no special pal," F.P.A. intoned, "plagiarism is plagiarism, whether her name is Kate Sproehnle or Lizzie Borden."

"Oh," said Douglas earnestly, "if her name had been Lizzie Borden I would have known *Aleck* said it!"

Woollcott's interest in famous crimes (especially Lizzie Borden's) was well-known enough to give this remark a cockeyed point, and it restored Fairbanks to favor. But Douglas, who thrived only on unbroken popularity with everyone, worried about the incident. When he talked to Father about it later he brought forth another artless quip which the Round Table never heard.

"Gee, Frank," he said, "it's a good thing I'm not a really *big* guy. I mean, like the President, or something."

"Why?" Father asked.

"Well, because . . . Gee, I don't know how to explain it. But those fellows at the Round Table certainly can make molehills out of mountains!"

The fact that everybody at the Round Table was fiercely concerned with the credit given his colleagues for a crack or a pungent comment may be one reason why so many thousands of witticisms have been attributed to

§ 223 §

THE VICIOUS CIRCLE

Dorothy Parker—more, possibly, than any one person could utter in a lifetime. Another reason is, obviously, that she did say a great many of them. Her one-line review of a play of Channing Pollock's called *The House Beautiful* has become a classic: *"The House Beautiful,"* Mrs. P. wrote, "is the play lousy." So has her remark when someone wondered aloud how a certain mutual female acquaintance had managed to break her leg while on a holiday in London. "Probably sliding down a barrister," Dottie opined.

One of her long succession of dogs was a mild-mannnered dachshund named Robinson, and one day Robinson unaccountably got into a fight with another dog and came off pretty well lacerated.

"Well, your dog started it!" the other dog's owner accused Mrs. Parker.

"Oh, certainly," Mrs. Parker retorted. "I have no doubt that he was also carrying a revolver."

When Woollcott and Benchley called on Dottie during one of her occasional hospital sojourns, she welcomed them cordially and then reached up and rang the bell beside her pillow. Did she want something? Could they fetch her anything? the two gentlemen inquired solicitously.

"No," said Mrs. Parker. "That bell is supposed to summon the night nurse, so I ring it whenever I want an hour of uninterrupted privacy."

When she was solvent—and frequently when she was not—Mrs. Parker was a great one for giving parties, and to one of these, at the Algonquin one night, came

§ 224 §

How To Be a Wit

Tallulah Bankhead, who had just made her first successess in *39 East* and *The Best People*. Under the influence of strong waters—she was not playing at the time—Tallulah did a few splits, threw a few bottles, and otherwise became so uproariously lighthearted that a committee of four gentlemen was appointed by the hostess to escort her away from there. As the clamor of their departure faded down the hall, Dottie poked her elfin face between the portieres of an adjoining room.

"Has Whistler's Mother left yet?" she inquired.

It was Tallulah herself who innocently topped this line—one of the few of Mrs. Parker's ever to be improved upon. Next day at lunch, she took a pocket mirror out of her bag and gazed ruefully at herself.

"Oh my," she mourned, "the less I behave like Whistler's Mother the night before, the more I look like her the morning after."

Tallulah was crowding seventeen when she arrived from Alabama, stage-struck, sultry-voiced, and brimming with a roseleaf beauty which she determinedly hid under the then-fashionable mask of white powder, blue eye-shadow, and beef-colored lipstick. She fondly believed that this made her look like Ethel Barrymore, who was her idol. Her distinguished family, including her father, Congressman William Bankhead, later Speaker of the House, and her Uncle John, a United States Senator, was comfortably off but not rich, and none of them was wild about the idea of Tallulah's going on the stage. However, her father agreed to finance a limited excur-

THE VICIOUS CIRCLE

sion to New York, and Tallu arrived in town chaperoned by her Aunt Louise who was plainly nervous about the whole thing.

Aunt Louise had chosen to stay at the Algonquin because it seemed modest and respectable, and because somebody had told her that Commander Evangeline Booth of the Salvation Army made it her headquarters when in town. Neither she nor her niece had any idea of the hotel's theatrical clientele when they registered, and when they went down to dinner the first night they each received a separate jolt. Stage stars were scattered over the dining room like planets over a planetarium ceiling. Laurette Taylor at one table, Jane Cowl at another, Elsie Janis at another, Walter Hampden across the room, Dennis King at the next table, Douglas Fairbanks (in the chandelier, no doubt), and . . . in one corner, Ethel Barrymore. Tallulah, after one gasp, decided she had died and gone to heaven. As she and her aunt sat down at their own table, Tallulah, with an air, pulled out a cigarette and lighted it. A great feminine voice boomed out just behind her.

"Take that cigarette out of your mouth, you infant," it said.

The voice belonged to Jobyna Howland, the six-foot comedienne who was then playing with Ina Claire in *The Gold-Diggers*. It was Tallulah's first meeting with a real actress.

Aunt Louise was called home to Alabama after a month or two and left reluctantly, first saying to Father, "You *will* keep an eye on our little girl?" Father readily

§ 226 §

How To Be a Wit

agreed—Tallulah was about the same age as me—and it was not until several months later that he was heard to murmur, "Either I keep an eye on Tallulah Bankhead or I run this hotel. No man does both." It is only fair to add that he had the greatest admiration for Tallu, and always denied having made this remark. Nobody actually heard him make it, except his immediate family.

Tallulah stayed on, gay, broke, and unemployed. When her money got so low that she owed a little back rent to the Algonquin, she made the true actress's gesture; she moved to a cheaper hotel. This is something that many actors and actresses do, and it is based on affection for the man they owe the money to. They honestly figure that they have mistreated him long enough and that they love him too much to do it any longer, so they move to some place where they can owe money to somebody they don't care so much about. It is a wholly sincere gesture, and the fact that Father understood it completely was probably one reason for his great success at the Algonquin. He was a courteous man, and recognized a courtesy when he met one.

When Tallulah's finances hit rock-bottom she went to stay with her uncle, Colonel Henry Bankhead, who was stationed on Governor's Island, and made the ferry trip twice a day, wearing her famous (and only) black satin dress. The ride was free for officers and their kin, and there is scarcely any doubt that Miss Bankhead was the dressiest deadhead on the Governor's Island ferry.

Tallulah's own wit came, in time, to be almost as dependable and widely quoted as Dorothy Parker's. Con-

§ 227 §

THE VICIOUS CIRCLE

sidering the fact that Tallulah talked all the time, whereas Mrs. Parker was given to moods of pensive silence, Tallu's average is possibly just as high. She is as friendly as a magpie, and as impossible to shut up. "WILL you LISTEN to me at the top of your lungs?" a friend trying to deliver an important message once shouted at her. She is warmhearted and sympathetic, as long as she can do the talking. "Darling, what a ghastly time you must have had," she said recently to a woman who had just had a serious operation; "now, sit down and tell me *all* about it."

"Well, I was on the table four hours . . ." the lady began.

"Oh, don't be such a blasted hypochondriac!" said Tallu, and she was off on an account of her latest play. I like best her remark as she came out of the theatre one night, after the preview of a particularly bad picture launched by an independent producer.

"What I don't see," Miss Bankhead observed, "is what that producer has got to be independent about."

Jests at the Round Table were usually at someone else's expense, and Woollcott was clearly the master at this kind of humor. "Hmm-mm," he murmured thoughtfully one day, gazing at the retreating back of a young pianist-composer who was generally disliked for his belligerent manner, "there is absolutely nothing wrong with Oscar Levant that a miracle cannot fix." Oscar Levant, mellowed by years and success, has grown up to be a popular character and a considerable wit himself, and I

§ 228 §

How To Be a Wit

must remember to call him up and ask him the latest thing he said, so I can put it in this chapter.

One thing many people didn't realize when they complained of Round Table humor being always at someone's expense was that the attack was not so much malicious as it was a healthy debunking. The Vicious Circle raked only those people whom they considered— according to their own standards—to be pretentious or phony. Sometimes they didn't have to reach outside their own circle to find those qualities, and they were equally merciless about them with one another. Whenever anybody at the Round Table made a pompous remark, for instance, the others would rise and bow to the speaker. (They had to give this up finally in the case of Aleck Woollcott, or they never *would* have gotten to eat their lunch.)

Louis Bromfield once felt the scorch of their hot breath, although in a friendly way. They admired Bromfield's early books—*Early Autumn* and *The Green Bay Tree*—and they liked and accepted Bromfield for what he was; a cosmopolite, a bon viveur, a bit of a social climber, and an exceptionally pleasant man. They liked him until, to their minds, Bromfield began to dither. On a trip back to Ohio, his home state, Louis had fallen in love with the earth and become a farmer. It was a confusing thing to happen to a man who had only wanted to be society's darling, and Bromfield's conversation suffered from it. He would talk about duchesses in one sentence, and mulch in the next. It was an honest confusion but the Round Table mistrusted it. It sounded

§ 229 §

THE VICIOUS CIRCLE

too much like an "act." Finally Edna Ferber spoke up, one day at lunch, after Bromfield had gone on at length about the Riviera season and what he fed his pigs.

"Oh, for godsakes, Louis," she said wearily, "brush the caviar off your blue jeans."

Puns were the most innocent form of Round Table humor, and the Vicious Circle loved them so much that they fell with delight on anyone who made a good one and instantly asked him to lunch. If the pun came from an unlikely person it was even better, as in the case of Jerome Kern, who was not a regular member of the Vicious Circle, and not generally considered to be a cutup.

Kern and F.P.A. were driving in Florida, one time, and stopped at an Indian reservation where they fell into talk with an ancient squaw. She was a Cree, she told them, and the very last one in that part of the country.

"Ah, la dernière Cree!" quoth Kern.

"Just Kern luck she didn't turn out to be a Cherokee," Adams muttered later, but he told it at the Round Table, and no song Kern ever wrote delighted the Vicious Circle more. It's a good guess that Kern felt pretty pleased, too. There was considerable competition among people offering puns to the Round Table, and the boy or girl whose pun was accepted was tapped for honors indeed.

Musicians are pretty comical people on the whole, as the Round Table gradually discovered. Ed MacNamara, the Singing Cop whom everybody loved, was a great friend of Enrico Caruso's. He was never a pupil of Ca-

§ 230 §

How To Be a Wit

ruso's (I believe Caruso took no pupils), but Caruso liked Mac, and occasionally took him up to his apartment in the Knickerbocker Hotel to give him a little coaching. One such session was something Mac never forgot, nor the Round Table either, when they heard about it.

Caruso stationed Mac at one end of his library and sat down at the piano at the other end. "Now, Mac," he said, "geeve *fortissimo*. Seeng loud!" Mac sang loud. "Louder!" Caruso shouted, "Louder!" Mac gave out full voice until the pictures waved on the wall. "LOUDER!" Caruso shouted. "Give fool voice fraahm staahmick!" Mac gave full voice from stomach until his eyes popped and (it is said) a crystal vase twenty feet away fell into splinters. Then Caruso rose and led him, reeling slightly, into the next room.

"Now," said Caruso, placing Mac at the end of the room and sitting down at another piano, "seeng softly. *Pianissimo*."

Mac song softly. Pianissimo.

"Softer . . . *softer*," Caruso directed.

Mac crooned, then whispered.

"*Softer!*" Caruso kept saying.

Mac finished his number in something like a murmur, and went immediately into battle. He had not been a cop for nothing.

"Hey, what's the big idea?" he said. "You take me into one room and make me bust my guts singing loud, and then you take me into the next room and make me whisper. What's the big idea?"

§ 231 §

THE VICIOUS CIRCLE

"Ah, Mac," said Caruso, patting him on the shoulder, "you weel onderstand. You see, in the room underneath the room where I ask you to seeng loud is Scotti—and he is seeck. I like to bother heem."

§ 232 §

CHAPTER TWELVE

As the Girl Said to the Sailor

SATURDAY WAS always a big day at the Algonquin Round Table, since it marked the weekly meeting of the Thanatopsis Literary and Inside Straight Club. This group of impassioned poker players would assemble after lunch, in a room Father had given them on the second floor of the hotel, and would play all afternoon and evening, generally all night, and frequently throughout the entire weekend. Sometimes one member or another would give up and go home before the game ended, pleading extreme fatigue—a condition which F.P.A. once described as "winner's sleeping sickness," lamenting that he himself was far more subject to loser's insomnia, or "Broun's disease."

F.P.A. had founded the Thanatopsis in Paris during the war, when he and his colleagues on the *Stars and Stripes* used to play at a bistro called Nini's. Stakes were modest in those days and even later when the players resumed the game in New York; but as the boys became more and more successful, and as new blood was ad-

§ 233 §

THE VICIOUS CIRCLE

mitted to the game, the stakes grew picturesque. Harpo
Marx joined, bringing with him a zany shrewdness and
a Hollywood idea of money; Raoul Fleischmann came
and went, often leaving with a noticeable nick in his
baking fortune; and Herbert Bayard Swope, then executive editor of the *World,* was, by nature, a man who
would bet five thousand dollars on the first name of the
next girl with knock knees to get out of a crowded
elevator. Five hundred dollars was a normal table stake
at the Thanatopsis, subject to the usual fluctuations. It
has been said that Harpo won thirty thousand dollars
one night, but he has always denied this, maintaining
that he never won more than "a few thousand dollars"
at one sitting. It is a fact, however, that the Thanatopsis
in one evening took from Johnny Weaver a sum amounting to his entire royalties from *In American.*

Women were not encouraged to play, with the exception of Viola Toohey, who was a good, tough poker
player, and was also the wife of John Peter Toohey, a
man so largely instrumental in reviving the Thanatopsis in New York that he was referred to by the other
members as "Our Founder." Each time they called him
"Our Founder" Toohey would rise gravely, and bow.
Neysa McMein, Jane Grant, and Beatrice Kaufman occasionally sat in, but it was only for a little while, the
way you would let a child have *one* piece of candy before dinner. Solvent male newcomers were usually welcome, as long as they were prepared to expect no
mercy.

"I hope you boys won't be too hard on me. I'm the

§ 234 §

FRANKLIN P. ADAMS

As the Girl Said to the Sailor

worst poker player in the world," a first-timer might say as the game started.

"We shall see," the boys would mutter grimly, and then proceed to prove, if possible, that his statement was correct.

Sometimes a stranger turned out to be something of a surprise. One night, Woollcott brought Michael Arlen, the Armenian-born writer who was New York's current glory-boy because of *The Green Hat,* in which Katharine Cornell was then starring. Though born in Armenia and christened Dikran Koujoumian, Arlen was excessively British in manner, with a kind of frosty elegance. Airily, he set about violating every rule of poker, drawing to inside straights and committing other crimes, and to the boys' amazed disgust, won every round. As the chips mounted in front of Arlen, H. L. Mankiewicz finally spoke.

"I move," he said wearily, "that next round, we kitty out for the Turks."

The Thanatopsis became a popular hangout with friends of the Vicious Circle who would drop in to kibitz after the theatre, and on nearly every Saturday night the crowd would include Ina Claire, Beatrice Lillie, Gertrude Lawrence, Roland Young, Alfred Lunt, Lynn Fontanne, and other theatre people who were playing in town at the time. Sometimes these friends brought other friends of their own, who were always plainly fascinated by the strange customs of the Thanatopsis. One such rite was to rise in unison around the table whenever anyone made a foolish play and, to the

§ 237 §

THE VICIOUS CIRCLE

tune of Gilbert and Sullivan's "He Remains an Englishman," solemnly warble:

"He rema-AINS a god-dam fool."

Another tradition was the phrase, "As the girl said to the sailor." This splendidly meaningless tag line was used as a comment on any and every remark that seemed to require no other answer. If Connelly complained of a losing streak, if Kaufman said he was hungry, if Woollcott remarked that they needed new cards . . . "as the girl said to the sailor" was considered adequate reply. Its origin was lost in some forgotten, bawdy A.E.F. joke, but its use at the Thanatopsis was mainly pure, until the night somebody brought along a young Southern actress who became increasingly mystified by the catchword as the evening wore on.

"My!" she said finally to F.P.A. "You certainly seem to be crazy about that ol' monkey business!"

"I never tire of that ol' monkey business," growled Adams.

"As the girl said to the sailor," a chorus of voices around the table instantly intoned.

On one occasion Adams had reason to suffer on account of the Thanatopsis Literary and Inside Straight Club. When he married Esther Root, in 1925, the Thanatopsis voted to give him—as a wedding present, for home use—the handsomest poker set obtainable, with ivory chips and all . . . on one condition: after his wedding in the afternoon, he must return and play poker with them that night. Adams agreed, and brought the bride along to kibitz, and both of them behaved so

§ 238 §

As the Girl Said to the Sailor

prettily that the boys let them go home around 2 a.m.

Each of the Thanatopsis players had idiosyncrasies of his own. George Kaufman was a great one for betting on low cards—or perhaps, as his fellow players sometimes surmised—a great one for thinking that a ten is a high card. He would bet on a pair of tens and take it calmly when someone came up with Jacks or better, merely remarking, "I will now fold my tens like the Arabs, and as silently steal away." Kaufman's collaborator, Marc Connelly, was a fierier sort. He once tore up his cards in a temper, after a ruinous run of losses. Marc's outburst is mainly remembered by former Thanatopsis men as one of the few occasions when Ring Lardner, who often sat in on the game and was playing that night, ever said anything.

"Childish!" said Lardner.

Ring Lardner was the most silent man in the world, and he looked even more mournful than most professional humorists. It is said that he once stared so long in silence at a man who came to interview him that the interviewer nervously came back twice in the five minutes after he had left, to see if Lardner was really there. This tale is apocryphal. The truth is that Lardner never looked like a man who might vanish; he merely looked like a man who knew some secret way of making everybody *else* vanish.

At the Thanatopsis, where everybody loved him for what he wrote as well as for his wordless and strangely appealing personality, Lardner was comfortably allowed to say nothing, except "Hello," "I raise," "I'm out,"

§ 239 §

THE VICIOUS CIRCLE

"Good night," and other technical expressions of good will. About the only other time he ever volunteered a remark, according to Thanatopsis members, was the night David Wallace turned up for an impromptu game wearing an Army shirt with the Infantry insignia on its collar tabs. Wallace, at that time publicity agent for William Harris Jr., had been a first lieutenant in the Infantry during World War I. The reason he wore the Army shirt, he says now, was that his laundry hadn't come back when the Thanatopsis pulled him out of bed to play poker, and he had to put on the first shirt that came to hand.

Woollcott began baiting him the minute he came in the door.

"I didn't know we were entertaining General Pershing," he said bitterly; and, "Do tell us all about your war experiences in the front trenches." Later, he said, "Tell me, are you related to General Lew Wallace, who wrote *Ben Hur?*"

It was Woollcott at his nastiest, but everybody in the room, including Dave Wallace, realized that it was also the Woollcott who had wanted to go to the war and had been turned down by the Army, Navy, and Marines as being near-sighted, flat-footed, and overweight, and had ended up as a kind of publicity man for the Medical Corps and a contributing editor of the *Stars and Stripes*. It was natural for Woollcott to hate an Infantry man; and, since he always took everything personally, it was natural for him to consider Dave Wallace's Army shirt a deliberate, personal insult.

§ 240 §

As the Girl Said to the Sailor

The Thanatopsis went on playing poker, with Dave Wallace taking a hand. But Woollcott was still simmering.

"It's too bad you're sitting down, General Wallace," he said presently, "or you might show us your battle scars."

At this, Dave Wallace lost his temper and threw down his cards. He glared across the table at Woollcott.

"At least I'm not a *writing* soldier!" he shouted.

There was a silence. And again Ring Lardner made his only remark of the evening.

"You sure swept the table that time, Dave," he said quietly.

Wallace followed Lardner's lazy glance around the table. The circle of poker players included almost every "writing" soldier who had been on the staff of the *Stars and Stripes* in France.

There are those who maintain that Lardner made two remarks that night, and that his next one was immediate and tactful.

"Roodles?" he said.

Dave Wallace was the most prominent of what might be called the "cushion" membership of the Vicious Circle. Like one or two other regular lunchers in the group who were themselves neither conspicuous nor famous, he was a good audience. He was usually the first to arrive at the Round Table, ready to laugh at the first thing Woollcott, or Adams, or Benchley, or Ross, or any of the other great men said. Dave's laughter

§ 241 §

THE VICIOUS CIRCLE

was genuine, if over-prompt, and one thing about him made it seem even more spontaneous; Dave had dimples. Somehow, a man with dimples can be a stooge and never look like one.

The Vicious Circle needed an audience like Dave and his one or two fellow claqueurs; it got to be a strain, sharpening their wits only on one another. Besides, they cherished Dave for another reason. As a theatrical press agent he knew many beautiful actresses, and nobody at the Round Table, or at the Thanatopsis, was ever averse to having a pretty actress at his side. The Vicious Circle treasured Dave for his wide acquaintance among beauties, for his ready laughter, and for his patent hero-worshiping . . . but they treated him, mostly, like a bunch of little boys kicking around a mud turtle to make it lie on its back.

One reason for this was that Dave, unfortunately, was an incurable social snob, the kind that dearly loves a Vanderbilt. Social snobbery was one of the things the Vicious Circle condemned . . . at least, until some time later, when they began to meet a few Vanderbilts and so on themselves. They never let Dave forget a remark he made the time a friend got married and Dave inquired about the bride.

"Who *was* she?" he wanted to know.

"Oh, just plain folks," they told him. "Her father was a grocer."

"*Wholesale,* of course?" Dave asked anxiously.

The Vicious Circle's bland distaste for pretentiousness once provoked one of George Kaufman's most-

§ 242 §

As the Girl Said to the Sailor

quoted sallies. A stranger, sitting in at the poker game, took to bragging of his ancestry back to the time of the Crusades. Finally Kaufman gave him a proud retort.

"I had an ancestor, too," he said, "Sir Roderick Kaufman. He *also* went on the Crusades! . . . As a spy, of course," George added thoughtfully.

Racial gags almost never caused any ill-feeling in the small, perfect democracy of the Round Table and Thanatopsis circle, perhaps because they were usually volunteered by someone belonging to the race or creed in question and were nearly always at the expense of something else—snobbery, pretentiousness,. phoniness, or any of the other qualities the boys derided.

"Did you fellows know that I have a little Jewish blood?" Herbert Bayard Swope inquired, one evening at poker.

"And did you-all know that I's. got a tinge of the tarbrush?" asked Paul Robeson, who was sitting in.

Another night, Raoul Fleischmann happened to remark that he was fourteen years old before he knew that he was a Jew.

"That's nothing," said Kaufman. "I was sixteen before I knew I was a boy."

Sometimes these mild ribaldries shocked Dave Wallace's notions of old-world decorum. Dave, a sedate and simple soul, took a fairly constant ribbing from the crowd anyway. For example, Kaufman, as banker of the Thanatopsis, handled all the checks and so knew that Dave's middle initial was "H." and that he was for

§ 243 §

THE VICIOUS CIRCLE

some reason fiercely secretive about it. After hazarding many uncouth guesses which Dave, no master of repartee, bore with patience, his cronies took to sending in squibs to the New Yorker, all credited to the well-known wit, David H. Wallace. These were either corny or perfectly pointless, and Ross gleefully published every one. " 'It,' quoth David H. Wallace, gnomic graybeard, 'never rains but it pours' " would appear at the bottom of a page; or, "As David H. Wallace says, 'Tea and coffee are good to drink, but tennis is livelier.' "; or, "David H. Wallace, the monologuist, convulsed his set with a good one the other evening. 'It seems there were two Irishmen,' Mr. Wallace began, but could not go on for laughing." Only once did they let him have a real joke, and he now recalls it with a shudder. "It raised my hair," says Dave, who is nearly bald. The joke went like this: " 'Once there were two Jews,' David H. Wallace related at a recent soirée, 'and *now* look!' " The authors of this line were later revealed to be George S. Kaufman and Raoul H. Fleischmann.

Naturally, Wallace was not the Vicious Circle's only target; a pleasant mockery tinged most of the remarks the boys exchanged with one another. One night Woollcott arrived wearing a bearskin coat he had bought for $200, before the war. "This coat was a smart investment," he boasted, preening himself. "I can sell it any day for as much as I paid for it."

F.P.A. glanced across the table at Heywood Broun, slumped in his usual rumpled and spotty heap.

"You couldn't get that much for your entire ward-

§ 244 §

As the Girl Said to the Sailor

robe, Heywood," he surmised, ". . . unless it was from a costumer."

Broun merely smiled his angelic smile. "Poor old Broun," he murmured. But it was easy-going, soft-spoken, "poor old Broun" nevertheless who was partly responsible for the only fist fight the Thanatopsis remembers. This was a battle between Broun and Joe Brooks, a stockbroker and member of the Thanatopsis, and it did not take place in the Thanatopsis clubroom; it took place chiefly in an even more interesting chamber, namely Heywood Broun's mind.

Thanatopsis members are not sure how it began. Some say that Joe Brooks refused to sell chips to Dorothy Parker; others say Mrs. Parker never played poker and the argument was about something else entirely. Mrs. Parker, interrogated, says "Ooh!" At any rate, one thing led to another and many questions were involved, including American womanhood, the Socialist Party, the Right to Strike, Censorship in the Theatre versus Decency in the Theatre, How to Make Ravioli, and Where Do You Get Your Suits Made, You Monster? Both men quit the poker game in a fury and went home separately at about two in the morning. A couple of hours later Broun, tossing in his bed and unable to sleep, suddenly sat up and addressed his wife, Ruth Hale.

"I'm going down and beat hell out of that son of a bitch," he announced.

Ruth tried to dissuade him, pointing out the lateness of the hour and the fact that Joe Brooks was a

§ 245 §

THE VICIOUS CIRCLE

trained athlete and a former all-American football player, but it was no use. Broun pulled on a pair of trousers and a coat, taxied dangerously from his house on West 85th Street to East 10th Street, where Brooks lived, and kept his finger on the bell until Brooks opened the door. He then pasted Brooks on the jaw.

There were no eyewitnesses to that battle, which raged all over the Brooks apartment, but it was later disclosed that Broun took a life-sized beating in which even his garments were ripped to shreds, and that he taxied home in the dawn with two black eyes and wearing a suit of gentleman's evening clothes lent to him by his recent adversary.

The final victory was Broun's, however. When he took off Brooks's coat he found in a pocket a fat address book crammed with the addresses and telephone numbers of innumerable fair women. Serenely, as the sun came up, Heywood sat at his window tearing up the pages of the address book, and watching the fragments drift away on the early morning breeze.

Although fisticuffs were not a general diversion of the Thanatopsis, the clubroom in the Algonquin usually looked, after a poker session, as though carnage had taken place there. Sandwich crusts, mayonnaise, cigar butts and fruit peelings were strewn everywhere, there were a dozen new cigarette burns in the carpet, and several chairs had come apart at the seams from too much tilting back to scrutinize the table. These damages represented a pure loss to Father, since the Thanatopsis was charged nothing for the room and never spent any-

§ 246 §

As the Girl Said to the Sailor

thing on food in the hotel on poker nights. When they got hungry one of the members would go down to a Sixth Avenue delicatessen and come back with a paper bag full of sandwiches and fruit. One hot summer night they ordered in from a neighboring caterer a whole ice-cream freezerful of strawberry and pistachio ice cream, which melted and ran all over the carpet. It was after that incident that Father gently caused a large sign to be hung in the clubroom in time for the next session. The sign read simply:

BASKET PARTIES WELCOME

The boys got a good laugh out of it, and even found it a handy thing to jot down telephone numbers on.

Not all of the poker games were held in the Algonquin, although that became the club's best-known meeting place. Sometimes one of the members would play host in his own apartment, and they would all "kitty out" for the refreshments; occasionally a literati-struck actress would invite them to meet in her penthouse or duplex and they would feast freely on a superb buffet and gratefully allow their hostess to sit in on the game. This was truly a courteous gesture, for they did not enjoy taking money from women. One time, Alice Brady, whom they had met through Dave Wallace—then press agent for her father, William A. Brady—asked them to come and play at her house in the Fifties, fed them royally on pheasant and champagne, and took a jovial hand in the poker game. She was so stimulated by the company that she made reckless bets all over the place.

§ 247 §

THE VICIOUS CIRCLE

and was soon seriously in the red. One of the boys took Wallace aside.

"Listen, for godsakes," he said, "tell her to go easy. Or better still, you sit beside her and tell her how to play her hand."

"If you insist," said Dave. "It made them feel more comfortable," he explains now. "My first instinct was to tell them the truth—that Alice could afford to lose more than all of 'em put together at that particular time. She had just signed a contract with Famous Players for forty weeks at four thousand a week, on a rising scale."

Many people who ought to know say that what finally ruined the Thanatopsis was the fact that the stakes became too high; they rose from one hundred dollars to two hundred and fifty, then to five hundred, and too often the sky was the limit. Too much money was involved, and the game degenerated into a cutthroat project rather than a friendly gathering. At least once the members tried to curb their own skyrocketing bets— they cut the value of the chips by fifty percent so that, although a chip was still called a dollar, it was worth only fifty cents. However, their minds remained geared to think in terms of fat round figures. One night, soon after the devaluation, Ross won $450.00 in real dollars. "Just think," said Toohey mournfully, "last week that would have been nine hundred dollars!"

What you gain on the swings you lose on the roundabouts, and the Thanatopsis boys proceeded to gamble on other games the money they saved by cutting the chips at poker. They never played any game except

§ 248 §

As the Girl Said to the Sailor

for money—anagrams, craps, cribbage, croquet. One or two of them grew peevish when they lost—Marc Connelly often flew into a temper, and Woollcott was a great one for kicking the cribbage board across the room—but mostly, they took their ups and downs philosophically. "None but the brave chemin de fer," sighed Bob Sherwood one evening, after losing a monumental sum at that sport, at Swope's.

As the Thanatopsis grew richer (and some of its members poorer), it moved its headquarters from the Algonquin to the Colony Restaurant, where its wealthy new members such as Swope and Joe and Gerald Brooks had been long and favorably known. Father did not grieve over its departure. His true love was the Round Table, and the Round Table still met at the Algonk. As for Gene Cavallero, that other master of diplomacy, who owns the Colony, he has only one comment to make on the Thanatopsis.

"It was an honor to have them," he says. With a shrug.

CHAPTER THIRTEEN

Merrily We Roll Along

SOME YEARS ago George S. Kaufman and Moss Hart wrote a play called *Merrily We Roll Along*. It was a serious drama concerned with the disintegration of a man on account of too much prosperity, and it was one of their few flops. Herman Mankiewicz saw it in New York and, returning to Hollywood, attempted to describe it to a friend.

"It's a problem play," he explained, "about this playwright who writes a play and it's a big success, and then he writes another play and *that* one is a big success, all his plays are big successes, and all the actresses in them are in love with him, all these beautiful women are in love with him, and he has a yacht and a beautiful home in the country and a penthouse in town, and a beautiful wife and two beautiful children, and he makes a million dollars. Now the problem the play propounds is this," Mankiewicz concluded, "how did the poor son of a bitch ever get into that situation?"

This vignette might well be used to describe the

§ 251 §

THE VICIOUS CIRCLE

members of the Vicious Circle at the top of their success. As their fame and fortune grew, so did their sensitiveness to trouble. If any group was ever wholeheartedly susceptible to Dr. Freud and his new-fangled psychiatry, the Vicious Circle was that little band of quiverers.

Oddly enough, the two greatest sufferers from neuroses at the Round Table were the two biggest and burliest men who ever sat there: John Peter Toohey and Ed MacNamara. They were the first to visit a psychiatrist, and they chose one with the surprising name of Dr. Dorian Feigelbaum.

Toohey's trouble, which he related freely at the Round Table, was mainly that he kept dreaming of a slut who tried to sell him violets. This was considered pretty sinister at the Round Table since Mrs. Toohey, a lady of irreproachable character, was named Viola. "It clearly means," said Woollcott gleefully, "that Viola was not all she professed to be when you married her." And the next time he met Mrs. Toohey at the Thanatopsis, he greeted her with a sympathetic throb in his voice. "Viola!" he cried, "I didn't *know!*"

It was odd—or perhaps it wasn't—that Woollcott, the one most in need of psychiatric treatment, was about the only one to scoff at it.

MacNamara's trouble was more real. Having studied and worked as a singer, he suddenly found he couldn't sing on account of a lump that kept coming up in his throat. This nervous ailment—said by psychiatrists to denote a fear or guilt complex of some kind—

§ 252 §

Merrily We Roll Along

persisted with Mac until he was forced to give up singing and take what jobs he could get as a straight actor; he never got over it. Frank Sullivan, who loved Mac, has an explanation. "Mac had one of the first inferiority complexes," Frank says. "He could never get over the wonder of being accepted into that magic circle, the Round Table. He used to say, 'What do they see in *me?* They're all such brilliant people—and me, I'm just a cop who can carry a tune.' . . . Mac really worried about it, and I guess it got to be a strain on him trying to be bright all the time instead of just singing as God made him to do," says Sullivan.

Perhaps this is the place to tell what finally happened to MacNamara, who was a good friend and a hero-worshiper to the end. A great pal of his was the movie actor James Cagney, another Irishman whom he often visited in Hollywood or at Cagney's place at Martha's Vineyard. Somewhere in this period Mac had developed angina pectoris, but nobody knew about it—from Mac, at least.

Cagney had some horses at Martha's Vineyard that he wanted shipped to the West Coast, so he asked MacNamara, who was visiting him in California, to go East and superintend the shipping. "Sure," said Mac, and took off for Martha's Vineyard. It was no sacrifice, really, for Mac had always said that Martha's Vineyard was the place he wanted to live and die in.

The horses were nervous, and Mac decided to ride with them on the ferry to the mainland, and in the freight car to New York. Sometime during the trip in

§ 253 §

THE VICIOUS CIRCLE

the freight car a frightened horse reared, and Mac had to yank it back into control. The angina caught up with him then. He died right there, in a minute, in the freight car, alone. It wasn't anybody's fault.

It wasn't anybody's fault, but sometimes I wonder what might have happened to MacNamara if he had never met any celebrated people. He might have been John McCormack or Morton Downey if he had stuck to singing; or he might have been Police Commissioner if he had stuck to being a policeman. He might be alive today if he hadn't done a favor for Jim Cagney.

On the other hand, of course, he might not be any of those things. As Joe Hergesheimer once said to me, "Some people are *addressed* to disaster."

For the people who were "addressed" to success, the Round Table was honeysuckle and roses during the 'Twenties.

"It must be a boom," Georges, the headwaiter, said to my father one day, "they order ice cream on top of everything!"

"Uh-huh," said Bob Benchley, when Father told him this glad news, "and then they grab their lollipops and pitter-patter over to their psychiatrists." How true it is that fame and fortune oft bring complications in their train.

The passion for being psychoanalyzed that flourished around the Algonquin in the middle and late 'Twenties was not, of course, restricted to the Round Table; but it did seem to affect writers, mostly. With

§ 254 §

Merrily We Roll Along

the success of *The New Yorker,* a malady called *"New Yorker* neurasthenia" developed among staff members and became so well-known in medical circles that only recently a pyschiatrist referred to it in an interview with a new patient who has been on the magazine since it started.

"How long you been with *The New Yorker?"* the doctor inquired.

"Twenty-five years," replied the patient.

The doctor stared in amazement. "And this is the *first* time you've been to a psychiatrist? Holy smoke! We *usually* get 'em in a year or two."

It is hard to say why *The New Yorker* staff were so peculiarly afflicted. Perhaps it was partly because many of them—except Ross, who, to my mind, has always been as normal as blueberry pie—were addicted to light wines and late hours, and too much introspection toward dawn. Perhaps it was also because none of them ever let any hangover, fatigue, or personal depression prevent them from showing up at the office next morning, and working harder than most people on any other magazine. This last statement will be challenged, I know, by any staff member of any other magazine who happens to read this, but there it stands. So kill me.

There was another reason, too, why people on *The New Yorker* began looking over their shoulders. *The New Yorker* office was always haunted by strange goings on. Hobgoblins were at work there. One day, Jim Thurber went into E. B. (Andy) White's office to see him about something, found White absent, and noticed

§ 255 §

THE VICIOUS CIRCLE

a memorandum White had scrawled on the wall. "THURSDAY, April 15th, 11 a.m." it read. Thurber casually circled the memo with a pencil, and wrote beside it "DER TAG." Then he left, thinking no more of his mild joke.

On Thursday, April 15th, at 11 a.m., a bank in Mount Vernon was held up by a gang of bandits, and it was discovered that they had used White's car for their getaway. The police traced the car to the New York garage where White kept it, and pretty soon two tough dicks turned up in White's office and grilled him. Why was his car used, they wanted to know, and—above all— what was the meaning of that memorandum on his office wall, naming the day and moment of the crime? Grilling Andy White is something like turning the heat on a young deer or on the first snowdrop; he is a poet, not very big physically, and patently a gentle and innocent man. In this case his alibi was good, too. The memorandum on the wall referred to a dentist appointment, he explained, and furthermore he had been at the dentist's at the time of the robbery and could prove it.

"That alibi is *too* good," the cops decided, and detailed a fellow policeman to keep an eye on Andy. For a week—until the real 'criminals were caught—this armed guard relaxed in White's office, engaging him in literary chitchat. "How did you ever get started in this writing business anyway?" was one of the things he wanted to know.

§ 256 §

Merrily We Roll Along

Another thing that has always seemed uncanny to *New Yorker* editors is the fact that admirers of Charles Addams—the artist who draws the family of wonderful monstrosities—are always coming up to them at parties and saying, "You know, my favorite Addams cartoon of all you've published is the one where a nurse outside the maternity ward is handing a baby to the terrible-looking father and saying, 'Will you take it with you or will you eat it here?' " The strange thing about this is that the drawing never appeared in *The New Yorker.* It was a sketch idly drawn by Wolcott Gibbs one day, on a wall near the water cooler, as a parody of Addams and a variation on the old gag about the S-shaped cake. *New Yorker* editors can't figure out how so many people who have never been in the office came to know about it.

Gibbs, a high-strung party who will not ride in self-service elevators because he expects them to keep on going right through the top of the building and out over the rooftops, is nevertheless cool and even hard-boiled, as an editor. "This writer has got to the point where he thinks that everything that happens to him is interesting," he once noted on a manuscript. When the galley proofs of *Enjoyment of Laughter,* Max Eastman's weighty analysis of American humor, came into the office for perusal and consideration, Gibbs's typed comment was negative but vague until the last sentence, which read, "All I know is that Eastman has got American humor down and broken its arm." Gibbs is also the

§ 257 §

THE VICIOUS CIRCLE

boy who remarked of the little girl in Lima, Peru, who had a baby at the age of eight, "She can't tell who did it until she learns to talk."

Although it was a nervous age, things were pretty much peaches and cream with the Round Table in the gilded 'Twenties.

Aleck Woollcott, prosperous with magazine and newspaper contracts—and, beginning in September, 1929, radio contracts as well—took an apartment in the Campanile, a co-operative apartment house on the East River where Alice Duer Miller lived. Installing himself there, he sent out invitations to his friends to give him a linen-china-and-silver "shower." F.P.A. obliged explicitly with three gifts: a handkerchief, a mustache cup, and a dime.

This was the same domicile that Dorothy Parker christened "Wit's End" . . . although there were some in favor of F.P.A.'s suggestion, "Old Manse River." At Wit's End Woollcott presided grandly. There were Sunday breakfasts with the Master in a dressing gown and Junior, the skeptical colored boy, serving one sweet dish after another . . . pancakes filled with jam, jelly doughnuts, French toast with powdered sugar and maple syrup —these were the things Woollcott liked to eat. Possibly as an antidote to this sugary fare, his conversation at the breakfast table was steadily acid.

"You," he said one fair Spring morning to a woman guest, "are married to a cuckold." It was simply a general, all-purpose insult, which he had probably

§ 258 §

Merrily We Roll Along

thought up in the dark of night, and in this case it meant nothing because the lady was happily married to her husband and neither had, nor wanted, any outside beaus. But Woollcott was a master of the unwelcome implication; he knew that you can almost never accuse anybody of anything without making that person wonder nervously what gave you that impression—and how many other people share it? This unwholesome truth Aleck grabbed onto and "milked" as riotously as a radio comedian "milks" a gag.

"It was as though he called people together just to exhibit their weaknesses to each other," one breakfast-table guest said recently.

Sometimes, at the Sunday gatherings, the host sulked openly, and on one occasion he was so nasty to John T. Winterich, a man beloved by all, that Winterich took him aside later that morning and said, half-seriously, "Look, Aleck, do you *hate* me?"

"You are unworthy of so noble an emotion as hate," Aleck yapped at him. This was a remark nobody in his right mind could take seriously about himself, so Winterich patted Aleck briefly on the shoulder and the two men remained good friends—in the precarious fashion that marked most people's friendships with Woollcott.

It is possible, of course, that Woollcott's remark to Winterich was a peace offering. It might very well have come from the heart and meant, "Gee, I think you're the greatest guy in the world." The deviousness of Woollcott's inner workings was something that not even his

§ 259 §

THE VICIOUS CIRCLE

close friends could always fathom. With Aleck, many an insult was a garland; partly because insult was his habit of speech, and partly because it was also his form of endearment. The only thing his friends had to figure out was which one—the true insult or the insulting endearment—he meant at the time. It kept them on their toes, it was good for them. I think it was one reason why people always flocked around Woollcott, and spoiled him so outrageously. He always gave them something, if only a furious question in the mind.

Peggy and Ralph Pulitzer lived in the Campanile, as did Woollcott and the Millers; Frank Sullivan had an apartment with Corey Ford in the next block, and Alfred Lunt and Lynn Fontanne lived not far away. It was a happy arrangement, and one that suited Aleck's love of cliques. In fact, the reason for a famous row he had with Herbert Bayard Swope was that Swope wanted a friend of his, John D. Hertz, the Chicago taxicab tycoon, to take the Joshua Cosdens' apartment in the building when it fell vacant after Cosden went broke. Woollcott didn't want Hertz and, since the apartments were run on a co-operative plan, managed to blackball him.

With all these activities Aleck found time for many trips to Europe, sometimes alone, sometimes in pleasant company. Charles MacArthur sailed with him once, on the *S.S. France*, and—two days out at sea—came on deck and stared around him in perplexity. "I can't get over the feeling that I'm on a boat," he confided to Aleck. Woollcott's departures were always the signal for his friends to arrive at the pier bearing *bon voyage* gifts of

§ 260 §

Merrily We Roll Along

a strange and baffling character. Benchley, wishing to give him something that he could not procure in Paris, once brought him a plate of wheatcakes. Another time, declaring that they desired to make the Master's cabin cosy for the voyage, Marc Connelly and Alexander Clark presented him with a bowl of goldfish and a two-foot bust of Schiller weighing about a hundred and twenty pounds.

Those were lighthearted days, indeed. In 1927, Father bought a black Rolls-Royce, a pear-shaped diamond for my stepmother, and a mink coat for me; and what was more important, he bought the Algonquin, the actual property, that is—he had owned the lease, the equipment, and the business for many years. Father was never much of a one for show, however. Fundamentally he remained the same man who had tried to instill notions of thrift in me when I was sixteen. At that time, I remember, I lost a twenty-dollar bill and, after a brief search, said casually, "Ah, well, it doesn't matter. I have another." Believe me, it was a long time before I saw another double sawbuck. Father stopped my allowance for a month, for that crack.

In the next couple of years the Round Table boys and girls did fairly well. George Kaufman wrote *Animal Crackers* with Morrie Ryskind, for the Marx Brothers, and *The Royal Family* with Edna Ferber, who was also writing her novel, *Cimarron;* Robert Sherwood wrote *The Love Nest* and *The Queen's Husband,* starring Roland Young; Deems Taylor composed *The King's Henchman;* Marc Connelly and Herman Mankiewicz wrote a

THE VICIOUS CIRCLE

comedy called *The Wild Man of Borneo;* Benchley wrote *The Early Worm* and innumerable magazine pieces, and started his famous movie "shorts"; Woollcott followed three popular books—*Shouts and Murmurs, Mr. Dickens Goes to the Play,* and *The Story of Irving Berlin*—with a fourth, *Going to Pieces;* Adams, Sullivan and Stallings were all on the *World;* Broun later went to the *World-Telegram,* and had also written two books, *Pieces of Hate* and *Gandle Follows His Nose;* and Dorothy Parker followed her first book of verse, *Enough Rope,* with a second, *Sunset Gun.*

Now that the Vicious Circle had come to know so many industrialists and stockbrokers, most of them (with that touching faith the artist always feels toward the businessman) invested their earnings in the stock market. In 1929 many of them are said to have had two or three hundred thousand dollars, on paper.

"It's really nothing," Marc Connelly remarked one day, with a shrug. "After all, Ed MacNamara has got the only really steady income in the bunch." Mac was playing in *The Ladder.*

The Ladder, generally conceded to be one of the worst, if not the worst play ever written, was a phenomenon of the 'Twenties along with *Abie's Irish Rose,* bathtub gin and Aimée Semple MacPherson. It seems that one Edgar B. Davis, a Texas oil millionaire, read something in the Bible one day that started him thinking about transmigration of souls. He commissioned a journalist, Frank Davis (no relation) , to write a play on this theme, and engaged a music teacher named Isadore

§ 262 §

Merrily We Roll Along

Luckstone to write incidental music for it. Edgar Davis then brought the manuscript to New York and persuaded Brock Pemberton to produce it. Brock called in Edward Knobloch, a well-known playwright, to work on it, but since Edgar Davis insisted on rewriting it himself at every rehearsal, Pemberton and Knobloch soon withdrew in a flurry of nerves. Edgar Davis proceeded on his own, the play actually opened at the Mansfield Theatre, and then began one of the strangest endurance tests New York has ever witnessed.

Nobody came to see it, of course. An average matinee audience consisted of about four people, three downstairs and one in the balcony. Evenings, attendance rose sharply to around sixteen people—or (said *The New Yorker*, pointing out that there were twenty-five actors in the cast), approximately one and one-third actor to each member of the audience. The weekly gross, in good weeks, was around $300, and the weekly cost to Edgar Davis around $11,000. But Davis believed in the transmigration of souls, and this play contained his message. He kept it running for two years, at a total cost to himself of $1,250,000.

During what may be called its "run" the play was shoved around to five different theatres; the Mansfield, the Lyric, the Waldorf, the Cort, and the Belmont. Davis paid the full rental on each theatre, and the moves were due to the qualms of theatre-owners who began to feel about *The Ladder* the way landlords feel about people who keep pet owls. This was the least of Davis's worries. He had discovered that actors do not like to play to an

§ 263 §

THE VICIOUS CIRCLE

empty house, even at a good salary, so his main problem was to fill the house. He chartered a train and brought a theatreful of people down from Boston to see the show (with orchids for all the ladies). He offered a weekly prize of $500 for the best letter about *The Ladder*— adding that the contestant need not have *seen* the play in order to win the prize. He gave away fans and other trinkets advertising the play. He announced that any customer who bought a ticket, saw the show, and didn't like it, would have his money cheerfully refunded with no questions asked. The last challenge was the most popular. The audience (what there was of it) almost pushed over the box office every night at 11 p.m., getting their money back, and it gave Davis his next idea. From then on, he charged no admission whatever.

The day after the announcement of free tickets 3000 people stormed the theatre, and one woman was hurt by being pushed through a glass door. It is clear that the great American public likes anything that is free, and liked it even in the 'Twenties, before radio giveaway shows were known.

Davis kept up the free admission policy until the end of the play's run, but after the first exciting day few customers availed themselves of it. The great American public, being skeptical as well as grabby, distrusts anything it gets free for too long. Audiences dwindled to the familiar three or four (I've always wondered who *they* were?) and finally Davis closed the show and went back to Texas, a relatively poor man.

He struck oil in Texas again, in 1932. Ten years

§ 264 §.

Merrily We Roll Along

later, at the age of 71, he was once more a million-aire. I can't help admiring Mr. Davis. He was lovely to actors, for one thing: he not only kept them steadily employed, but he also circulated among them almost weekly handing out a twenty-dollar gold piece to each one as a private token of his own surprise at finding them still there.

Besides, he was a man who believed in something and was willing to spend a million dollars to convince the public that it was true. If there is anything in his notion of transmigration of souls, I rather hope that the soul of Edgar B. Davis will inhabit the body of some equally dogged but more successful producer . . . say, Mike Todd.

CHAPTER FOURTEEN

How To Run a Fortune Into a Shoestring

ONE FINE October day in 1929 Groucho Marx was playing golf with Max Gordon, the producer, at a Long Island country club. Gordon was suddenly overtaken by sensations of bliss.

"Marx," he said, strolling down the fairway and twirling his club, "this is the life! Why should we do any work at all? Here I am, a nobody, my real name is Salpeter, I am a kid from Rivington Street, but I can spend a fine day playing golf because I already made three thousand dollars in the stock market this morning. Marx," Gordon demanded, hitting a ball and running happily after it, "how long has this been going *on?*"

A few days later, on the morning of the crash, Groucho's telephone rang. It was Max Gordon, and his voice was hollow. "Marx?" he said. "This is Salpeter. The jig is up."

Gordon went to a hospital soon afterward, with ulcers and no money, and it is pleasant to report that all four Marx Brothers called on him frequently and that

§ 267 §

THE VICIOUS CIRCLE

Harpo entertained him with his famous sleeve trick—the one where he tilts an arm and lets a thousand knives and forks run out of his cuff. Only this time it wasn't knives and forks; it was cash—tens, twenties, fifties, and one-hundred-dollar bills contributed by the Marxes and other friends of Gordon's. Enough to help put him back in business again, so that he could produce *Three's A Crowd* with Fred Allen, Clifton Webb, and Libby Holman, and *The Band Wagon* with the Astaires, Frank Morgan, and Helen Broderick. Gordon, an unaffectedly sentimental man who went on to produce such distinguished plays as *Design for Living, The Shining Hour, Dodsworth, Othello,* and others, likes to recall how generous his friends were in hard times, and declares that George Kaufman, for instance, lent him $1,500 of the $1,600 cash that Kaufman possessed in the world at that moment.

It was true generosity because the other boys had taken a bad beating in the stock market as well. The day of the crash Groucho Marx hurried around to Morris Ernst, his attorney, with his investment list. It was a tragic document. In a few hours the most reliable stocks had fallen from 122 to 2, from 130 to 1½, and so on. Ernst asked Groucho a few questions as he read the list.

"Where did you get this recommendation?" he asked, pointing to an item.

"From Bernard Baruch," Groucho told him, truthfully.

"And this one?"

"Holy mackerel! From Gerard Swope himself!"

§ 268 §

How To Run a Fortune Into a Shoestring

Finally Ernst came to a single item standing alone and proud upon the page. It was a stock Groucho had bought at 31, and it now stood at 30. In all that morning's holocaust it had dropped only a point.

"For God's sake! Where'd you get *that* tip?" Ernst demanded.

Groucho peered over his shoulder at the item.

"Oh, *that*," he said. "I got that one from a wardrobe woman in the Shubert Theatre in Chicago."

It would be silly to say that a financial panic is good for anyone, but the truth remains that an unexpected loss of money is usually a boon to writers. Writers seem to write best when they have to worry about paying the rent.

Immediately after the stock market crash Marc Connelly wrote *The Green Pastures*, George Kaufman (with Moss Hart) wrote *Once in a Lifetime* and also wrote *The Bandwagon* with Howard Dietz, and *Dinner at Eight* with Edna Ferber. Robert Sherwood turned out *Waterloo Bridge* in 1930, and *Reunion in Vienna* a year later. During the depression Woollcott wrote his best book, *While Rome Burns*, and made his great success as radio's Town Crier. Dorothy Parker wrote "Big Blonde," her O. Henry Memorial award story, during the depression, and Edna Ferber wrote *Cimarron* and *American Beauty* —the last being one of her finest novels, to my mind, although it attracted less attention than the others.

The actors and actresses who were playing in the Round Tabler's shows were doing nicely, too, and for

§ 269 §

THE VICIOUS CIRCLE

the theatre kids who couldn't get a job in the depression
there was always Heywood Broun, the big brother of
every little guy who was kicked around. In 1931, with
some borrowed money and some of his own, Broun produced a show called *Shoot the Works*, in which he was
featured as an actor, at the George M. Cohan Theatre.
His friends now agree that his chief motive in staging this
production was to help the starving young actors, but a
few skeptics have pointed out that Broun himself was
memorably stage-struck.

"What I mean," one of them has put it tersely, "he
would have let 'em starve if he hadn't been stage-struck
too."

Shoot the Works, a revue, played about eighty-seven
performances and was mainly notable for a bedroom
scene in which Broun was discovered hiding under a
bed. He didn't look much different than usual when he
finally emerged.

"It isn't true that Heywood always looks like an un-
made bed," a friend in the audience remarked on opening night. "What he really looks like is a one-man slum."

For the first performance the Marx Brothers made
an appearance on the stage and did a number together.
They did it for love and without pay, and Broun gratefully rewarded them with one of his own paintings—
an Early Broun, as all of his works of art were called.
Groucho stared at the painting in silence for some seconds. "Hmmm," he said at length. "It was bad enough
having to do the show for nothing."

Broun's acting and his painting were only two of

§ 270 §

How To Run a Fortune Into a Shoestring

that driven man's endless efforts to find emotional security and inner peace. He was literally a man who tried everything, and all with utter sincerity. He seemed happier after his marriage to Connie Madison, the widow of Johnny Dooley, the vaudevillian, and a good, bright, levelheaded little Catholic girl; and at length, like most inwardly tortured people, he too turned to religion and became one of Monsignor Fulton J. Sheen's celebrated converts. Before he took the final step he consulted his friend, Morris Ernst, about the advisability of joining the Catholic Church. Morris is always sympathetic, but sometimes not very. "Why don't you join the Jews instead? Then you could *really* suffer," he suggested.

When Broun was dying, in 1939, the last words he spoke, although pious, were not concerned with religion and may have startled the priest who was attending him. He sighed and murmured, "Ring Lardner died a happy man because he wrote what he *wanted* to write."

Eight years earlier, in 1931, the Round Table had lost another old friend when the Pulitzers sold the *World* to Scripps-Howard, which absorbed it into the *World-Telegram*. Since I started writing this book, Scripps-Howard has also taken over *The Sun* (Frank Ward O'Malley's old paper, of which he was the star reporter), and incorporated it into *The World-Telegram and Sun*.

The death of a newspaper as an entity is a tragic thing to almost anybody who can read and write. To the Vicious Circle the end of the *World* was a shattering personal blow. Most of them worked, or had at some time

§ 271 §

THE VICIOUS CIRCLE

worked, on its famous "page-opposite-editorial" which was easily the most talked-of feature of any newspaper of that period. F.P.A., Woollcott, Sullivan, Deems Taylor, and Laurence Stallings mourned the loss of their columns and, being true newspapermen with a fondness for their fellow workers, lamented even more the loss of many jobs for many an anonymous toiler, when Roy Howard failed to pick up a contract or rehire a certain man. Their truest grief was for a more intangible loss, however. *The World,* particularly the "page-op-ed," had become a kind of banner of liberal thought for its writers and its readers; and now the banner was taken from them.

Probably no other newspaper was ever so deeply mourned in its passing. Although its final edition announced on Page One the sale (or sellout, depending on how you look at it), some six thousand bereft readers telephoned its offices on Park Row next day, demanding to know where the hell their morning paper was; and F.P.A., sitting sadly at home that morning, got seventy-one more calls at his house, from strangers wanting to know the same thing.

Subconsciously, they must have known that the end of the *World* was the end of an era.

PENSIVE INTERLUDE BY AUTHOR

I just got a crick in my back sitting at the typewriter, so I rose and had a good stretch, then went into my living room, turned on the radio, and lay down on the couch for a few minutes' relaxation with music.

What I got was not music but a radio drama called

§ 272 §

How To Run a Fortune Into a Shoestring

Portia Faces Life, and if you think I relaxed for a second you are mad. Here is this woman lawyer (Portia, get it?) who is forever having to defend her husband (he is not Bassanio, like in Shakespeare, he's just little old Walter), and even in the fifteen minutes I heard, Portia was right more times and Walter Bassanio was wrong more times than you would believe possible in one quarter of an hour. This was obviously a show designed to prove radio's iron conviction that all women are pillars of wisdom and all men just lovable fools. A popular notion with housewives, I have heard.

So I started to shut the thing off, but was arrested by the fact that Portia was praying to God, and it didn't seem respectful to dial her out in the middle of prayer. I was rewarded for waiting.

Among the credits at the end of the show, the announcer said, "The story is written by Mona Kent. The chapter quoted from the Bible is by Ezekiel."

I bet that's the first time any Old Testament prophet ever got even second billing on a radio show, right under Mona Kent.

Thinking about this I dozed off, forgetting to shut off the radio, and was awakened presently by a great yammering. Leaping to my feet, I turned off the machine and went back to the couch to enjoy the silence.

Friends, I have never heard anything more beautiful than that silence. I just lay there and soaked it up. Then it occurred to me that the Round Table people were all able to enjoy silence like that; there was no radio, to speak of, and there was no television. When

§ 273 §

THE VICIOUS CIRCLE

they wanted to think something out, they sat down quietly and thought it out. Which may be one reason why so many of the thoughts they had were so very good. For all its surface giddiness, the Nineteen-Twenties was a quiet and reflective age.

End of Pensive Interlude and Back to
The World . . .

The World had grown great under many men, but none more vivid than Herbert Bayard Swope, its last executive editor. Swope, long-legged, red-haired, loud-voiced, snap-eyed and jumping, has held so many positions of authority, from Racing Commissioner to Peace Emissary, that writers contemplating his biography have been known to shrink away from the idea in sheer fatigue, and the Information Department of the New York Public Library has been compelled to make a new ruling known as "The Swope Ruling." I myself discovered this new stricture recently when, lacking a *Who's Who*, I called up the Public Library and asked Information to read aloud, from *Who's Who*, a list of the official positions held by Herbert Bayard Swope from, say, 1930 to date. There was a shocked silence, and Information faded away from the telephone for a while—but returned to state quite gravely:

"I am sorry, we cannot help you. Owing to our present rush of business we have been instructed not to give out answers that require more than ten minutes."

Swope is also a very elusive man, owing to his habit of suddenly taking off for Europe, Bermuda, Thailand,

§ 274 §

How To Run a Fortune Into a Shoestring

or the like. When I first wrote him that I would like to see him in order to get his own recollections for this book, he replied charmingly that if I would call his office he would be pleased to make a date. I called, but he had left for Saratoga or South Carolina, I forget which. For the next few weeks I continued to call diligently, and also sent him a couple of telegrams expressing quiet desperation, but still failed to make any connection; so, in the press of seeing other people, I gave up temporarily and let Mr. Swope slide for a while.

One afternoon my telephone rang, and Mr. Swope's secretary was on the wire.

"And where are *you?*" she demanded.

"I'm home. Why?" I said.

"You were expected in Mr. Swope's office at two o'clock today," she informed me.

"Oh no!" I gasped. "Surely you're mistaken? This is the first I've heard of it."

"Not at all," she insisted. "Your name is right on Mr. Swope's pad for two p.m. today, and it's now after four."

Well, I was staggered. I have never forgotten an appointment in my life, and I certainly wouldn't be apt to forget one I had been trying to make until my teeth fell out.

"I feel terribly about it," I stammered to the secretary, "but I give you my solemn word that this is the first I have heard about any appointment with Mr. Swope for today, or any other day."

"Well, no matter," she said coolly, "I just called you

§ 275 §

THE VICIOUS CIRCLE

to tell you that Mr. Swope wouldn't be able to make it anyway."

When I told this to Frank Sullivan, he said it was the perfect Swope story, illustrating all of that gentleman's powerful drive and airy unconcern.

Some people wonder why Swope, the big, noisy go-getter, was such a success with the little group of introverts that composed the Round Table. The answer seems simple: they admired him for the way he romped all over the place and accomplished something, and he admired them for the way they just sat still and accomplished something. This is the eternal love affair between extroverts and introverts.

Besides, Swope afforded the Round Table endless entertainment; he was always doing *some* damn thing, and there was always a story about him. For instance, when he learned that Broun and other members of the Vicious Circle were regularly visiting a psychiatrist, Swope also discovered psychiatry. He got the name of their doctor (I think by this time it was Dr. Barach), made an appointment, and told his secretary to cancel all office appointments for that morning.

"But——" she said.

"Oh, well, if there's anything urgent you can get me at this number," said Swope, giving her the doctor's telephone number. Then he went uptown and reclined expectantly on the psychiatrist's couch.

"Do you dream much, Mr. Swope?" the doctor asked.

"Do I dream much!" shouted Swope, bouncing to

§ 276 §

How To Run a Fortune Into a Shoestring

a sitting position. "Why, just let me tell you what I dreamed only last night!"

"Lie down and tell me, Mr. Swope," the doctor suggested. At that moment the door opened and the doctor's secretary appeared.

"A telephone call for Mr. Swope," she announced. "Governor Smith on the wire. They say it's urgent."

"I'll take it in here," said Swope.

He talked for several minutes on the doctor's private phone, then flopped back on the couch. "Now, doctor," he said.

"*Now*, Mr. Swope," said the doctor.

The door opened. The doctor's secretary said, "I'm sorry, doctor, but they say it's urgent. Mayor Walker on the phone for Mr. Swope."

". . . *Now*, doctor," said Swope, getting back on the couch a few minutes later. The door opened again and the secretary appeared.

"Doctor," she whispered, "Washington is on the wire for Mr. Swope. It's the White House, and they *say* it's the President calling."

"I'll take it in here," said Swope again, and after he had chatted for a while he made for the doctor's couch once more. The doctor stopped him in mid-air.

"Mr. Swope," he said, "your case is easily diagnosed. Obviously your only trouble is that you are suffering from delusions of grandeur."

Although Swope undoubtedly acted as a stimulus to the Round Table group, he was also partly responsible for its gradual disappearance from the Algonquin.

§ 277 §

THE VICIOUS CIRCLE

Through this human dynamo and the people who surrounded him the quiet denizens of the Vicious Circle were introduced to a system of high life that included yachts, horse racing, swimming pools, Long Island houseparties, croquet at $1,000 a side, and navy-blue dinner clothes. It was all fine fun, and probably it did them no harm; but they would never be quite the same as in the days of their spontaneous and simple youth.

One of the more soigné emanations of the latter-day Vicious Circle was their very own night club, called the Elbow Room. There is a tinkle of tired wit in that name, but unfortunately the Elbow Room fell flat on its face. I say "unfortunately" because I was a charter member of the club (it didn't last long enough to have any other kind) and I had some good times there. The Elbow Room was what is now the Barberry Room, a part of the Berkshire Hotel which was, and is, owned by George Backer, a delightful man and a good friend of Woollcott's and the rest of the Round Tablers'. George was also the wealthy Socialist who later married Dorothy Schiff (now Dorothy Thackrey) and published the New York *Post* for a while. Woollcott and Beatrice Kaufman, afire with the notion of a private night club for their own group, obtained the room from Backer and got Norman Bel-Geddes to decorate it—all in blue mirrors and blue glass.

"Whee," observed Gerald Murphy, president of Mark Cross, viewing it for the first time, "just let the water in, and it'll make a great swimming pool."

§ 278 §

How To Run a Fortune Into a Shoestring

The club asked a modest initiation fee and nominal dues, but charged fancy prices for food and drink to keep out the riffraff. Unhappily, the high prices kept out a good many members in good standing as well. Another thing that hastened its decline was Woollcott's steely insistence on excluding all newspaper columnists except those who belonged to the Vicious Circle; Winchell, Leonard Lyons, Lucius Beebe, Elsa Maxwell, all were barred. "Even Elsa Maxwell?" someone once asked Aleck. "*Especially* Elsa Maxwell!" he snorted. Not unnaturally, these exclusions caused the outcast columnists to gang up in print against the Elbow Room and badger and ridicule it to a standstill, but it might have withstood such attacks had it not died of its own splendor.

While it lasted, though, there were some fine parties there. I remember one in particular, given by Robert and Madeline Sherwood after the opening of Sherwood's play, *Abe Lincoln in Illinois*. Two of my vivid recollections of that evening are both connected with the short flight of steps that led into the room. The first is a mind's-eye picture of Lynn Fontanne flying down those steps, wearing a gold-colored satin gown and very little underneath it, and looking as beautiful as I ever saw anyone look—like a winged victory in gold. The second, by contrast, is one of the homeliest little scenes I ever witnessed—when Raymond Massey, the star of the play, came in and hesitated for a moment at the top of the steps. The whole room, moved by his superb portrayal of Lincoln earlier in the evening, broke into spontaneous applause, and Mr. Massey, honestly taken aback,

THE VICIOUS CIRCLE

executed a true Lincolnian bow—long arms hanging loose, feet shuffling, head and shoulders humbly bent. It was enough to give you a turn, seeing what looked like Abe Lincoln in the flesh standing gawky and diffident against that lush Norman Bel-Geddes décor.

My nicest memory of that party is one of Bob Sherwood himself. When I arrived, he and his wife were welcoming their guests in the doorway. I shook hands, murmured something heartfelt about the play, and started to move on, but Bob held onto my hand.

"Say," he said earnestly, as though it were the most important thing in the world, "that was a good piece you had in *The New Yorker* this week."

That I have never forgotten. Here it was, *his* night, *his* play, *his* party—his triumphant hour, in fact—and he had time, not only to have read some piece of mine, but to remember it and to say something about it. For my dough, he is a wonderful guy.

He is a truly modest man, as everyone who knows him will attest. Lynn Farnol, former publicity director for Samuel Goldwyn, likes to tell about the time Sherwood won the Motion Picture Academy Award for writing the movie, *The Best Years of Our Lives.* Lynn and some other Goldwyn executives sat up in New York, the night of the Award Dinner in Hollywood, anxiously waiting to hear whether their picture had won anything or not. The news that the picture had taken nine awards—for writing, acting, direction, photography and so on—came through by telephone at about two in the morning and, in the midst of the rejoicing, Lynn sud-

§ 280 §

How To Run a Fortune Into a Shoestring

denly thought of Sherwood, who was also in New York. "I wonder how Bob feels about this? Think I'll call him up," he said. He called Sherwood's apartment and a sleepy voice answered.

"Bob?" said Lynn, excitedly, "how you feel, boy? You got it! The Academy Award!"

"Say! . . . That's . . . great . . . news," Sherwood's slow voice came over the wire. He always speaks as though articulation were a new and dangerous experiment he is trying out for the first time.

"Look, I didn't wake you up, did I?" Lynn asked.

"Uh . . . yes. . . . But that's . . . perfectly . . . okay."

Movie executives were staggered when they heard this story. "Can you figure that fella?" they demanded. "Going to bed and going to *sleep* the night he wins the Motion Picture *Academy* AWARD?"

Aleck Woollcott, a man who was less than modest, carried his love of cliques to the island he, with Neysa McMein, Janet Flanner, and Raymond Ives, bought on Lake Bomoseen in Vermont. Neshobe Island was to be another club, with community organization, but—as often happened with any plan nurtured by Woollcott— he soon became its impresario and führer, with Joseph Hennessy, his business manager, as club manager. The guests, who paid $7.50 per day, included all of the Round Table and Thanatopsis crowd, and the diversions were swimming, eating, talking, cribbage, anagrams and croquet. Probably the only visitor who never cared much

§ 281 §

THE VICIOUS CIRCLE

for Neshobe was Frank Sullivan. "I don't play games, and I get claustrophobia on islands. I always want to get *off*," Sullivan explains.

Samuel Hopkins Adams, in his biography of Woollcott, and Charles Brackett, in a novel called *Entirely Surrounded*, have both given entertaining pictures of life on the island, and, since Neshobe was a later development of the Round Table (with which this book is concerned) I shall not go further into details. But there is one "Swope story," which seems to have eluded the above gentlemen, that is worth telling here.

Croquet, as played by the Vicious Circle, was no gentle, meandering pastime; it was a cutthroat game, involving long shots into the rough, and the idea was not merely to defeat your opponent but to murder him. Stakes were regularly $10 a wicket, and sometimes rose as high as $1,000 a side. Swope, playing one day with Gerald Brooks, an indifferent player, as his partner, became so enraged by Brooks's flubbing that he ordered him not to make a single shot until he, Swope, told him exactly how to make it. Brooks agreed, and from then on, whenever it was his turn, Swope stood over him and said, "Now, Brooksy, you shoot for position. That's it! Now you go through this wicket. Fine!" Finally, at a crucial point in the game, Swope hovered anxiously over his partner and directed, "Now—watch it, this is vital—you hit that ball up here in the road. Good! *Now* you put your foot on *your* ball and drive the other one to hell and gone over into the orchard. *That's* it! Perfect!"

It was only then, from the convulsed spectators,

§ 282 §

How To Run a Fortune Into a Shoestring

that Swope discovered it was his own ball which had been driven to hell and gone.

The best player among the women who came to Neshobe was considered to be Kathleen Norris, a good friend of Woollcott's with whom, however, he did not fail to have at least one tiff. In this mild affair Woollcott was, for once, clearly innocent. He wrote, and published in *Cosmopolitan,* an admiring piece about her containing the seemingly inoffensive sentence, ". . . you did not chance to see our Mrs. Norris on that night when she and I missed the entire first act of *The Black Crook* because we had become involved in a singularly bitter cribbage game with Madge Kennedy and Harold Ross in a Hoboken saloon." When the Profile came out, Woollcott received a sharp letter (it is said, on good authority, to have come from Charles G. Norris, the novelist, and not from his wife), pointing out that the millions of Kathleen Norris readers who revered her as a respectable and God-fearing woman would be outraged to think of her sitting in a saloon. Woollcott replied that this was a lot of damn nonsense, that they had scarcely been carousing, merely playing cribbage before the performance of Christopher Morley's revival, and that this fact was plainly stated in the article. However, Aleck truly wished to offend neither Mrs. Norris nor her teetotaling readers, so when the Profile reappeared in book form, in *While Rome Burns,* he added a footnote saying, in part: "The insensate cribbage players could find a table only in the bar of one of the more teeming restaurants. If soaped mirrors

§ 283 §

THE VICIOUS CIRCLE

and brass rails can make a saloon, I suppose it *was* one, but if any members of the W.C.T.U. were present that evening, they can testify that, when it comes to a question of liquor having soiled any of the players' lips, the game might as well have been played in the basement of the First M.E. Church."

This was undoubtedly true, all of the players being notably on the abstemious side. But the thought does cross the mind that the restaurant, or saloon, must have been teeming indeed, to let four people occupy a table for a couple of hours without buying a single drink.

Although her sentimental stories seldom disclose it, Mrs. Norris has a pretty wit. Frank Sullivan, walking down Fifth Avenue one day, happened to see her looking in a shop window and, thinking himself unnoticed, eased up behind her and gave her a playful tap on the arm. But Mrs. Norris had seen his reflection in the plate glass. Instantly, she turned on him, shaking her fist, and raised her voice to a clarion pitch that soon collected a crowd.

"Not one penny more, Frank Sullivan!" she shouted. "You've had the last cent you'll get out of me! Gambling and drinking it all away like the worthless scamp ye are! Only last week I gave you a hundred dollars for your poor old sick mother, and what did ye do? Drank it all up, and they found ye in the gutter again! NO, Frank Sullivan, you'll wheedle no more money from me!"

Sullivan—than whom no man is more decorous and solvent—turned and fled, pursued by the boos and hisses of the mob.

§ 284 §

How To Run a Fortune Into a Shoestring

At dinner that evening, he told the story to Woollcott, and later regretted slightly that he had done so. "Son of a gun had my own story in print before I had a chance to tell it to anybody else, at all," Frank says, now.

§ 285 §

CHAPTER FIFTEEN

Whatever Became of Tootsie Rolls?

ONE DAY, at lunch, the members of the Round Table fell into a reminiscent mood, recalling great events they had witnessed, great books they had read, great plays and performances they had seen. One dimly remembered the San Francisco fire, another remembered the first publication of Dreiser's *Sister Carrie,* another had seen Bernhardt in a revival of. *Camille,* and quite a few grew nostalgic over Bert Williams, and (in a different way) Marie Doro. Through most of this little Mary Brandon, then the bride of Robert Sherwood, sat silent, made helpless by sheer youth. Suddenly she piped up.

"*I* remember Tootsie Rolls!" she proclaimed.

I think of Mary every time anyone younger than I says to me, "Why, *I* remember the Round Table!" Or, more frequently, "Whatever became of the Round Table?"

Well . . . whatever became of Tootsie Rolls? (Tootsie Roll manufacturers, don't write. You're

§ 287 §

THE VICIOUS CIRCLE

probably back on the market by now, but you *were* gone
for a long, long time.)

Father, during the thirteen or fourteen years he
continued to run the Algonquin successfully after the
gradual dissolution of the Round Table—until he died,
in 1946—had a much better answer for people who kept
asking him, "Whatever became of the Round Table?"
Father just said, gently, "Whatever became of the city
reservoir at Fifth Avenue and 42nd Street? It gave place
to the Public Library. These things do not last forever."

The Algonquin Round Table did not die suddenly: it faded away as imperceptibly as it had come into
being. Even its own members were not conscious that it
was drawing to a close. Edna Ferber wrote me recently,

> "I didn't even know that the group had sort
> of melted away and one day, having finished
> a long job of work, and wishing to celebrate,
> I flounced into the Algonquin dining room, sat
> down at an empty place at the Round Table—
> and found myself looking into the astonished
> and resentful faces of a family from Newton,
> Kansas, who were occupying the table on their
> New York stay. I mumbled an apology and left."

Miss Ferber is using a writer's license in citing this
fictional family from Newton, Kansas. I am told that
the Algonquin, under the ownership of Mr. Bodne, to
whom we sold it after Father died, still has plenty of
celebrities. In fact, they do say that Mr. Bodne is pro-
moting a *second* Round Table, with none other pre-

§ 288 §

Whatever Became of Tootsie Rolls?

siding than that old gypsy from Newton, Kansas, Konrad Bercovici.

But, as all bad writers always say, I am anticipating myself.

The year 1932 was a grim one for the Case family. What with strikes, prohibition, depression and all, Father was losing not only his shirt but his tail coat and his Rolls-Royce in the hotel business. I had had Socialist leanings myself, but when I saw what happened to Father that year, I became a lifetime partisan of what my father stood for—namely, Individual Enterprise.

Father, who had worked up from being a hotel night clerk to owning the Algonquin, a house in the country, a couple of cars and nearly a million dollars in the bank—sheerly through his own enterprise and guts—would be *summoned* to see the head of the cooks' union, or the waiters' union, somewhere downtown; and he had to go. He always went with a good grace, but he always came home looking white and desperate. I understood why, when he finally told me what happened on at least one of those visits.

The union head, a big, tough-looking guy, made Father walk the full length of his office to the desk where he sat, and kept him standing there while he turned his swivel chair and spat into a cuspidor at his side. Then he leaned back, folded his hands over his fat stomach, and stared up at Father.

"Well, Case," he said, "they tell me you run a hotel."

§ 289 §

THE VICIOUS CIRCLE

(I suppose that ought to be funny by this time, but somehow it isn't. I still can't write calmly about it.)

The ironic thing is that not one of Father's employes wanted to join the Union. They had all been with him twenty or thirty years, they loved their jobs, they loved Pa and the Algonk, and they were satisfied with their hours and pay. The Union managed to frighten them, however. One telephone operator said to me, in a panic, "If we don't join, they'll close the hotel!"

Union delegates filled the back halls, and threatened employes entering and leaving. I am proud to say that the Algonquin employes held out until the last gasp. But the Union finally insisted on a poll of employes, and the Union won—by one vote. I have always thought that that one vote was cast by the hotel cat.

Then, of course, came the waiters' strike. In our family the roses always come right along with the thorns, and this was a chance for Father's friends to show what they thought of him; it turns out they loved him to pieces—especially the Round Table.

The waiters walked out at one o'clock, just as the three dining rooms were filling up with hungry luncheon customers. Without a second's hesitation every man at the Round Table put on a waiter's white jacket, every woman at the Table donned a frilly apron, and they all set about serving lunch to the other patrons. Quite a few out-of-towners got a pleasurable jolt that day when they looked up from their menus to find George S. Kaufman or Ina Claire waiting politely with pad and pencil to take their orders. They all served pretty deftly, too,

§ 290 §

Whatever Became of Tootsie Rolls?

and got through the entire luncheon hour without a hitch.

Father always felt warmly grateful about this incident, and the hotel also received a good deal of valuable and entertaining publicity when the newspapers got wind of the goings on and sent their reporters hurrying over. Only one note of discord intruded upon the happy scene. It came from Aleck Woollcott, and not without provocation. Woollcott wanted to help too, but although the staff frantically supplied him with all the jackets belonging to the fattest waiters on the payroll, he couldn't get into any of them. He threw the last one down in disgust.

"Damn things aren't properly tailored!" he snorted, and stormed out of the hotel in a huff.

Later, an echo of disapproval arrived from Heywood Broun, who was picketing somewhere in Pennsylvania at the time of the strike, and who wrote his friends of the Table Round calling them scabs and renegades for deserting the waiters' cause and coming to the rescue of Case, the capitalist.

To add to Father's troubles at this time, I was suddenly stricken with a volvulus and rushed to St. Luke's Hospital in an ambulance in the middle of one night. I mention this painful fact only because of a couple of fairly fascinating incidents that occurred when, after several months and four different embroideries by the great Dr. John F. Erdmann, I began to bet better. Father had taken a room in the hospital next to mine, and one day Dr. Erdmann (who was close to seventy) came into

§ 291 §

THE VICIOUS CIRCLE

my room looking peculiar, and said to my nurse, "Maybe old age is creeping up on me after all . . . or else I need to get my glasses changed. When I came down the hall just now, I thought I saw Mary Pickford sitting in Frank's room reading the Bible."

It wasn't old age, and his glasses were all right. Mary Pickford, a devout and devoted friend of the family's, was in there all right, reading the Bible and praying for me to get well. All of Father's friends were wonderful during that tough time. Dennis King, who had a singing radio program then, telephoned one day to ask what I would like above everything.

I said, "Sing 'Trees' for me on the radio." (You may think I was running a temperature, but actually "Trees" was new then, and highly esteemed.)

"Done and done," said Dennis. "I'll sing it for you on tomorrow's program."

The next day, I had visitors or treatments or some darn thing, and when I looked at the clock it was six-thirty. The Dennis King program with my special request was over, and I hadn't even turned on the radio. I had to thank Dennis for his kindness, of course, and I was too craven to admit that I hadn't heard him; so I wrote him a profuse note thanking him for the song and saying how beautifully he had sung it. Weeks later, after I was out of the hospital, I ran into Dennis one day in the Algonquin and he looked at me strangely.

"I say, that siege of yours didn't affect your mind, did it, dear?" he asked gently.

You've guessed it. They had had to cut the program

§ 292 §

Whatever Became of Tootsie Rolls?

at the last minute, and what they cut was "Trees." Dennis simply had not sung the song for which I had thanked him, and thanked him, and thanked him.

Interesting things are always happening to me in hospitals. Not too long ago, immured in another one with something called ileitis (same as colitis, only affecting the ileum instead of the colon) I was able to brand as forever false the fashionable accusation that Bennett Cerf, of Random House, is not an original wit. It is the popular thing to say that Bennett, in *Shake Well Before Using* and his other joke anthologies, has made a fortune out of "lifting" everybody else's gags—that he is a kind of vulture, preying upon the wit of others. He is an anthologist, to be sure, but I am in a position to state that he has a very pretty repartee of his own. Bennett called me up at the hospital to ask me what books I wanted and, incidentally, asked me what ailed me. I told him it was ileitis and, not unnaturally, Bennett said "What?"

"Well," I started to explain, "do you know what the ileum is?"

"Certainly, I know what the ileum is," said Bennett. "We publish it, and the Odyssey, too."

Come good times or bad, the Round Table was always ready for a gag, and nothing was too much trouble for any member of that lighthearted crew when he set out to prepare one. Bob Benchley and his wife once asked my father and stepmother to spend a weekend at their house in Scarsdale. When the Cases arrived and were shown to their room to freshen up for dinner they

§ 293 §

THE VICIOUS CIRCLE

were a little taken aback to find that every towel in the
bathroom was neatly inscribed HOTEL ALGONQUIN
in familiar, flowing letters. Some inner reticence prevented each from mentioning, even to the other, that
anything seemed unusual (the Benchleys were such
nice people, surely it was just some accident?), and as a
result they held a remarkably stilted conversation for
a few minutes on the subject of the view from the
window. When they went downstairs for cocktails the
cocktail shaker bore the name HOTEL ALGONQUIN,
and when they sat down to dinner every piece of table
linen and silver was marked HOTEL ALGONQUIN.
Still the Cases politely said nothing, until they went up
to bed about midnight, courteously accompanied by
their host. The twin beds were trimly turned down to
reveal HOTEL ALGONQUIN on the sheets and pillow
cases. Father could keep silent no longer.

"I see you've been staying at the Commodore lately,
Bob," he said.

It had taken Benchley a couple of days of devious
plotting with me, and, through me, with the Algonquin
housekeeper, to succeed in borrowing a carload of hotel
supplies for the weekend.

The Vicious Circle's pranks on one another were
not always so deliberate; sometimes they had the artless-
ness of sheer lunacy. One summer, after the New York
run of *The Man Who Came to Dinner*, its stage-struck
authors, George Kaufman and Moss Hart, were inspired
to put it on for a summer-theatre engagement at the
Bucks County Playhouse, with Kaufman playing the role

§ 294 §

Whatever Became of Tootsie Rolls?

of The Man and Hart in the Noel Coward part. Both of these boys belong to the ambitious, but severe, type of actor. Kaufman, by nature gloomy of countenance, is so nervous on the stage that he tends to withdraw into himself until he resembles one of the embodied strokes of doom in a Russian tragedy. Hart, intrinsically a merrier man, nevertheless admires underacting so much that he plays in a monotone to the first three rows only, and sounds, in the opinion of many of his friends, like some kind of Chinese actor. Fortunately—or perhaps not—the part of Harpo Marx in the Bucks County production was played by Harpo Marx. Harpo turned up with a pocketful of candles and his cane with the automobile-horn attachment and, throughout the play, appeared wildly in unexpected corners of the stage, eating candles and honking his cane. Upon both of his co-stars he had the effect of a particularly lively alkali on a couple of litmus papers; both Kaufman and Hart turned blue.

Such antics became less frequent as the Round Table boys and girls grew older. For one thing, they were working harder than ever; and for another, the emotional lives of many of them had grown so complex as to interfere with their gags. Benchley, Kaufman, the Pembertons and Toohey remained married to their original wives, and Broun and F.P.A. were long settled into happy second marriages (F.P.A. to Esther Root, after a divorce from Minna Schwarz); but not all of the Vicious Circle were so matrimonially serene. Woollcott, of course, died an unwilling bachelor; Ross remarried

THE VICIOUS CIRCLE

twice after his divorce from Jane Grant; Sherwood is now happily married to Madeline Hurlock, whose former husband, Marc Connelly, is still single. Frank Sullivan, the group's happy bachelor, is still a happy bachelor.

As for the Round Table girls, life kept biting at their heels too, and they did their share of marrying, unmarrying, and remarrying—for the most part satisfactorily, except for Destiny's stepchild, Dorothy Parker. Mrs. Parker, long divorced from Eddie Parker, married Alan Campbell, a writer, and divorced him some years later. One night, when the bloom was beginning to wear off this union, Tallulah Bankhead came upon Mrs. Parker (as she continued to be known throughout her marriage to Mr. Campbell) sitting alone and mournful in the Algonquin lobby. The sorrow of the ages dwelt in her eyes, and Tallulah sat down to cheer her up.

"Look, Dottie," she said briskly, "you've got a fine husband. Alan is good-looking, attractive, faithful, devoted, and he just worships you. What *more* do you want?"

Dottie raised tearful eyes.

"*Presents!*" she wailed.

Presumably she got them, for she remarried Mr. Campbell only a few months ago.

Tallulah herself took a brief fling at wedlock, with John Emery, the actor. Shortly after her marriage, I ran into her in the Algonquin and she said, "Well, Maggie, I'll bet you never in your born days thought I would haul off and do such a thing as get *married!*" I said no, and behaved with astonishment because it seemed to

§ 296 §

Whatever Became of Tootsie Rolls?

please her, but personally I had always thought of Tallu as a girl who would try everything.

Dorothy Parker, after her divorce from Alan Campbell, reacted to her marital troubles in her usual feminine way, employing that small gesture of defiance that women used to express with a fan and now express by joining a political party. Mrs. Parker went in for politics. She now lives in California most of the time, and still uses her glorious talent chiefly in a valiant and lifelong effort to get out of writing anything whatever. Donald Ogden Stewart went in for politics, too, and so (in a bigger, more unfortunate way) did Paul Robeson.

Perhaps it was politics, and a broadening sense of public issues, that helped to break up the Round Table. In the Nineteen-Twenties public issues were mainly simple—votes for women, John S. Sumner, censorship, prohibition and the like. You could take them or leave them; and, with the exception of Broun the crusader, the Round Table largely left them alone and concentrated on the (to them) more vital business of writing and acting.

However, as the small, independent worlds we all used to live in gradually expanded and fused into One World with its one vast headache, there was no longer any room for cosy little sheltered cliques of specialists. Any writer who had any sense was obliged to know what was going on in this new world around him, and even actors found their own private concerns more and more mixed up with national and even international affairs. The day of the purely literary or artistic group was over,

§ 297 §

THE VICIOUS CIRCLE

and so was the small, perfect democracy of the Algonquin Round Table.

Besides, the boys and girls had grown pretty well scattered. Stallings, Mankiewicz, and Donald Ogden Stewart moved, more or less permanently, to Hollywood. F.P.A., Ross, Kaufman, Benchley, Broun and Sherwood —all with wives and growing children—went to live in the country and took to staying home whenever possible, now that they had homes to stay in. Dave Wallace lives in Syracuse, and Frank Sullivan in Saratoga Springs. Edna Ferber spends increasingly less time in New York, and more at her place in Connecticut, whence an occasional pleasant if apocryphal anecdote drifts in to her friends and admirers in town. The newest one concerns an afternoon when Edna came into the house, threw herself luxuriously on the couch, and said to her mother:

"Well, Mother, I just sold the new book to Hollywood for five hundred thousand dollars."

"Edna! Your skirt!" admonished Mrs. Ferber.

Many of the Vicious Circle—far, far too many—are gone forever. Woollcott, Benchley, Broun, Bill Murray, Johnny Weaver, Brock Pemberton, Ruth Hale, Beatrice Kaufman and Neysa McMein . . . all of these died too soon, and too young. Only one of them had reached sixty, and most were a good deal younger than that.

While I was writing this book I used to go down to Princeton now and then to see my son, who was in his senior year there. (He is all educated now, and is teach-

§ 298 §

Whatever Became of Tootsie Rolls?

ing English at Lawrenceville.) His classmates got wind of what I was doing, and showed an interest in it that surprised me. It hadn't occurred to me that kids of that age would be even slightly concerned about a group of people that had its heyday while they were still in their cradles. But they peppered me with eager and evidently sincere questions, and the people who interested them most were, in this order: Alexander Woollcott, Heywood Broun, Robert Benchley, Dorothy Parker and, of all things, Ina Claire. After all, Miss Claire married one William Ross Wallace, retired from the stage and went to live in San Francisco some eleven years ago, when these Princeton seniors were in knee pants.

"What on earth do you boys know about Ina Claire?" I asked.

"Oh, I don't know," said one, "she's always just seemed to embody everything that was glamorous about the stage in the 'Twenties."

They had not read much of Heywood Broun's writing, I found—to them, he was more of a legendary figure, a crusader, than a writer—but they had read all of Woollcott, Benchley, and Parker. "And I'll tell you one thing," said another boy, "there's nobody writing today, except Thurber, who can touch them.

"The trouble with the new bunch of young writers today," he went on, seriously, "is that they're too *limited.* They're good, yes—Arthur Miller, Truman Capote, Tennessee Williams—but they can't write anything but the *stark* stuff, the *grim* stuff. They can *only* write tragedy. They're in a rut, they have no variety . . . I'll tell you

§ 299 §

THE VICIOUS CIRCLE

what," he concluded after a thoughtful pause, "they got no sense of humor, that's what!"

"Maybe the world isn't as funny today as it was in the 'Twenties," I suggested.

He looked at me scornfully.

"Shucks," he said, "a sense of humor doesn't depend on the world being funny. It just depends on how it looks to *you*."

And that's as good a description of the Round Table's enduring quality as any I could think up myself.

§ 300 §

Index

Index

ADAMS, FRANKLIN P., 5, 11-12, 19, 30, 34, 36-37, 40, 42, 51, 53-54, 67, 77-78, 81-83, 87, 89, 90, 92, 97, 100, 103, 105, 106, 111, 112, 113, 145-46, 157, 161, 171, 172, 198, 206, 208, 210, 212-13, 221, 222, 223, 230, 233 (cartoon, 235), 238-39, 241, 244, 258, 262, 272, 295, 298

ADAMS, MRS. FRANKLIN P. *See* ROOT, ESTHER; SCHWARZ, MINNA

ADAMS, SAMUEL HOPKINS, 282

ADDAMS, CHARLES, 257

ADLER, ELMER, 180

ALLEN, KELCEY, 91

AMHERST, EARL. *See* HOLMESDALE, JEFFREY

ANDERSON, MAXWELL, 13, 39

ANGELL, KATHERINE. *See* WHITE, KATHERINE

ARDEN, ELIZABETH, 182

ARLEN, MICHAEL, 237

ARNO, PETER, 191-92

ATHERTON, GERTRUDE, 21, 199-201

BACHRACH, ARTHUR, 91

BACKER, GEORGE, 278

BALDRIDGE, C. LEROY, 118, 119, 172, 173, 214-15

BANKHEAD, TALLULAH, 48-49, 91, 225-28, 296-97

BARACH, DR., 276

BARAGWANATH, JOHN, 140, 216-17

BAROCINI, RANDOLFO, 128

BARON IRELAND. *See* SALSBURY, NATE

BARRYMORE, ETHEL, 4, 99, 113, 200, 225, 226

§ 303 §

INDEX

BARRYMORE, JOHN, 4, 32

BARRYMORES, THE, 22

BARTON, RALPH, 175, 179, 207-08

BEEBE, LUCIUS, 279

BEL-GEDDES, NORMAN, 278, 280

BENCHLEY, ROBERT, 5, 8, 11, 14, 15-16, 19, 29, 31, 42, 52, 60-66 (cartoon, 63), 67, 81-83, 87, 88, 89, 91, 97, 100-01, 103-04, 105, 106, 113, 180, 205, 224, 241, 254, 261, 262, 293-94, 295, 298, 299

BENCHLEY, MRS. ROBERT, 293

BENNETT, ARNOLD, 8

BERCOVICI, KONRAD, 289

BERLIN, IRVING, 87, 92 (cartoon, 93), 156, 189-90, 211

BERNAYS, EDWARD L., 139, 141, 142

BLACKMER, SYDNEY, 96

BODNE, BEN B., 288

BOLITHO, WILLIAM, 68

BOOTH, COMMANDER EVANGE-LINE, 4, 226

BRACKETT, CHARLES, 181, 282

BRADY, ALICE, 247-48

BRADY, WILLIAM A., 53, 247

BRANDON, MARY, 45, 89, 91, 287

BRENON, JULIET ST. JOHN, 91

BROMFIELD [CHARLES], 150-51

BROMFIELD, LOUIS, 150-51, 229-30

BROOKS, GERALD, 249, 282

BROOKS, JOE, 245-46, 249

BROUN, HEYWOOD, 5, 8, 11, 13, 20, 47, 51, 55, 67-76 (cartoon, 71), 87, 89, 91, 98, 101, 102, 103, 105, 108, 113, 126, 127, 128-31, 138, 139, 142-43, 146, 157, 160, 179, 205, 207, 233, 244-46, 262, 270-71, 291, 295, 297, 298, 299

BROUN, CONSTANCE. See MAD-ISON, CONSTANCE

BURKE, BILLIE, 14-15

CAGNEY, JAMES, 254-55

CAMPBELL, ALAN, 296

CASE, CARROLL, 23, 28

CASE, FRANK, 7 (cartoon, 9), 21, 23, 24, 26, 27, 28, 29-31, 33-34, 35-37, 51, 74, 81-83, 102, 108, 109, 112, 129, 150-52, 160-61, 162-63, 187, 202, 208, 219-20, 222, 223, 226-27, 246-47, 249, 254, 261, 288, 289-92, 293-94

CARUSO, ENRICO, 230-32

CAVALLERO, GENE, 249

CERF, BENNETT, 293

CHASE, ILKA, 6

CLAIRE, INA, 22, 41, 49-51, 237, 290, 299

CLARK, ALEXANDER, 31, 261

CLARK, FRANCES, 125-26

COBB, IRVIN S., 4, 32, 202

COLLIER, CONSTANCE, 4, 22

§ 304 §

Index

CONNELLY, MADELINE. *See* HURLOCK, MADELINE

CONNELLY, MARC, 4, 11, 12, 20, 40, 42-43, 88, 89, 90, 91, 92 (cartoon, 93), 95, 97, 98, 99-100, 103, 105, 153-54, 155, 156, 161, 163, 165-67, 179, 206, 215, 219-20, 238, 239, 249, 261, 262, 269, 296

CORNELL, KATHARINE, 41, 47, 86, 129, 237

COSDEN, JOSHUA, 260

COWARD, NOEL, 46, 85, 145, 162

COWL, JANE, 4, 156, 226

CROUSE, RUSSEL, 164

CROWNINSHIELD, FRANK, 185-87

CUKOR, GEORGE, 101

DALY, BILL, 211

DAVIS, EDGAR B., 262-65

DAVIS, FRANK, 263

DEVERAUX, BEE DREW, 28-29

DEVERAUX, JOHN DREW, 28-29

DIETZ, HOWARD, 77, 269

DOOLEY, JOHNNY, 271

DRAGE, LUCY CHRISTIE, 122

DREW, JOHN, 4, 22, 23, 28, 41, 140, 200, 204

DUFFY, EDMUND, 8, 12

EASTMAN, MAX, 257

EARLY, STEPHEN, 172, 173

EMERY, JOHN, 296

ERDMANN, DR. JOHN F., 291-92

ERNST, MORRIS L., 74, 268-69, 271

F.P.A. *See* ADAMS, FRANKLIN P.

FAIRBANKS, DOUGLAS, 24-27, 28, 45, 152, 222-23, 226

FAIRBANKS, DOUGLAS, JR., 23-24

FARNOL, LYNN, 280-81

FAULKNER, WILLIAM, 113

FEIGELBAUM, DR. DORIAN, 252

FERBER, EDNA, 11, 13, 47, 78, 109-10, 113, 144, 145 (cartoon, 147), 155, 157, 179, 206, 208, 230, 261, 269, 288, 298

FERBER, MRS., 298

FISKE, MRS., 8

FLANNER, JANET, 213, 281

FLEISCHMAN, DORIS, 138, 139, 141, 143

FLEISCHMANN, JULIUS, 176, 188

FLEISCHMANN, RAOUL, 176, 179, 188, 234, 243, 244

FONTANNE, LYNN, 42, 86, 156, 237, 260, 279

FORD, COREY, 181, 260

GABRIEL, GILBERT W., 181

GANNETT, LEWIS, 75

GAIGE, CROSBY, 121

§ 305 §

INDEX

GEORGES, 7, 8, 160, 208, 254

GERSHWIN, GEORGE, 43, 211

GIBBS, WOLCOTT, 155, 190, 191, 257-58

GILLMORE, MARGALO, 11, 13, 41, 47-48, 129, 149, 157, 205, 209

GILLMORE, RUTH, 90, 96, 99

GLASS, MONTAGUE, 105

GORDON, MAX, 267-68

GOULD, HAROLD, 89

GRANT, JANE, 11, 13, 43-45, 47, 91, 92, 114-19, 125, 126, 127, 134-37 (cartoon, 135), 139, 141-43, 144, 146-49, 175, 212, 214, 215, 234, 296

GRIFFIS, STANTON, 109-10, 133

HALE, LOUISE CLOSSER, 95

HALE, RUTH, 11, 13, 47, 67, 69, 103, 127-31, 134-37 (cartoon, 135), 138-39, 143, 144, 245-46, 298

HAMPDEN, WALTER, 226

HAMPTON, MYRA, 84-85

HARRIS, JED, 49-50

HARRIS, SAM, 43

HARRIS, WILLIAM B., 125, 137

HARRIS, WILLIAM, JR., 240

HART, MOSS, 156, 251, 269, 294-95

HAWLEY, HUDSON, 172, 173

HAYES, HELEN, 86, 91, 96, 99, 211, 214

HEIFETZ, JASCHA, 84-85, 87, 92, 96, 99, 100, 211

HELBURN, THERESA, 202, 203-04

HENNESSY, JOSEPH, 281

HERGESHEIMER, JOSEPH, 254

HERTZ, JOHN D., 260

HOLMESDALE, JEFFREY, 193-94

HOPKINS, ARTHUR, 13

HOROWITZ, CHARLIE, 68

HOWARD, ROY, 272

HOWLAND, JOBYNA, 226

HUFFAKER, LUCY, 139

HURLOCK, MADELINE, 215, 279, 295

INGERSOLL, RALPH, 174

IRVIN, REA, 175, 179, 181, 192

IVES, RAYMOND, 281

JANIS, ELSIE, 4, 22, 189-90, 226

KAUFMAN, BEATRICE, 11, 13-14, 47, 84, 91, 144, 181, 234, 298

KAUFMAN, GEORGE S., 11, 12, 13-14, 20, 30-31, 40, 42-43, 47, 49, 51, 68, 89, 90, 91, 92, 96, 97, 98, 99-100, 103, 105, 106, 107, 109, 144 (cartoon, 147), 153-54, 155-56, 161, 168-69, 171, 179, 206, 209, 238, 239, 242-43, 244,

§ 306 §

Index

251, 261, 268, 290, 294-95, 298

KAUFMAN, S. J., 4, 6, 7, 14

KEENE TWINS, 186

KENNEDY, MADGE, 283

KENNEDY, MARY, 91, 92

KERN, JEROME, 78, 230

KERRIGAN, J. M., 87, 89, 92, 95, 96, 104

KEYNES, JOHN MAYNARD, 128

KING, DENNIS, 226, 292-93

KING, MURIEL, 146

KIRBY, ROLLIN, 68

KNOBLOCH, EDWARD, 263

KRAMER, DALE, 74

LADY GREGORY, 22, 23

LA FOLLETTE, FOLA, 139, 140

LACKAYE, WILTON, 102-05

LARDNER, RING, 105, 106, 155, 239-41, 271

LAWRENCE, GERTRUDE, 237

LEECH, MARGARET, 11, 13, 145-46, 149, 164, 260

LENIHAN, WINIFRED, 40-41, 91

LEVANT, OSCAR, 226-27

LILLIE, BEATRICE, 237

LINDSAY, HOWARD, 164

LIPPMANN, WALTER, 68, 70

LITTELL, ROBERT, 68

LIVERIGHT, HORACE, 14

LONG, LOIS, 181-82, 185, 192

LOPOKOVA, LYDIA, 128

LUCKSTONE, ISADORE, 262-63

LUIGI, 7, 8

LUNT, ALFRED, 86, 156, 237, 260

LYONS, LEONARD, 279

MACARTHUR, CHARLES, 211-12, 214, 215, 260

MACNAMARA, EDWARD, 126-27, 129-31, 230-32, 252-54, 262

McINTYRE, O. O., 4

McMEIN, NEYSA, 11, 13, 85, 87, 88, 91, 92, 95, 99, 139, 144, 146, 156, 160, 162, 209-18, 222, 234, 281, 298

McMULLIN, JOHN, 186

MACKAY, ELLIN, 189, 190

MADISON, CONSTANCE, 271

MALONEY, RUSSEL, 197

MANKIEWICZ, HERMAN J., 11, 19-20, 181, 237, 251, 261, 298

MARX BROTHERS, 88, 155, 267-68, 270

MARX, GROUCHO, 267, 268-69, 270

MARX, HARPO, 84, 234, 262, 268, 295

MASSEY, RAYMOND, 279-80

MAXWELL, ELSA, 279

MELONEY, MRS. WILLIAM BROWN, 172, 173

MERWIN, SAMUEL, 5

MILLER, ALICE DUER, 86, 91,

§ 307 §

INDEX

MILLER, ALICE DUER (*cont.*) 92, 112-13, 128, 140, 189, 191, 258, 260

MILLER, HENRY WISE, 47, 89, 164, 260

MOATS, ALICE-LEONE, 213-14

MURPHY, GERALD, 278

MURRAY, BILL, 5-6, 11, 298

NICHOLS, ANN, 60-66

NORRIS, CHARLES G., 283

NORRIS, KATHLEEN, 283-84

O'MALLEY, FRANK WARD, 22, 23, 28, 202, 271

PARKER, DOROTHY, 11, 14-19 (cartoon, 17), 20, 45, 46, 67, 78, 87, 91, 105, 111, 113, 134, 139, 144, 145, 157, 168-69, 179, 192, 224-25, 227-28, 245, 258, 269, 296, 297, 299

PARKER, EDWIN, 16, 296

PEMBERTON, BROCK, 5, 11, 13, 40, 46, 91, 111-12, 156-57, 160, 263, 295, 298

PEMBERTON, MURDOCK, 5, 6, 11, 20, 40, 69, 91, 180, 295

PENNINGTON, ANN, 4

PERELMAN, S. J., 196

PERSHING, GENERAL JOHN J., 130

PICKERING, RUTH, 139

PICKFORD, MARY, 45, 292

PULITZER, MARGARET. *See* LEECH, MARGARET

PULITZER, RALPH, 70, 145, 260

PULITZERS, THE, 271

ROBESON, PAUL, 87, 243, 297

ROOT, ESTHER, 238, 295

ROSS, ARIANE, 126

ROSS, HAROLD, 5, 11, 13, 19, 20, 40, 43-45, 51, 56-57, 84, 95, 96, 113, 114-21, 122, 125-27, 139, 142-43, 160, 165-67, 171, 172-82 (cartoon, 183), 188, 189, 190, 191, 192, 194-98, 208, 214, 215, 244, 248, 255, 283, 295, 298

ROSS, MRS. [GEORGE], 113-14

RYSKIND, MORRIS, 43, 107-09, 155, 261

SACCO AND VANZETTI, 66-67, 70-73, 75

SALSBURY, NATE, 90, 97, 103

SAMUELS, ARTHUR, 5, 11, 90

SCHWARZ, MINNA, 295

SCHIFF, DOROTHY, 278

SHAW, G. B., 203-04

SHEEN, MONSIGNOR FULTON J., 271

SHERWOOD, MADELINE. *See* HURLOCK, MADELINE

SHERWOOD, MARY. *See* BRANDON, MARY.

Index

SHERWOOD, ROBERT, 11, 14, 15, 29, 42, 45, 51, 87-88, 91, 92 (cartoon, 93), 156, 205, 215, 249, 261, 269, 279, 280-81, 287, 296, 298

SPROEHNLE, KATHERINE, 180, 221-23

STALLINGS, LAURENCE, 5, 11, 13, 20, 39, 46, 67, 179, 262, 272, 298

STEIN, GERTRUDE, 149-152

STEVENS, DORIS, 139

STEWART, DONALD OGDEN, 78, 89, 297, 298

STONE, LUCY, 134-143

STRYKER, LLOYD, 175

SULLIVAN, FRANK, 67-68, 78, 157, 162, 164, 165, 253, 260, 262, 272, 276, 282, 284-85, 296, 298

SUMNER, JOHN S., 297

SWOPE, HERBERT BAYARD, 67, 73, 84, 108, 234, 243, 249, 260, 274-77, 282

TAYLOR, DEEMS, 5, 11, 42, 67, 87, 91, 100, 153, 157, 158, 261, 272

TAYLOR, LAURETTE, 4, 32, 41, 97-102, 226

THACKREY, DOROTHY. See SCHIFF, DOROTHY

THURBER, JAMES, 190-91, 255-56, 299

TOOHEY, JOHN PETER, 3, 5, 7, 11, 89, 90, 92, 95, 98, 160-61, 175, 234, 248, 252, 295

TOOHEY, VIOLA, 234, 252

TRUAX, HAWLEY, 114-17, 118, 119, 120, 121, 125, 175

TYLER, GEORGE C., 42

ULRIC, LENORE, 91

VANZETTI. See SACCO AND VANZETTI

VICTOR, SARAH, 3, 4

WALKER, JUNE, 91

WALLACE, DAVID H., 11, 240-44, 247, 248, 298

WALLACE, WILLIAM ROSS, 299

WALLGREN, A. A., 172, 173

WEAVER, JOHN V. A., 11, 13, 31, 45-46, 50-51, 76, 91, 234, 298

WERRENRATH, REINALD, 87, 91, 100

WHITE, KATHARINE, 190

WHITE, E. B., 190-91, 255-56

WHITEHOUSE, MRS. NORMAN DE R., 130

WINCHELL, WALTER, 76, 279

WINTERICH, JOHN T., 172, 173, 259

WOOD, PEGGY, 11, 13, 45-47, 86, 157, 221

WOOLLCOTT, ALEXANDER, 3, 4, 5, 6, 7, 8, 11, 32-33, 44-45,

§ 309 §

INDEX

WOOLLCOTT (*continued*)
46, 47-48, 51-52, 52-53, 54, 55, 67, 69, 76, 77, 84, 85, 86-87, 89, 90, 91, 92, 96, 97, 98, 101, 105-07, 109-10, 112, 113, 114-25 (cartoon, 123), 126-27, 133, 146-49, 156, 157, 160, 161-69, 172, 173, 179, 192, 193-95, 205, 207, 208-09, 214-18, 223, 224, 228, 229, 237, 238, 240-41, 244, 249, 252, 258-61, 262, 269, 272, 278, 279, 281-82, 283-84, 291, 295, 298, 299

YOUNG, ROLAND, 153, 154, 237, 261

ZIEGFELD, FLORENZ, 15

CPSIA information can be obtained
at www.ICGtesting.com
Printed in the USA
LVHW110159121219
640241LV00007B/40/P